CIUDAD REAL
1500-1750

CIUDAD REAL
1500-1750

Growth, Crisis, and Readjustment in the Spanish Economy

CARLA RAHN PHILLIPS

HARVARD UNIVERSITY PRESS
CAMBRIDGE, MASSACHUSETTS, AND LONDON, ENGLAND • 1979

Library of Congress Cataloging in Publication Data

Phillips, Carla Rahn, 1943-
  Ciudad Real, 1500-1750.

  Bibliography: p.
  Includes index.
  1. Ciudad Real, Spain (City)—Economic
conditions. 2. Ciudad Real region, Spain—
Economic conditions. I. Title.
HC388.C58P5   330.9′46′45   78-9293
ISBN 0-674-13285-8

To my mother
and the memory
of my father

PREFACE

It is one of the paradoxes of scholarly activity that the longer you work, the more indebted you become. In the years since this book began as a dissertation, many persons have given me advice and encouragement, and I am grateful to them all. Nicolas Sánchez-Albornoz of New York University supervised the dissertation and has always been a source of helpful criticism and friendship. The professional and technical staffs of the Archivo General de Simancas have helped me in ways too numerous to mention, from the beginning to the end of my research; I can only add myself to the ranks of scholars in their debt. The late Isabel Pérez Valera was the director of the Casa de Cultura in Ciudad Real, which houses the provincial archive, when I began my dissertation research. Her lively interest in the history of La Mancha and her scholarly contributions to the field were an inspiration to me, and I am heartened to know that others are carrying on her work. The staffs of the ecclesiastical and municipal archives in Ciudad Real were also kind and generous with the materials in their care.

American Hispanists form a small group, and the support and criticism of scholars within that group have been very important to me. Conversations with Richard L. Kagan of the Johns Hopkins University, Michael Weisser of the University of South Carolina, and Helen Nader of Indiana University, among others, have helped me clarify thoughts on diverse topics. I particularly wish to thank David R. Ringrose of the University of California, San Diego, for his careful and perceptive reading of a draft of the manuscript. He has an unusual ability to write lucidly and well about economic history; I am grateful to have had the benefit of his criticism. Finally, I am indebted to my husband, William David Phillips, Jr., of San Diego State University, for love, friendship, and scholarly criticism—a rare and wonderful combination. All of these persons have contributed to any strengths the book may have; the weaknesses are my own.

Copyright holders in Europe and the United States have generously allowed me to use material for this book. In particular, I would like to thank the editors of *Societas* for permission to draw on material that first appeared in their journal for chapters 3 and 5. All of the illustrations were adopted from their original sources by Urve Daigle of the University of Minnesota.

The notes to chapters often include general secondary works as well as archival sources, to aid readers outside the field. To that same end I have included in the bibliography works dealing with Spanish history in general, and other works of a comparative nature, even though they may not have been cited in the notes.

CONTENTS

CIUDAD REAL
1500-1750

THE PHYSICAL
AND HISTORICAL SETTING

I

The rise and fall of Spain as a world power have concerned historians for hundreds of years. At its peak in the late sixteenth century, Spain controlled the first empire upon which the sun never set and exercised a powerful influence in European affairs. By 1600 thoughtful Spaniards knew that something had gone terribly wrong, and by 1650 the rest of Europe knew it too. Other powers rose to prominence—the United Netherlands, France, England—and Spain fell to a secondary role in European politics. Many historians have ignored the complexity of this process, especially the continual interplay between the economic base of Castile (including American treasure) and the political role of its sovereigns. I will examine this interplay in one Castilian city, Ciudad Real, from about 1500, when the city began a period of economic growth, to about 1750, when it had become a classic example of subsistence economy. In the interim its inhabitants had adapted to the changing international economy and to internal changes in the economic base of Castile. Before turning to Ciudad Real, however, I will review developments in Spain as a whole, especially in its Castilian heartland.[1]

In the early sixteenth century, the Castilian population rise and settlement in the Americas together created an increased demand for agricultural and manufactured goods. At the same time, Spain and its Habsburg kings were drawn into a long series of dynastic and religious struggles in Europe which, among other things, also fueled internal demand for goods and services. The economy of Castile responded with higher production, and many areas enjoyed real growth. When large profits began to arrive in quantity from the Americas, they contributed to Spain's ability to wage war, and—to a point—also stimulated the economy.

Unfortunately, Castile's economy had a number of structural weaknesses which became increasingly apparent as the sixteenth century progressed. Good arable land was scarce, and much potentially good grain land suffered from inadequate rainfall. In addition, herding often took precedence over agriculture under the law, especially the transhumant herding under the jurisdiction of the Mesta, the organization of livestock owners.[2] There was some expansion of farmland at the expense of pasture in the early and middle sixteenth century, as growing demand pushed prices up for grain and wine and made agriculture a profitable investment. But any fundamental changes in land-use patterns ran into strong opposition from the Mesta, especially from its powerful aristocratic members. As landowners as well as livestock owners, they combated proposed changes from agriculturalists or from native industry that might lower their incomes from wool exports. Successive kings could not risk alienating the Mesta while Spain was at war, and besides, the flocks provided a steady source of foreign exchange, taxes, and pasture rental fees to the crown. Limited agricultural land thus combined with entrenched interests at home and the need to present a united front abroad to hamper agriculture's efforts to meet the demands placed on it.

In industry as well, internal and external forces combined to restrict growth in the sixteenth century. Artisanry was well developed in many areas of Castile, particularly where there was a weak return from agriculture. Stimulated by market demand in the early sixteenth century, some areas expanded production for local consumption, and some began to gain international reputations for their products. The swords of Toledo, the leather goods of Córdoba, the gloves of Ocaña and Ciudad Real, the broadcloths of Segovia, and the silks of Granada all became justly famous. As luxury goods they could sustain the high cost of land transport to link with the network of international trade. But a shortage of skilled workers and guild intransigence held down production, and the guilds were protected by the crown in return for subsidies and for their role in preserving social peace in Castile. At the same time, powerful individuals involved in the import trade turned to foreign goods to fill demands from the colonies and from Spain itself. Private treasure from the Americas paid for the goods from abroad and stimulated economic activity in France, the Netherlands, and England. In Castile, on the other hand, industrial production could not change, or change fast enough, to absorb additions to the money supply. Instead, American treasure came to cause more inflation than growth in the Castilian economy, and eventually helped to price many of Castile's goods out of the international market, and even out of the national market.

By the fourth quarter of the sixteenth century, population, agriculture, and industry were approaching a crisis in Castile; Spain as a whole was well on its way toward becoming a raw-materials producer for the more advanced parts of Europe and an importer of foreign manufactured goods, paid for in part by American treasure. The country was also involved in the eighty-year struggle against the rebellious Netherlands and was more or less waging open war at sea with England. In other words, just as Castile needed help from the crown in the form of tax relief and effective protection for industry, the crown was forced to raise taxes beyond the level of inflation in order to pay for foreign wars.

In the seventeenth century frequent harvest failures and epidemics and the expulsion of the Moriscos (Spain's converted Moslems) lowered the population of Castile from about 7.5 million to about 6.0 million inhabitants. The drain of men in foreign wars and in search of riches in America also contributed to the absolute decline in population. Theoretically, the population losses should have relieved demographic pressure and established a new balance between population and resources. Cultivators should have withdrawn from marginal lands, leaving them as pasture. Prices should have dropped, especially for agricultural products, and people should have been able to afford more and better food and still have money for manufactured goods. That, at least, was how it should have happened. In fact the beneficial readjustments to a lower population were somewhat blunted by Spain's continuing involvement in foreign wars and, in the 1630s and 1640s, by rebellions at home and in other areas of the monarchy. There is some evidence that cultivation and herding did establish a new balance, but prices continued to rise until about 1650, fueled in part by the government's currency manipulation. Aggregate taxes managed to keep up with inflation, and then some, even though in many areas the taxpaying population had fallen considerably. Moreover, the majority of Castilian taxes were regressive excises on basic consumer goods. Only at the end of the seventeenth century did taxes fall, when Spain had ceased to be a major force in European politics. Then in the reign of the unhappy Charles II, last of the Spanish Habsburgs, there were signs of a limited recovery in the internal economy of Castile and considerable growth in Catalonia. Modest progress in Castile continued during the reigns of the first Bourbons in the eighteenth century.

Though Spain was by then too far behind to compete in industry with the United Netherlands, France, and England, local manufacturing flourished in many areas of Castile, especially those which could not afford manufactured goods from abroad. In those often isolated areas, in other words, a subsistence economy had reemerged during the seventeenth century, consolidating production and markets within a regional network and providing tolerably well for its citizens, at least in good years. We can see this process quite clearly in the economic evolution of Ciudad Real from 1500 to 1750. I have used a variety of documentation from both national and local archives that covers the 250-year period, but for most detailed analyses I will focus on the late sixteenth and seventeenth centuries, when the subsistence economy took shape. Even before 1500, however, the city's physical and historical background had set limits to its economic potential.

The city of Ciudad Real lies on the plains of La Mancha in New Castile, the largest area of flat land on the Iberian Peninsula. Modern visitors have no difficulty in imagining the countryside as the scene of Don Quixote's surrealistic adventures. Like him, they can find in this "elemental landscape a rest for the eyes and a torture for the imagination."[3] Most of La Mancha lies in the modern province of Ciudad Real, which touches Toledo, Cuenca, and Albacete on the north and part of the forbidding Sierra Morena on the south. Journeying north from Andalusia, one traveler's first impression of La Mancha was of its "terrible rocks, intermixed with a great quantity of rushing streams, which are such that one cannot enter [the plain] through more than one place where they have carved an aperture through a mountain of prodigious height."[4] Once on the Manchegan plain, a traveler might look in all directions without seeing a hill, a gully, or even a sign of human habitation. The climate too was given to extremes, unlike the temperate south. Isolated by its mountainous borders, the plains of La Mancha experienced cold winters, very hot summers, and a notable lack of precipitation.[5]

The discerning traveler, nonetheless, could appreciate the real and potential sources of wealth behind La Mancha's desolate exterior. The soil was very hospitable to vines, grain, and olive trees, and natural grasses flourished on all but the worst lands. In addition, La Mancha was the southern terminus for several of the famous sheepwalks of Castile, where herds of the Mesta rented fall and winter pasture for fees reputedly worth 200,000 escudos each year to the king in the mid-seventeenth century.[6] The arable lands were even greater sources of wealth and remain so today.

The best description of La Mancha in the Habsburg period is contained in the *Relaciones topográficas*, an inquiry first ordered by Philip II in 1575 which gives topographical profiles of each locale polled, in addition to a wealth of other information. Unfortunately, there is no response extant from the city of Ciudad Real,[7] but a fair picture of its terrain emerges by examining relaciones from a few of the neighboring towns.[8] La Cañada del Moral lay 3 leagues southwest of Ciudad Real (each league being 5.6 kilometers), separated from it by two small *aldeas* (villages). The temperate and healthy land, free of extremes of topography, provided the citizens with farmland and with ample supplies of firewood from its wooded areas. Nearby flowed the Guadiana, Ciudad Real's

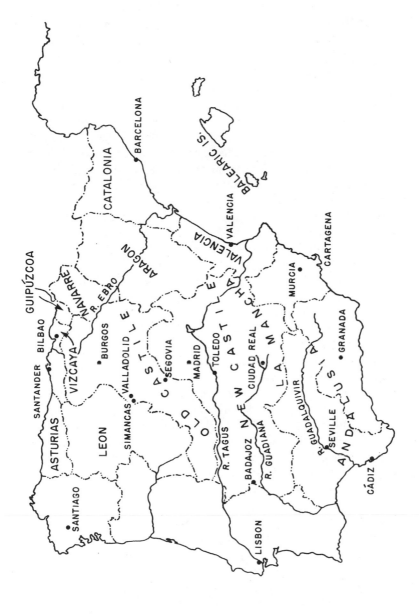

Figure 1.1. The Iberian Peninsula.

river, with abundant water throughout the year, and the smaller Jabalón, which tended to dry up every summer. The Guadiana periodically flooded the plains around Ciudad Real, and in 1508 the swollen river damaged more than three hundred houses in the southwest corner of the city.[9] But the river also provided power for the mills needed by the area around Ciudad Real, and most of them were in the hands of city residents by the time of another government inquiry in 1751.[10] From its source east of La Mancha, the Guadiana meanders through the center of the province, passing to the north and west of Ciudad Real before resuming its westward flow through Extremadura and Portugal. Much of the resident livestock in Extremadura and New Castile, as well as some transhumant sheep of the Mesta, were able to forage along its banks the better part of each year.[11] For example, nearly all of the livestock owned by householders of Ciudad Real pastured by the Guadiana in the fall and winter months, and some found forage there all year.[12]

Northwest of La Cañada and 4 leagues southwest of Ciudad Real lay Los Pozuelos de Calatrava. The land under its jurisdiction (its *término*) was also level, healthy, and well-supplied with firewood, but residents suffered from a chronic shortage of drinking water. Due west of Ciudad Real lay Alcolea de Calatrava, at a distance of 3 leagues. Like its neighbors, Alcolea had healthy land, about half of its término in open land and half in wooded areas with abundant firewood. Farther northwest was Piedrabuena, 4 leagues from Ciudad Real by a direct road. Here the topography began to change. Although part of Piedrabuena's término was on the Manchegan plain, the western part extended to the Montes de Toledo, whose hills teemed with wolves, foxes, wild boar, and deer, all harmful to grazing livestock. Smaller animals and birds often attacked the grain crop. Closest to Ciudad Real on the plain lay Miguelturra, 0.5 leagues to the southeast. In addition to grain, the land was good for vineyards, but residents had to travel great distances for firewood and kindling. Drinking water was plentiful though, and many householders were able to sink spring wells on their property.

For the most part, the population centers of La Mancha were far apart and nucleated near the sources of fresh water. Farmers could commute fairly easily from the towns to their scattered parcels of land, but for seasons of heavy agricultural labor, the more prosperous farmers maintained shelters in the fields (*casas del campo*). The towns of La Mancha often found favor with travelers who otherwise despised the area. Almagro, 3 leagues southeast of Ciudad Real and sometime seat of the military order of Calatrava, was "a large town, whose streets are rather handsome." Ciudad Real won fainter praise as "A small town, rather pretty for this region."[13] Many visitors made unfavorable comparisons between Almagro and Ciudad Real. Even after its appointment as pro-

O CITY
• TOWN
+ DEPENDENT VILLAGE

Figure 1.2. Urban jurisdictions in the Ciudad Real area. (Adapted from María Dolores Marcos González, "Castilla la Nueva y Estremadura," pt. 6 of *La España del Antiguo Régimen*, ed. Miguel Artola, Salamanca, 1971.)

vincial capital in 1691, Ciudad Real never exercised an attraction for the casual visitor. Access to the city, located about 200 kilometers south of Madrid, was by a secondary trade route to Andalusia. Isolated on the vast Manchegan plain, a few tall buildings stood out above the general two-storied construction. In the government inquiry in 1751, the city proper was estimated at 1.5 leagues east to west, 2 north to south, and 4.5 in circumference,[14] or about 47 square kilometers by modern reckoning. Today Ciudad Real contains over 40,000 people, but it rarely, if ever, exceeded 10,000 in the Habsburg period. Even in the mid-nineteenth century, there was still plenty of room in the city proper for fields and pastures. Beyond the city boundaries lay its término, which included 30,000 fanegas or about 19,500 hectares.[15] Some 17,000 fanegas were devoted to sown crops; another 6,000, to olives, grapes, and various other items; about 6,000, to common and private grazing lands, and the remainder was waste, suitable only for occasional pasture.[16] Though the city's término could vary in size, these figures are representative of the whole early modern period in Ciudad Real. Today it contains over 29,000 hectares, and other términos in La Mancha are even larger.[17]

Ordinarily a major city in that underpopulated region would have been given fiscal and judicial supervision over an area much larger than its término alone. But the administrative area of Ciudad Real (its *partido*) was the same as its término. This situation arose because Ciudad Real had not developed naturally as a market center or a commercial crossroads. Instead, the city had been founded by Alfonso X of Castile as a royal counterbalance to the noble military orders. Castile's intermittent reconquest of territory from the Moslems lasted for several centuries, until the final Moslem surrender of Granada in 1492. In the process aristocratic Christians formed local crusading orders similar to the Knights Templar and the Knights of Malta. They fought for the kings of Leon and Castile as well as for the King of Heaven, and it was only natural that the secular kings would reward them with land grants as the Moslems were pushed ever farther to the south. In return for guarding the frontiers of New Castile, the orders of Santiago, Alcántara, and Calatrava gained effective ownership of much of the land of La Mancha. Once given, the land could hardly be taken back, but the growing power of the military orders posed a threat to royal authority. This is a familiar story to students of Europe's eastern border history, and the tug-of-war between crown and nobility was practically universal in Renaissance western Europe. Castilian monarchs faced the problem in La Mancha in part by founding royal towns in the wake of Christian military victories. That was the origin of Ciudad Real, established in the middle of lands granted to the order of Calatrava.

The order began in the mid-twelfth century, named after a Moslem fort on the Guadiana River that Alfonso VII of Castile captured in 1147. Thereafter Calatrava steadily increased its power by conquest and by additional land grants, and the order brought new settlers south from Navarre to populate the land. In 1195 Alfonso VIII suffered a major defeat by the Moslems at the battle of Alarcos, and the old fort and its surrounding area fell to the victors. When the Christians won back the area at the battle of Las Navas de Tolosa (1212), the order moved its headquarters closer to the southern frontier, though it remained the principal landowner in the area. Both Alfonso VIII and his successor tried to repopulate Alarcos, but every attempt failed because of its unattractive and unhealthy character.[18]

Alfonso X, called the Wise, preferred Pozuelo de Don Gil, a nearby settlement, as the site of a "great and good town, that would be ruled in all things by [the usages laid down in the town charter] and that would be the head of all that region . . . and [he] gave it the name of Real."[19] The challenge to Calatrava was clear and unmistakable, since the site was in the heart of the order's lands. The new royal town was to be a frontier outpost of the crown, not against the Moslems, who were far to the south, but against the overweening power of the military orders. Later on, as the Reconquest and the repopulation of Christian Castile were consolidated, the new town would become an administrative center as well, closer to the action than the towns of Old Castile, but not so far away from them as to lose touch.

Even at its foundation Alfonso's town was designed for the dual purpose of protection and growth. The large *casco de la villa* (town proper) was to be surrounded by an impressive wall set with 130 towers and either six or eight gates.[20] Local legend has it that Alfonso X himself traced out the boundaries of the wall and the location of the main streets. Then, as now, the boundaries were pear-shaped, with six streets leading from a central plaza to the city walls.[21] To attract settlers to Villa Real, its nobles were to be governed by the usages of Toledo, exempting them from all ordinary taxation, among other privileges. Commoners were to be governed by the usages of Cuenca, often considered the model for municipal self-government.[22] In addition, all residents were given land and exempted from transit and port taxes everywhere in the kingdom except Toledo, Seville, and Murcia. The town as a whole received jurisdiction over several nearby villages and their lands.[23] In fact, the legal position of Villa Real was attractive enough to lure nobles of the military orders to live there, although the mere existence of the new town was a source of irritation to their leaders. Ordinary settlers were harder to find. The most enthusiastic were the Jews and Moslems who had formerly lived nearby and who were only too happy to become residents of the new town, particularly since it offered them royal protection.[24] More

Figure 1.3. Lands of the military orders. (From Herman Kellenbenz, *Die Fuggersche Maestrazgopacht (1525-1542): Zur Geschichte der Spanischen Ritterorden im 16, Jahrhundert*, Tübingen, 1967.)

Figure 1.4. Administrative divisions in La Mancha. (Adapted from María Dolores Marcos González, "Castilla la Nueva y Estremadura" pt. 6 of *La España del Antiguo Régimen*, ed. Miguel Artola, Salamanca, 1971.)

Moslems were invited in 1279, forming the basis of the large *morería* (Moorish quarter) in Villa Real.[25]

It soon became clear that whatever prosperity the town might someday enjoy would be due to royal favor and not to its natural growth and development. Instead of a "grand villa é bona," Alfonso X had created a useful but weak pawn in his struggle with the order of Calatrava. To make Villa Real viable economically the king granted it many privileges in the years after the foundation, but almost always these privileges set the residents against the knights of Calatrava. For example, when Alfonso ordered the citizens of Villa Real to build an *alcázar* (fortress) at the same time that they raised their own houses, he gave them the right to gather necessary wood and to "cut green and dry firewood from the hills, and drink the water, and graze their animals" on Calatrava's land (the Campo de Calatrava).[26] Predictably the forceful leadership of the order refused to accept the town's privileges and instead followed "a sinister plan of enclosing the new population in a circle of iron."[27] Calatrava founded several fortified towns—Miguelturra, Peralvillo, las Casas, and Benavente—on the very borders of Villa Real's término, and during the turbulent minority of Alfonso XI, royal weakness encouraged Calatrava to deny the town's residents access to firewood and other necessities. Royal troops did demolish the unauthorized castle of Miguelturra, but quarrels over the regency prevented any sustained royal assistance to Villa Real. Instead the residents had to rely upon a town militia of one hundred horsemen and two hundred archers, and upon the internal squabbles of Calatrava's knights to gain compliance from the order.

At one point rebellious knights under the command of Don Juan Núñez de Prado abandoned the leadership in Miguelturra and sought refuge in Villa Real. A series of skirmishes led to a major war in 1328 between the two factions, the residents of Villa Real and Miguelturra joining in. When the rebels won and retired from the area, their supporters from Villa Real took the opportunity to attack Miguelturra and massacre its remaining residents, mostly women, children, and old men. This seriously damaged the town's credibility as an innocent victim of Calatrava's oppression. Following up its advantage, the *consejo* (town council) of Villa Real seized several settlements belonging to Miguelturra, as well as dependent villages of other towns in the Campo de Calatrava.[28] Each time the king ordered the return of these illegal seizures, and in addition he transferred to Calatrava control of the village of Villar del Pozo, which had belonged to Villa Real since its foundation. It was clear that the town could no longer hope for special treatment from the crown against Calatrava; the order was too valuable in the Reconquest.

When Alfonso XI attained his majority the kingdom was wracked with civil disturbances and threatened by a major offensive from the Moslems of Granada, led by Abul Hasan, emir of Morocco. To defend Castile, Alfonso needed the political and military support of Calatrava and the assurance that the kingdom would be secure in his absence. Perhaps that is why he imposed a settlement of the rivalry between Villa Real and the order of Calatrava. Gathering together the numerous legal cases pending between Miguelturra and Villa Real, Alfonso reaffirmed the rights of Villa Real's residents to use water, firewood, and pasture in the Campo de Calatrava. On the other hand, he denied the claim of Villa Real's residents to be exempt from taxes to Calatrava on land they had purchased in Miguelturra. In a decree issued in January 1339 the king ordered that residents of the rival towns had to live where they owned land, on pain of its expropriation. This decision harmed Villa Real much more than Miguelturra; it meant a temporary end to agricultural expansion in the former town and forced its residents to turn more toward artisanry.[29]

Curiously, the standard histories do not say much about the Black Death in Castile, even though Alfonso XI died of it, nor do they reveal much of Villa Real's history in the turbulent fourteenth century. The new Trastámara dynasty took the throne in 1369, but royal policy toward Villa Real did not change. In 1380 the king affirmed Calatrava's possession of Miguelturra and of various other towns to which Villa Real had at one time or another laid claim.[30] Still, the town had no real alternative to continued loyalty to the crown, and under the Trastámaras it was again a useful arm of royal power. In 1421 the town's sizeable militia responded to a call for help by King John II, who was under siege by the powerful Infante Henry of Aragon. For its aid, Villa Real won the title of city, thereafter to be known as Ciudad Real. In 1476 the city proved its loyalty to the crown in the civil war that broke out between Joanna (daughter of Henry IV) and her supporters and Ferdinand and Isabella, the anointed sovereigns. Calatrava, under its young master Rodrigo Téllez Girón, favored Joanna and launched an attack on Ciudad Real, which remained loyal to Ferdinand and Isabella. Lope de Vega immortalized the attack as a subplot in his play *Fuente Ovejuna* (1619), and although he allowed himself poetic license in dialogue and character motivation, he generally followed the account of the sixteenth-century chronicler of Calatrava, Rades y Andrada.[31]

In the play Rodrigo, the master of Calatrava, decided to invade Ciudad Real, encouraged by one of his men.[32]

> Few forces will be needed. As their soldiers
> They only have the natives of the place
> And some few gentry who support the cause
> Of Isabella and King Ferdinand.
>
> (I.92-95)

At Almagro the forces of Calatrava gathered for the assault.

> Against that city which we call
> The Royal City, our young Master
> Of Calatrava raised his troop,
> Two thousand infantry, to swoop,
> And carry slaughter and disaster
> Together with three hundred horse
> Of seculars and monks and friars—
> For even priests must join the force
> When our great Order so requires.
>
> (I.463-471)

Attacked by Calatrava,

> The city rose in the King's name
> Since for the Crown they all proclaim
> Their loyalty to the King's succession.
> They made resistance worthy fame.
>
> But in the end, their strength to tame,
> The Master entered in possession,
> And those who had denied his right
> He had beheaded upon sight.
> As for the common people there,
> He had each snaffled with a bit,
> And, having stripped their bodies bare,
> He flogged them in the public square
> Till they could neither stand nor sit. (I.514-526)

Two aldermen of Ciudad Real managed to carry news of their plight to the *Reyes Católicos* Ferdinand and Isabella. Ciudad Real is a small city, they said, and it has few people. Most of them are modest commoners, unable to challenge the power of Calatrava, which surrounds and intimidates them. They asked for aid almost apologetically, explaining that "though we fought/Opposing bravery to violent force,/Till the blood ran in streams, we lost the war" (I.677-679). Ferdinand and Isabella, well aware of the danger they faced from Calatrava's powerful opposition, ordered royal troops to Ciudad Real to recapture it. Even this early, the city's walls were in disrepair, offering little protection to those within or opposition to those without. The battle took place on the city streets, and eventually Rodrigo lost to the royal army, which remained in the area for some time to prevent Calatrava from aiding the crown's enemies further.[33]

By absorbing the military orders as part of royal administration, the Reyes Católicos largely ended the actual fighting between Calatrava and Ciudad Real.[34] Order in the countryside was further improved by the Santa Hermandad Vieja, one of the rural police forces formed in the principal towns of Castile and operating under the auspices of the crown. In the late fifteenth century the organization in Ciudad Real was particularly powerful, and, as one of the original three hermandades, it enjoyed considerable autonomy in its functions.[35] The reign of the Reyes Católicos was the apex of Ciudad Real's administrative importance. Partly as a reward for its loyalty and partly because of its location, the city became one of the seats of the newly established Inquisition in 1483. Its prime target in Ciudad Real was the community of converted Jews, or *conversos*.

Jews were very early residents of the city, where they seem to have prospered despite restrictions placed upon them by successive sovereigns. Technically forbidden to own land or to loan money at excessive interest to Christians, the Jews of Ciudad Real were in the same anomalous situation as their coreligionists elsewhere in the kingdom.[36] In 1391 a vicious pogrom broke out in a number of Spanish cities, eventually spreading to Ciudad Real, where many died in the senseless violence. A fire in the Jewish neighborhood (*judería*) in 1396 finished the destruction begun by the pogrom; the judería of Ciudad Real never recovered its former prosperity or its cultural identity. The great synagogue became a Dominican convent in 1407, and most residents of the neighborhood converted to Christianity, hoping their new religion would shelter them from further persecution.[37] They were disappointed. As New Christians (conversos) they suffered from an inferior legal status, and because of their connection with tax collecting and money lending, they came to be distrusted and even hated by the Old Christian community as well as being viewed as traitors by the remaining Jewish community.

Matters came to a head in July 1449, when news spread to Ciudad Real of a pogrom against the conversos of Toledo, followed by the imposition of further legal restrictions against them. The Old Christians of Ciudad Real raised a mob and, aided by the knights of Calatrava, subjected the converso neighborhood to armed attack and pillage. The converso numbers must have been quite large, since they sent three hundred armed men into the city streets to defend their homes. Even when peace was restored, mutual resentment persisted, and the Old Christians increasingly had official sanction on their side. For their loyalty to Henry IV against rebels supporting the king's half-brother Alfonso in 1468, the Old Christians won a continuation of the prohibition forbidding conversos to hold offices.[38]

By the reign of Ferdinand and Isabella, the Jewish community of Ciudad Real seems to have disappeared altogether, although a large body of conversos remained in the city. It was this group that the Inquisition sought to punish for suspected Judaizing. For the nearly two years that the tribunal sat in Ciudad Real it collected evidence, some of dubious merit, against the city's conversos. In several autos-de-fe 52 "obstinate heretics" were turned over to secular authorities to be burned, 220 fugitives were condemned in absentia, and 183 received penances for their crimes against the faith; nearly all of the first group and about half of the second seem to have been residents of the city.[39] This is not the place to debate the justice or wisdom of the Holy Office and its procedures; suffice it to say that the punctilious observation of legal formalities by the Inquisitors does not make the Holy Office any less repugnant to modern readers. The Reyes Católicos, in instituting the tribunals and in keeping them firmly under royal control, were responding to the racial hatred that had been growing for at least a century and, at the same time, were using religion as a force for political unity. Whatever group was most responsible for persuading the sovereigns to establish the Inquisition, it seems to have been an acceptable, and even a popular, expression of Christian religiosity at the time.[40] It is difficult to assess its effects on Ciudad Real's development, but its removal to Toledo in 1485 was surely a blow both to the wealth and to the prestige of the city.

Similarly, the brief sojourn of the Chancillería (high court of justice) from 1494 to 1505 raised Ciudad Real's fortunes and its hopes only to dash them again when it moved on to more fertile fields, in this case to Granada.[41] Bypassed as a major administrative center for southern Castile, the partido of Ciudad Real remained part of the fiscal and judicial province of Toledo, which represented it in the Cortes, or Castilian parliament.[42]

Despite the withdrawal of royal favor from Ciudad Real, the "very noble and very loyal" city rebelled against the crown only once, in the famous *comunero* revolt in 1520 against the new government of Ferdinand and Isabella's grandson Charles of Ghent and his Flemish appointees. It was no accident that this was almost exclusively a revolt of urban communes and that textile workers were among the most prominent rebels. The young king's upbringing in the Netherlands and his recent election as Holy Roman emperor (Charles V) bred fears that Castilian interests would be subordinated to those of the empire, and especially the Netherlands. Flemish textile centers already bought most of the best Spanish wool; local producers in Castile had to make do with the poorer sorts. In Ciudad Real the guilds of weavers, carders, and fullers supported the comuneros of other Castilian cities. They raised a mob in the main square and forced the *corregidor* (king's representative) to flee the city. Eventually the nobles of Ciudad Real calmed the rebels and reestablished the city's loyalty by sending twenty-five horsemen and fifty foot soldiers to help the royal forces restore order elsewhere. For its aid Ciudad Real received a reconfirmation of its privileges from the emperor and a tax rebate to use for municipal needs.[43] Then, like other Castilian cities, Ciudad Real returned to its habitual loyalty to the monarch—shamed, penitent, and without political power.

Charles and his successors were free to continue the broadening of Spanish interests begun in the late Middle Ages. From the late fifteenth century the scale of operations of the Castilian monarchy changed rapidly. In the foreign policies of Henry IV and the Reyes Católicos, Castile moved closer to the rest of Europe and to a diplomatic interdependence with the other great powers. Charles I and his son Philip II were able to make Spain the center of the European political order. This meant that the traditional cities of Castile—Valladolid, Segovia, Burgos, and Ciudad Real—lost importance to the cities of the expanded Habsburg monarchy—Naples, Milan, Antwerp, Vera Cruz, México, and Potosí. And within Spain, continued exploitation of the New World began to shift Castile's center of gravity toward the coasts, especially the southwest coast.[44] Cities and towns in central Castile could retain their importance only if they could make the transition from being local producers serving local markets to becoming international producers serving a world market.[45]

In Ciudad Real the resources to make such a transition did not look very promising on the surface. The city controlled only a limited land area, surrounded by the vast territories of the order of Calatrava. Because much of the land was more suitable for pasture than for farming and rainfall was unpredictable, residents could not rely on agriculture alone to sustain them. Paradoxically, these very sources of economic weakness were also sources of the city's potential economic strength. Inadequate natural resources and the impossibility of expansion into Calatrava's lands pushed many residents into part-time artisanry and into the local market network. The city's location on a trade route between Madrid and the south also bolstered the tendency toward a diversified economy of agriculture, industry, and trade. The city's residents were mostly free peasants and artisans, and many of them owned at least some land. Up to a point, then, they were free to decide how best to earn their livings, and the insecurities of life in La Mancha forced them to make those decisions carefully.

José Gentil da Silva saw in these characteristics a strong potential for growth in the region as a whole, and his analysis applies a fortiori to Ciudad Real.[46] Yet this potential was not realized. Growth in the early sixteenth century stalled before 1600, and thereafter a series of misfortunes hampered economic development until late in the seventeenth century, when a functioning subsistence economy reestablished itself.

POPULATION:
STRUCTURE AND TRENDS

II

The number of men, women, and children who make up a society is a necessary starting point for a study concerned with economic and social change. It was also a matter of concern for rulers and statesmen in early modern Europe, when the size and well-being of the population was considered an important index of a country's power. From all that we now know, it seems that the kingdoms of Spain suffered from the Black Death in the fourteenth century and from the economic dislocations that accompanied it.[1] The population began to recover near the middle of the fifteenth century, and after 1500 it began the rapid rise that was typical of most of Europe during the early sixteenth century. Felipe Ruiz Martín, carefully picking his way through the official government reckonings of the population, found that Spain increased from 5.7 million inhabitants in 1530 to 8.1 million in 1591.[2] By the latter date, however, the population had probably stopped growing. González de Cellorigo noted in 1600 that a lack of people was already diminishing both the armed might and the prestige of the Spanish crown in relation to its European neighbors.[3] Cellorigo was premature with this gloomy analysis, but it is probable that Spain's rising population approached the limits of the food supply by about 1580. This Malthusian crisis was not unique to Spain, but its resolution was particularly dramatic there. Between 1580 and 1650, Spain lost 1.5 million people, most of them from Castile. Famine, epidemics, and declining fertility—including the much-criticized increase in clerical vocations—accounted for about half the losses. The other half was due to external drains such as foreign wars, emigration to the Indies, and the expulsion of the Moriscos.[4] After reaching its nadir about 1650, the population was stable until the end of the century, when it slowly began to grow again. This time, however, the gains were not wiped out, and Spain, like the rest of western Europe, continued the demographic growth that characterizes the modern era.

The Spanish population was hardly a homogeneous entity. The economy of each region affected the rhythms of its normal demographic patterns and of its behavior in a crisis, just as the size and distribution of the population affected the economy of the area. Some regions, too, might have suffered from famine and escaped other Malthusian correctives. There is no reason, therefore, to expect that Ciudad Real's population mirrored the national trends, but it would be surprising to find no similarities between them.

In La Mancha the inhabitants tended to group themselves in middle-sized towns and villages, several of them clustered in the same general area. This is a lucky configuration for the student of demography. Middle-sized urban enclaves such as Ciudad Real do not have the floating population of larger cities, segments of society that are often overlooked in census estimates. Nonetheless, there are still serious inaccuracies in some of the overall counts of the city's population, which ranged between about 1,200 and 2,500 households during the period under study. The most reliable indicators of the city's population are two sets of parish registers, discussed in Appendix A. They are not sufficiently complete to allow family reconstitution, but simple aggregative analysis can tell us a great deal about the seasonal rhythms of life and death in Ciudad Real. Long-term trends of vital events will help us judge the accuracy of official counts, and more importantly, they will identify crisis points in the population history of the city.

Two powerful forces influenced the seasonal patterns of vital events: the Catholic church and the agricultural year. Together they explain most of the monthly variations in the parishes of San Pedro and Nuestra Señora del Prado shown in Table 2.1. Marriages were few in March and April, which generally include Lent. The December marriage totals, roughly concurrent with Advent, were also lower than other months. The ecclesiastical calendar does not account for the low marriage totals in summer, however, which can be explained better by the rhythm of the agricultural year. Since the calendar year does not fall easily into seasons, I have chosen an agricultural year: March to May, June to August, September to November, and December to February. Although it is as arbitrary as the calendar year, it makes a great deal more sense for an economy organized around the grain harvest.[5] This raises certain difficulties when the calendar year changes during the winter season, but keeping this in mind should ease any confusion.

In a typical year, marriages in both parishes reached a moderate level from March to May, dropped sharply from June to August, hit the year's high point from September to November, then declined slightly from

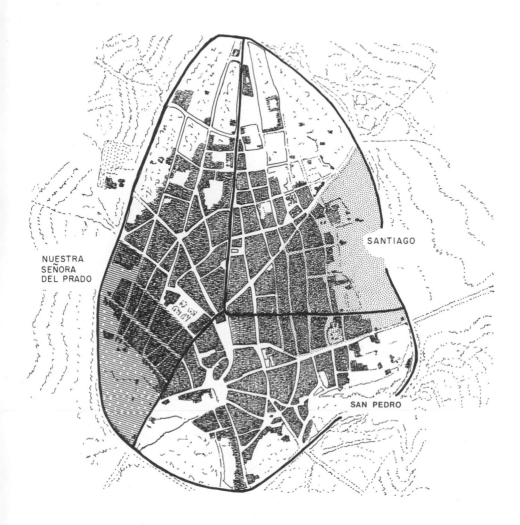

PARISH NAMES AND BOUNDARIES
EARLY LIMITS OF THE JEWISH AND CONVERSO NEIGHBORHOOD
EARLY LIMITS OF THE MUDÉJAR AND MORISCO NEIGHBORHOOD

Figure 2.1. City plan of Ciudad Real, showing parish boundaries and early limits of the Jewish and Moslem neighborhoods. (Adapted from Francisco Coello, *Atlas de España*, Madrid, ca. 1845.)

Table 2.1. Monthly pattern of vital records, 1660-1699.[a]

Month	San Pedro		Nuestra Señora del Prado		
	Marriage	Conception	Marriage	Conception[b]	Burial[c]
Jan.	166	492	170	361	212
Feb.	156	419	224	307	189
Mar.	111	443	103	315	209
Apr.	123	570	108	367	170
May	180	671	146	433	175
June	128	652	114	469	170
July	109	535	114	365	214
Aug.	114	501	96	317	281
Sep.	203	420	185	279	367
Oct.	191	336	189	246	434
Nov.	190	452	263	246	319
Dec.	180	553	135	334	216

a. The eighteenth century followed a nearly identical pattern. See Jerónimo López-Salazar Pérez, "Evolución demográfica de la Mancha en el siglo XVIII," *Hispania* 36 (1976):233-299.

   b. 1600-1627, 1664-1699.

   c. 1649-1699.

December to February (see Table 2.2). The high February total in Nuestra Señora del Prado is somewhat puzzling at first glance, but it, too, fits within the framework of ecclesiastical and agricultural influences. February is between Advent and Lent; it is also a month of little agricultural activity. Overall, the year's high season for marriages thus coincided with the aftermath of the harvest and the low point with the season just prior to and during the harvest. This is hardly surprising. Prospective marriage partners needed the assurance of a food supply before beginning a new family unit, and the early summer was often a period of high prices and food shortages, especially when the previous year's harvest had been scanty. The summer low point in marriages, then, can be explained by economic insecurity as well as by the rigors of agricultural labor. Similarly, the fall peak in marriages was related to a sufficient supply of food immediately following the harvest, enhanced perhaps by the lack of religious restrictions against marriage.

The seasonal pattern was even more striking for conceptions.[6] Spring was the traditional high point of conceptions in the demographic Old Regime, and Ciudad Real was no exception to the rule. April, May, and

Table 2.2. Seasonal pattern of vital statistics: percentage of total years counted in which each season registered the highest seasonal totals, 1600-1699.

Season	Marriages		Conceptions		Burials
	San Pedro	Nuestra Señora	San Pedro	Nuestra Señora[a]	Nuestra Señora[b]
March-May	20	13	31	29	13
June-Aug.	13	8	40	42	8
Sept.-Nov.	44	46	5	2	57
Dec.-Feb.	23	33	24	27	22

a. 1600-1627, 1664-1699.
b. 1649-1699.

June generally had the most conceptions in both parishes from the sixteenth through the eighteenth centuries. The fall months, plus February and March, had the fewest. Using the agricultural year produces a slightly different result, since its division point separates the months of peak conceptions. Thus, June to August had a higher number of conceptions than March to May. Conceptions, like marriages, followed a seasonal progression, but in the opposite direction. Whereas marriages decreased from a fall peak to a summer low, conceptions increased from a low point in the fall to a peak the following spring and summer. In the absence of proof, we can only speculate about the causes of this phenomenon. The end of winter, the lull in the agricultural work schedule, even the uncertainty of the coming harvest, could all help to explain the conception peak in late spring and early summer. Once the heaviest work of the year began, in July and August, conceptions would naturally fall, regardless of the promise that the harvest held for the future. In La Mancha, workers often lived in temporary dwellings near the fields and away from their families during the harvest season, and this would further lessen the opportunities for intercourse. The fall marriage peak, following the early summer conception peak, suggests that many brides were pregnant before marriage.

The agricultural year also influenced mortality figures, especially in times of famine, and the mortality curve often showed violent fluctuations from year to year. The only usable burial records for Ciudad Real during the Habsburg period begin in 1649 in Nuestra Señora del Prado. Happily the records are nearly complete in both parishes from 1700 to 1750. Like marriages, burials showed the highest monthly totals in September, October, and November, with the lowest figures appearing from April to June. If we use the agricultural year, the peak came in the fall season. Plague and other insect-borne diseases flourished in warm weather; filth and ignorance of proper nutrition and hygiene increased their potency. In years of heavy spring rains and hot summers, the danger from malaria would also increase toward the late summer in plains areas such as Ciudad Real, and a poor harvest could add the danger of famine at this time of year. In general, infants and children were more susceptible than adults to these fall-season hazards. The adult death season tended to be the winter with its "chills" and "grippes."

The seasonal pattern of burials was even stronger than those of conceptions and marriages. There is a striking regularity in all these patterns, with the similar marriage and burial cycles complementing the conception cycle. Nuestra Señora del Prado's seasonal pattern is more extreme than San Pedro's for both marriages and conceptions. If the figures are sufficiently representative, the difference could be due to an economic or social disparity between the two parishes. Nuestra Señora del Prado was the poorer parish overall, and its residents would have been more affected by monthly and yearly economic changes. They also might have adhered more closely to the dictates of the church.

If we turn to long-term trends of vital events, Ciudad Real shows a pattern similar to that for all Spain, at least in its overall shape. Baptismal records suggest a rising population from about 1525 to about 1575. In both parishes baptisms faltered in the last decades of the sixteenth century and experienced a sharp and jagged downward trend in the first quarter of the seventeenth century. Although the two trends are markedly similar, Nuestra Señora del Prado hit its nadir in 1610, recovered briefly, and had a further setback in 1620; San Pedro showed a more or less steady downturn until 1625. After 1625 San Pedro experienced a rising birth curve during the 1630s, 1640s, and 1650s, although marked by wide fluctuations from year to year. This upward trend peaked about 1660, to be followed by a downturn lasting a decade. The records for Nuestra Señora del Prado resume in 1664 after a hiatus of thirty-seven years. In the interim, the parish had increased considerably in size, so that its births equaled the level of the first years of the century. Both parishes showed a marked rise in births between 1679 and 1683, and severe declines in 1684 and 1685. After 1685 both parishes recovered, Nuestra Señora del Prado beyond its early-century figures, San Pedro nearly to its third-quarter level.

It is likely that the overall population of the city followed these broad trends, though that cannot be inferred from the baptismal figures alone. Fertility in the total population may have fluctuated over the years, but this cannot be precisely calculated without firm figures for the total population and without registers complete enough for family reconstitution. I have relied on a simple ratio of births to marriages as an indicator of marital fertility. Using overlapping ten-year spans,[7] I divided total births by total marriages—for example, births from 1605 to 1614 divided by marriages from 1600 to 1609. Unfortunately, the first calculations possible coincide with the arrival of over 3,000 Moriscos relocated from Granada in 1571. Since many of the arrivals were young married couples, they would have immediately added to recorded baptisms (assuming they registered their children) without adding to marriages. Predictably, the ratio for the one parish with complete data shows very high fertility, close to thirteen births for every marriage from 1577 to 1586. The Moriscos may have had a higher fertility ratio than the rest of the population, certainly a charge made against them by their detractors. It is also possible that this period saw higher overall fertility in the city's population, in response to a local economic boom. The fertility ratios in both parishes were at moderate levels in the 1580s and 1590s, and they dipped below what I defined as a crisis point—3.10—in the decade 1598-1607. They would hold at this low level for the early decades of the seventeenth century. Since the Moriscos were not expelled until 1610, it is unlikely that their expulsion was the only cause of the fertility decline of the early seventeenth century.

San Pedro's fertility ratio again fell below 3.10 from 1644 to 1655 and those of both parishes fell again several decades later—between 1682 and 1692 in San Pedro and between 1677 and 1690 in Nuestra Señora del Prado. Since the rest of the figures for the century were relatively stable, these drops in the fertility ratio probably denote times of demographic crisis in Ciudad Real in the seventeenth century. Fertility ratios in the first half of the eighteenth century were generally stable between 3.50 and 5.50 in both parishes, according to the figures compiled by López-Salazar.[8] Only in the five-year period 1710-1714 did they fall below my designated crisis point of 3.10.

Altogether, then, baptismal curves and fertility ratios suggest several probable distress periods in Ciudad Real, defined broadly as 1600-1625, 1644-1655, 1677-1690, and 1710-1714. The mortality curves provide further evidence. The obvious peak years for mortality in the seventeenth century were 1653, 1660, 1667, 1678, and 1684-1685 for the only records we have. In the early eighteenth century the obvious peak years were 1708-1710, 1726-1727, and 1739-1740, with lesser peaks in 1720, 1735, and the mid-1740s. Infant and child mortality generally followed the same trends as adult mortality, but with wider year-to-year variations.[9] According to Pierre Goubert, periods of demographic distress of any sort cannot be called true crises unless they show a doubling of mortality and at least a one-third drop in conceptions. For Jean Meuvret, however, a negative ratio of births to deaths was sufficient to indicate a subsistence crisis, and such ratios are also good indications of other di-

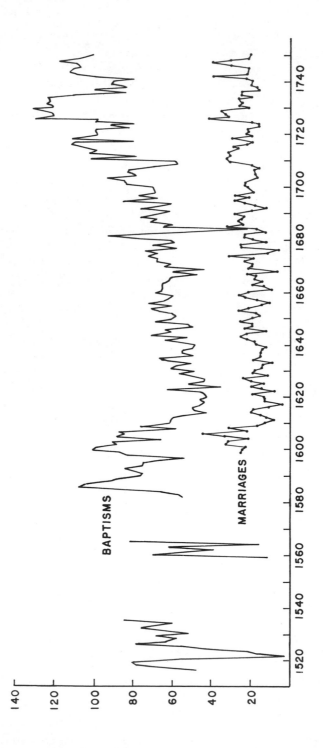

Figure 2.2 Marriages and baptisms, San Pedro.

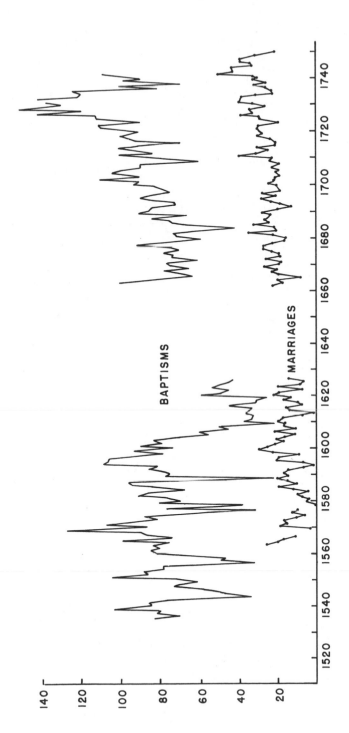

Figure 2.3. Marriages and baptisms, Nuestra Señora del Prado.

sasters in the population.[10] In the years for which birth and death information both exist, eleven show a negative ratio in the parish of Nuestra Señora del Prado: 1667-1668, 1684-1685, 1708-1710, 1726, and 1738-1740. There are three such years in San Pedro (1708-1710), and several other years approach unity in both parishes. In general, then, the burial registers support the existence of crises in many years I have identified, and they also direct our attention to various years in the 1660s, 1720s, 1730s, and 1740s as probable distress periods.

The parish registers, unfortunately, are not complete for the entire period, and they cover only two of the city's three parishes. Nonetheless, their general trends agree well with the few reliable estimates we have of the city's total population. Elsewhere I have discussed the plausibility of fifteen official estimates of Ciudad Real's population between 1527 and 1751.[11] Here I will use only the most trustworthy ones, listed in Table 2.3. The figures agree with the changes in population indicated by the parish registers from 1530 to 1621, but they provide no help for an analysis of the periods of distress I have identified. There is ample reason to investigate these periods more closely, however, for the light they may shed on Ciudad Real's economy.

Even with very high fertility rates, the tendency of an Old Regime population was to replace itself and no more, thus balancing the total population with the food supply. This balance often resulted from extremes of hardship and privation, and if ordinary people were aware of the symmetry of nature, they could hardly have been comforted by it. Many, perhaps most, demographic crises were related to scarcities of food, usually called subsistence crises. In the work of Pierre Goubert and Bartolomé Bennassar, the marriage figures tended to fall sharply during the first phase of a subsistence crisis; then they recovered and rose higher than normal as survivors of the crisis remarried.[12] Conceptions (or viable, fruitful conceptions, since we have figures only for those conceptions that resulted in live births) behaved rather differently. Early in a crisis, viable conceptions fell drastically, sometimes by as much as two-thirds or more, and minimum conceptions nearly always coincided with maximum deaths. Since conceptions recovered much faster than marriages, they probably occurred within already established families, rather than in the recent crisis remarriages.

Many things affected the ability of women to reproduce during hard times. Even a limited food shortage might curtail new marriages and perhaps limit conjugal relations as well (although this is far from clear). A real famine would limit the ability of women to conceive and would increase the numbers of natural abortions, stillbirths, and infant deaths— all of which would lower the conception figures as I define them. They would recover quite rapidly once the worst was over; infant deaths and

Table 2.3. Estimated number of householders in Ciudad Real.

Date	Taxpaying householders	Total householders	Note numbers
1527	1,146[a]	(1,252)	12
1557	—	1,810[b]	13
1591	1,865[c]	(2,037)	14
1621	—	1,200[d]	15
1751	1,549[e]	1,200	16

a. AGS, *CG*, leg. 768. The figures for total householders, when they appear in parentheses, are calculated by the method used in Ruiz Martín, "Población española." Otherwise they are given in the source cited.

b. AGS, *CG*, leg. 2304.

c. Ruiz Martín, "Población española," table following p. 202. The same figure is given in AMCR, doc. 344 for 1735.

d. Inocente Hervás y Buendía, *Diccionario histórico geográfico . . . de Ciudad Real* (Ciudad Real, 1890), p. 221.

e. Isabel Pérez Valera, ed., *Ciudad Real en el siglo XVIII* (Ciudad Real, 1955). This is a tabular summary of local responses to the *Catastro de Ensenada*. Before her tragic death in 1976, Isabel Pérez was engaged in a detailed analysis of these local responses.

natural abortions during the crisis, by shortening the normal period of pregnancy and lactation, would enable women to conceive again in a shorter time than usual.

Conscious birth control could also lower marital fertility, and indirect evidence suggests that at least part of the population of Habsburg Spain voluntarily limited marital fertility at one time or another. Tomás Sánchez (1550-1610), a Spanish Jesuit, listed several practices that were condemned by the church. Among them were coitus interruptus, potions to induce sterility, and the use of unnatural positions for intercourse. Although Sánchez recognized the need to avoid procreation during bad times, it was still a venial (minor) sin if the sex act was not consummated to avoid conception. On the other hand, it was a mortal (serious) sin for a man to intentionally waste the semen or release it anywhere but in its natural receptacle or for a woman to try to expel the semen after intercourse, whether by urination or any other means. Nothing, not even economic necessity, could excuse such acts. It is obvious that the Roman Catholic church had a fully elaborated and explicit doctrine against contraception by the early seventeenth century, and possibly even earlier. Philippe Ariès wrote that this doctrine was for the sake of theoretical formulation alone and not to combat existing practices.[13] It is more logical to assume that the forbidden practices did exist and that they were sufficiently widespread to alarm the church. In numerical terms, we cannot be certain what this meant, but the possibility of contraception as early as the seventeenth century in Spain cannot be lightly dismissed, particularly when we are analyzing times of demographic crisis.

Pestilence provided the most dramatic and terrifying scourge of Old Regime populations. Disease often followed in the wake of harvest shortages, but historians still have not proved that there is a necessary connection between them. That each played roles of varying importance in particular crises, however, is well established. I will try to take all contributing causes into account in analyzing demographic crises in Ciudad Real.

The first quarter of the seventeenth century is the first major period of distress for which we have good records. There was no single nexus of crisis, but rather a recurrence of bad years and conditions unfavorable for the recovery of the population once a downward trend had begun. The first sharp decline in marriages and conceptions occurred in both parishes about 1604-1605. The monthly conception figures from San Pedro experienced a sharp decline in 1604, roughly from May until year's end. The figures recovered sharply in January 1605 and remained strong. Conceptions showed a new downturn in 1608, again beginning in May. Thereafter the trend was steadily downward until 1625. San Pedro's marriage curve hit low points in 1612, 1618, and 1623, with the losses spread more or less evenly throughout the year. In Nuestra Señora del Prado, the conception figures declined from 1604 to at least 1615, with an absolute low point in 1612. Again in 1614, 1617, and 1619, the conception figures returned nearly to their 1612 nadir. Low totals were particularly noticeable in months that would normally have shown a substantial number of conceptions. After 1619, the conception curve of Nuestra Señora del Prado began what appears to have been a recovery before the gap in the registers. Marriages hit lows in 1613, 1614, 1617, 1623, and 1625 in a downward trend dating from about 1606. In the low years, losses were heaviest in the summer and fall.

What accounts for this unmistakable pattern of demographic distress? In the absence of mortality figures for either parish in this period, there is no way to know if the plague of 1596-1602 affected Ciudad Real. Its incidence was heaviest in northern and central Castile, and Antonio Domínguez Ortiz estimates that 500,000 people died in all.[14] In the south, Seville was so hard hit by this plague that Ruth Pike calls it the turning point in the demographic history of Andalusia's greatest port.[15] The plague could have spread inland from Seville, arriving in Ciudad Real in 1604. There is, however, no evidence that it did. In both parishes marriage and conception totals were strong until 1604, and the decline thereafter was more steady than the abrupt drop we would expect from an epidemic.

Short-term climatic events and harvests are more suggestive. Unusual winters (1603-1604 and 1604-1605) in Old Castile and Andalusia might indicate poor harvest conditions all over Spain.[16] We do not have wheat prices for 1605, but those for 1606 and 1607 were high enough to indicate harvest failures in New Castile, including Ciudad Real. A royal letter to the corregidor in 1606 mentions a harvest failure the previous year, and there is also evidence of distress in the large number of grain loans from the public granary (*pósito*).[17] At least in part, the demographic distress of the city from 1604 to 1607 can be attributed to poor harvest conditions and consequent grain shortages and high prices.

The single most important ingredient in the city's quarter-century distress was the expulsion of the Moriscos, decreed in 1610 and carried out over several years. Before the expulsion there were 612 Morisco households in Ciudad Real (2,000-3,000 persons), according to local officials, and in 1581 there may have been as many as 3,263.[18] Inocente Hervás claimed that 5,000 Moriscos were expelled from Ciudad Real by 1613, and since "they were all farmers, the fields lay fallow and uncultivated, and the population [was] reduced to great austerity and poverty."[19] It seems more reasonable that the loss was between 2,000 and 3,000, and it is highly debatable that all the Moriscos in Ciudad Real were farmers. Nonetheless, their expulsion was a sharp blow to a city with fewer than 10,000 persons.[20] By 1621, houses in the neighborhood near Nuestra Señora del Prado had been vacant "many years . . . through a lack of inhabitants that is notorious and they are on the point of being lost through not having anyone to inhabit them and through the city having few householders since the expulsion of the Moriscos."[21] Whether or not the lament was true, it was common in the decades after the expulsion.

The decline in marriages and conceptions in Ciudad Real from 1610 onward also related to adverse agricultural conditions. In 1609 there were scores of grain loans from the pósito during the late spring and fall, indicating short harvests in 1608 and 1609.[22] In 1615-16 an extreme drought hit Spain, accompanied by locust plagues in some areas. Valladolid suffered a subsistence crisis, and Earl J. Hamilton found substantially higher wheat prices in New Castile from 1615 to 1617.[23] In Ciudad Real locusts were a chronic problem from 1618 to 1622, and in 1619 they were responsible for a harvest failure.[24] The very low marriage totals in the city's parishes in 1617-18 and again in 1623-1626 may also have been related to local agricultural distress. We know, for example, that flooding and high winds visited Ciudad Real and other parts of New Castile and Andalusia in February 1626. If that was followed by a cold, humid spring and summer, as one author reported, the harvest might have been severely curtailed.[25]

The danger of harvest failure was habitual, of course, and short harvests can often explain fluctuations in the vital curves in Ciudad Real. In general, however, it was the presence or absence of pestilence that separated a major population crisis from a lesser one. The mid-century distress in Ciudad Real—from 1644 to 1655—did not lack any of the elements of a major crisis. The harvests of 1647 were the worst of the century in relative terms, and a terrible epidemic began in that same year in Valencia, eventually spreading all over the Levant and Andalusia. Its virulence and geographical extent are well documented.[26] Because of the memory of earlier plagues, an attempt was made to seal Andalusia off from its northern neighbors across the Sierra Morena, and, except for a few isolated incidents, central Castile was reputedly saved from the 1647-1652 contagion.[27] This is difficult to prove or disprove for Ciudad Real, since continuous mortality records do not begin until mid-1649. It is interesting to note, however, that in the five months reported for 1649 (August-December), the parish of Nuestra Señora del Prado had a suspiciously high number of deaths; the toll for 1653 was also elevated. San Pedro's marriage curve fell off noticeably throughout 1646; conceptions dropped also, beginning in the summer and fall of 1647 and recovering only in 1650. In Nuestra Señora del Prado marriages fell considerably in 1648 in all months and recovered briskly in the following year.

If the pestilence did reach Ciudad Real, the effects were much less severe than in Andalusia. Even so, the city was affected after 1645 by locusts and by the high prices for commodities that attended poor harvests, quarantine restrictions on commerce, and the depreciation of *vellón* (copper coinage).[28] Many short-term loans from citizens of Ciudad Real to residents of the surrounding countryside in early 1651 indicate the economic distress of the area.[29] Therefore, the mid-century demographic distress in Ciudad Real appears to have been related to hardship in all of Spain, aggravated by the dread, and perhaps the real presence, of pestilence.

About the middle of the seventeenth century, European agriculture began a slump that lasted for a century,[30] with increasingly frequent bad harvests and ruinous variations in prices. In Spain the situation was made worse by local restrictions placed on the internal grain trade and the low state to which agriculture had already sunk since the end of the sixteenth century. Nonetheless, the 1650s were relatively good times for Spanish agriculture, which accelerated a downward movement in all prices. Price and harvest data, therefore, do not explain why marriages in the two parishes showed a cyclical low point in 1657, why adult mortality was exceptionally high in the winter of 1659-60, or why the conceptions for both parishes were unaffected in that same winter. That these were adult winter deaths suggests pneumonia or even typhus, but this is only a guess.

The early 1660s experienced generally stable prices, despite official alterations in the money supply. Between 1664 and 1669, on the other hand, prices rose to their highest level since 1650 in both Castiles and in Andalusia, largely due to harvest failures.[31] This corresponds to the symptoms of demographic distress that appeared in the parish registers during the 1660s. Marriages declined at San Pedro in 1662, especially from early spring through summer. Conceptions dropped in 1663, with a particularly low count in April. Marriages slumped again from late 1668 through 1669, and conceptions uniformly declined in 1667 (spring to fall) and 1669 (spring) to their lowest points since 1624. By 1672 the conception figures had substantially recovered. The data for Nuestra Señora del Prado indicate that marriages and conceptions were adversely affected earlier than burials. The low point in marriages came in 1666 with a decline of more than half, spreading throughout the year; the curve recovered by 1667 to near its former level. Conceptions declined by about 31 percent in 1666—the losses affecting every season but spring—recovered briefly by 1671, then returned to the lower level until 1678. Mortality figures were unchanged until 1667 when they jumped a dramatic 120 percent (late summer and fall) and continued at higher than normal levels through the following year. The widely reported harvest failures between 1664 and 1669 were no doubt related to the altered vital curves in the city's parishes. Diverse local records mention short harvests from 1667 to at least 1671, and the mortality figures in Nuestra Señora del Prado for 1667-1668 suggest that this was a subsistence crisis. San Pedro seems to have been less affected, perhaps because of its greater wealth.[32]

The last distress period in the seventeenth century has the broad limits of 1677-1690. Like the first quarter-century, it contained a succession of demographic setbacks rather than a single unified crisis. The vital curves were stable after 1672 until late 1676 in San Pedro, when marriages dropped slightly, then sharply, until the spring of 1678. Conceptions fell in 1677 with declines from April through October. Marriages dipped again from fall 1679 to fall 1680. Conceptions also dropped in 1679 and 1680 to a point nearly 25 percent below the 1678 level. After recovering in 1681-1683, San Pedro's marriages fell again throughout 1684, returning to higher levels by about 1687. The conception curve was much more drastically affected, with an 81 percent drop in 1684, primarily from spring to fall. The curve recovered early in 1685 and maintained a relatively uniform level until the century's end.

In Nuestra Señora del Prado, marriages declined somewhat from May 1674 through fall 1675, recovered, and declined again from spring 1680 until fall 1681. Conceptions fluctuated widely during the earlier period, with frequent lows from March through October 1675. After a period of wide yearly variations Nuestra Señora del Prado's conceptions fell 50 percent in 1684. Thereafter, recovery was strong and relatively steady.

The burial curve provides the most dramatic evidence of distress in this period. Deaths rose 67 percent from 1677 to 1678, largely due to increased tolls in October and November. They remained relatively stable at a more normal level in 1679 and 1680, rising somewhat in the fall of 1681 and the summer and fall of 1682, and staying at this new high level in 1683. In 1684 the toll more than quadrupled for the year, with very high counts in summer and fall. The following year the mortality level remained high during the fall but it was considerably lower than in 1684. After 1686 mortality fell back to normal levels until the end of the century.

The reasons for this period of distress can be found in the Spanish economy. A series of harvest disasters in New Castile and Andalusia during the 1670s inflated prices for foodstuffs. Henry Kamen calls 1674-1676 the worst harvest period of the century in the south, particularly in Huete Province, La Mancha's eastern neighbor.[33] The climate contributed to these harvest failures on a year-to-year basis. Villalba described the 1670s and early 1680s as having a certain inversion of the normal seasonal climate pattern. Cold, dry springs; cold, wet summers; and hot, humid autumns were highly detrimental to grain and most other crops. Hamilton found that poor harvests continued from 1675 to 1679 in both Castiles and in Andalusia. Grain was so scarce in Andalusia in 1678 that officials refused to release any of the local supply to help other stricken areas. The peak of the seventeenth-century vellón inflation occurred in this period as well, ruining many people who were just able to get by in good times. Hamilton's commodity price index for Andalusia rose from 93.2 in 1676 to 124.7 in 1678. The general rise in New Castile was less striking, but wheat prices soared. In Ciudad Real a fanega of wheat sold for 50-55 reales in August 1678, which matched the rise shown by Hamilton.[34] Scarcity elsewhere in La Mancha was also severe. Almadén reported a very scanty harvest in 1677 and a disastrous one in 1678, continuing a long spell of bad times.[35] Pedro Galindo, a contemporary observer, complained that "in La Mancha, where not many years ago the price of two pounds of bread was three *cuartos* [12 maravedís], today a pound and a half costs ten *cuartos* [40 maravedís], and many persons, unable to afford it, content themselves with only garden stuff [*hierbas*], like carob beans and other similar vegetables."[36]

This situation was transformed into a major disaster by the arrival of a new pestilence—probably the worst of the century—between 1676 and 1685. The first wave started in Cartagena and lasted from 1676 to 1681; from Cartagena it spread all over Spain. According to one report, "the voracity of the epidemic . . . was of such an evil disposition that it extended to the lands of Castile, where the cold climate and the fineness of the atmosphere have been a powerful fortress that other epidemics have not been able to assault."[37]

We know that the disease was in Ciudad Real and its neighboring villages in August 1677. The local clergy and religious lay groups turned out in force to beg heavenly intercession in the city's distress, proceeding through the streets behind a cart which bore the image of Nuestra Señora del Prado, patroness of the city. Shortly thereafter, the epidemic ceased for a time. It had returned by November 1678, and the religious procession on that occasion was hampered by heavy rains. Once again, the citizens' prayers were answered. The plague passed from the city and many of the faithful claimed that a miracle had taken place. In August 1679 another procession pleaded for the patroness's help against the plague; this time it was in Granada and Antequera and did not spread to Ciudad Real.[38] The several visitations of plague in Ciudad Real agree well with observed variations in the city's vital events.

Unseasonably bad weather and the consequent ruin of the grain harvests continued. Severe flooding and hailstorms were reported all over Spain in 1680 and 1681, alternating with extreme drought in La Mancha, Andalusia, and Catalonia. The earthquake that hit southern Spain in October 1680 added to the misery.[39] The years 1679 and 1680 produced particularly bad harvests in Ciudad Real, which contemporaries blamed on the extreme drought. The king's representative in the city government, Don Francisco Velázquez, purchased 4,800 fanegas of wheat from Extremadura for the municipal granary, which sufficed to feed the city during the crisis.[40] Ciudad Real's vital statistics responded to the hard times with lower marriage and conception figures, but the prompt action of the corregidor had saved the city from widespread famine.

A severe monetary crisis in 1680 further exacerbated the situation. To combat counterfeiting and inflation, the vellón minted in 1661-1664 was deflated to one-half of its face value in February 1680. Since it had already been reduced to one-fourth of its minted value in 1664, this meant that vellón was lowered to one-eighth of its minted value by the deflation of 1680. Price ceilings were set by the government before the end of the year to forestall yet another inflation, but this hurt the rural sector of the economy even more grievously and dislocated the remaining industry in Castile.

It was in this atmosphere of worthless money, bad weather, and worse harvests that the second wave of late-century plagues hit Spain. The years 1683-1685 have been called the "decisive watershed" of the late seventeenth-century crisis.[41] There were successive crop failures in 1683 and 1684. Many people who had borrowed grain from the municipal granary in Ciudad Real could not pay it back because of the continuing crisis and "the barrenness of the seed grain."[42] The city's population, weakened by hunger, was susceptible to the spreading pestilence, and La Mancha was one of the areas most affected by this second great wave of the disease, a fact borne out by the mortality figures in Ciudad Real. In 1684, 283 people died in the parish of Nuestra Señora del Prado. In the following year the toll was 116, in a parish that usually registered between 40 and 50 deaths yearly.[43] Marriages had fallen off several years earlier, at the start of the agricultural crisis, but conceptions dropped sharply in 1684, coinciding with the highest death toll. Marriages and conceptions in San Pedro followed a similar pattern.

There is no doubt that the epidemic was responsible for the severity of this last crisis in seventeenth-century Ciudad Real. Pleading its loss of people, the city joined with Toledo, Madrid, Soria, Burgos, and Valladolid to beg the central government for a remission of taxes. In a group of towns that suffered substantial losses in the epidemic, Henry Kamen listed Valdepeñas (Ciudad Real Province), whose population fell from 1,140 householders in 1683 to 708 householders in 1687.[44] The notarial records showed almost no land transactions in 1684, 1685, and 1686, and the overall volume of notarial transactions from 1677 to 1690 was extremely small in comparison with other times. Notwithstanding the short-term severity of this crisis, however, its long-term effects were not as serious as we might suspect. Ciudad Real's vital curves had begun a gradual recovery after 1625, and the 1677-1690 crisis interrupted their upward trend only for a short time.

The same pattern of slow population growth and periodic setbacks continued in the first half of the eighteenth century. In 1708-1710 much of Europe experienced bad weather, but the precise sort of bad weather varied from place to place. In Ciudad Real an excess of rain in January 1708, for example, caused flooding in the city and prevented the operation of grain mills on the Guadiana River.[45] High grain prices and excess mortality during the summer confirmed 1708 as a year of demographic crisis in Ciudad Real, related much more to climate and disease than to the War of Succession going on at the same time.[46] The winter of 1708-1709 was bitterly cold and wet, and the following harvest was very short in many parts of Spain, including Ciudad Real, where a fanega of wheat sold for 66 reales in July.[47] The war may have helped to raise prices, though bad weather was certainly the most important cause of the poor harvest.[48] It is unlikely that the weather had much to do with the high death tolls in 1720 and 1726-1727, however. Baptisms and marriages were not as much affected as deaths, which would indicate that disease rather than harvest shortage was the cause of the demographic distress in those years.

After about a decade of impressive population growth in the late 1720s and early 1730s, demographic crisis returned to the city. Again the difficulty was a shortage of food (perhaps caused by drought) and a serious epidemic.[49] The population was once again approaching the level of the late sixteenth century, close to 2,000 households, which seems to have been a maximum for Ciudad Real in this period, given the city's natural resources and landownership patterns. Although this would be very difficult to demonstrate conclusively, we do know that by the mid-eighteenth century, the population of Ciudad Real had reached the end of another upward cycle, such as it had done in the late sixteenth century. Then, growth had been succeeded by crisis and decline, and finally by a slow recovery to its former level. In the eighteenth century, the population would not be cut back but instead would stagnate at a level close to what I have suggested was its natural maximum. It would remain there until fundamental changes in the economy allowed it to grow again, but that, as the saying goes, is another story. What concerns us here is the early modern period and its cycle of growth, crisis and decline, and slow recovery, both in the population and in the city's economy as a whole.

THE RURAL ECONOMY

III

The key to the economy of Ciudad Real, and therefore to its ability to recover from bad times, lay in agriculture. In addition to noble and ecclesiastical landowners, well over half of the city's householders worked the land on a full-time basis, perhaps 25-30 percent of them as *labradores* (farmers) who owned at least one parcel of land and a pair of draft animals.[1] Some labradores, such as Dorothea's father in *Don Quixote*, might even be a good deal wealthier. In favorable circumstances, the labrador, like the English yeoman farmer, was ideally placed to be in the vanguard of agrarian change, but the circumstances were far from ideal in Ciudad Real.

The rest of the nonnoble agricultural householders were *jornaleros* (day laborers). Rarely owning land of their own, they had nothing to market except their labor and were vulnerable to the changing fortunes of the annual harvest. In Ciudad Real, this group was less numerous than elsewhere in Castile. Noël Salomon found that jornaleros often headed over 50 percent of the total households of an area, not just a majority of the agricultural households.[2] For the city of Ciudad Real, day laborers were 57 percent of the agricultural householders in 1751, but only 35 percent of the total secular householders. In a city, some landless laborers could find enough work in a craft to qualify as artisans rather than day laborers, even though they probably worked in agriculture for part of the year.[3]

The land that they worked, the término of Ciudad Real, had much in common with other plains areas in the western Mediterranean. Fernand Braudel stresses the unity of Mediterranean agriculture, with its trinity of wheat, vines, and olives on the limited arable land and migratory flocks on the extensive grazing land.[4] There is amazing diversity of soil, climate, and topography in the Iberian Peninsula—conditions that represent most of the variations of western Europe, not just the Mediterranean.[5] But Ciudad Real, the southernmost province of New Castile, is clearly within the Mediterranean world. Since Ciudad Real has a less continental climate than the plains of Old Castile, its winters can support the vines and olives, as well as the cereals, of the Mediterranean. An enthusiastic French traveler (1672) wrote that La Mancha produced a "great quantity of wheat in the beautiful level countryside that covers it, and such a great quantity of wine, of game, of chickens and of fruit, that they carry them daily to Madrid."[6] According to Rodrigo Méndez Silva (1645), the city of Ciudad Real was also "very abundant in bread grain (pan), aromatic wine, livestock, game, honey, fowl, fish, [and] fruit."[7] He was undoubtedly misinformed about the quality and quantity of a few of these items —notably game—but grain and wine would lead any list of the city's products. The evidence from neighboring towns reinforces the picture of a farming community devoted largely to cereals and wine.[8]

As a whole, the immediate environs of the city of Ciudad Real were stronger in cereal grains than in wine, with olive oil occupying a poor third place. The relative poverty of much of the land led to its use as pasture and to the special importance of hides and wool in the area. With these nuances, Braudel's augmented trinity of wheat, wine, and olives, plus animal products, is a useful framework for the agricultural economy of Ciudad Real.

CEREAL GRAINS

Wheat was the grain most commonly cultivated in both Old and New Castile. Next in order was barley, which was often mixed with wheat in baked bread. Though inferior in quality to wheat, barley could be grown on poorer lands and often gave a yield three times that of wheat. Rye, the third major cereal grain, did not match the other two in importance. Made into bread, these grains formed the mainstay of the Castilian peasant's diet. Their overall importance to the rural economy of both Castiles can hardly be overrated.

In the late sixteenth century, the largest centers of grain production in New Castile were in the provinces of Toledo and, above all, in the Manchegan plains around the city of Ciudad Real. "It is clear," Noël Salomon tells us, "that La Mancha was a veritable granary."[9] Classifying and extrapolating data from the Relaciones topográficas, Salomon defined grain centers as first rank if they produced more than 50,000 fanegas a year. In La Mancha, the cities of Malagón, Daimiel, Manzanares, and Membrilla, among others, qualified as first-rank centers. Closer to the city of Ciudad Real was a cluster of second-rank producers (10,000-50,000 fanegas a year): Alcolea de Calatrava, Miguelturra, Carrión de Calatrava, Torralba, and Fernán Caballero. Grain centers of the third rank (less than 10,000 fanegas a year) included Pozuelos, Bolaños, Luciana, and Caracuel de Calatrava.[10] Although there is no relación for Ciudad Real, the available tithe records (diezmos) indicate that the city produced 10,000-20,000 fanegas of wheat a year in the early seventeenth century, and a comparable amount of barley.[11] Thus it was easily a second-rank producer of grain by Salomon's definition.

The término of Ciudad Real contained about 30,000 fanegas of land in this period, about 23,000 of it cultivated. Cereal land accounted for nearly 74 percent of the cultivated land in 1751, the rest going to other plants.[12] To aid in analyzing agriculture in Ciudad Real's término during the Habsburg period, I examined about 800 land sales in the notarial records of the city for the seventeenth century.[13] Over half of the sales and 74.5 percent of the land sold was grain land—categorized as either tierra (literally, land) or quiñones (shares in parcels of grain land)—which agrees very well with the proportions of land use described in the Catastro. Of the tierra, 3,662 fanegas in 489 parcels changed hands over the century, for an average of 7.5 fanegas per parcel. Eliminating the fifteen largest sales left an average size of 5.0 fanegas per parcel. Quiñones were predictably smaller, about 3.85 fanegas in average size. Since there were only 136 sales of quiñones, the average size of all grain parcels sold was still large, much larger than those in Valladolid, for example.[14] The grain land had a very wide range in market price, reflecting the varied land quality in Ciudad Real. The best quality tierra could sell for as much as 14,000 maravedís per fanega, but the overall average was only 1,900 maravedís per fanega. The quiñones, which had a uniformly higher quality, sold for an average price of 6,000 maravedís per fanega.

Harvest yield is the best indication of intrinsic land value, but there are problems in calculating it. Five-year averages, or more, are needed to avoid the distortions caused by wide differences in harvest volume from year to year, and these are rarely available. Even when data are plentiful, we often do not know if production costs have been deducted, and the figures given may not be accurate. Were they deliberately falsified? Do they represent the maximum possible yield or do they perhaps reflect changes in the demand structure? The information available for Ciudad Real, even from a reliable source, can seldom be trusted.

With this in mind we can glean some idea of the output of the land in Ciudad Real from the general responses to the Catastro de Ensenada. The following yield ratios for 1751 are based on five-year averages of production, as estimated by leading citizens, and on the amount of seed reported sown. The ratios agree well enough with the overall estimates of Pierre Goubert, who found that yields hardly ever exceeded 11 to 1 on the best lands in the Beauvaisis during the Old Regime; during the seventeenth century they probably hovered around 8 to 1.[15]

First quality land (1,500 fanegas) produced every other year (año y *vez*) in a six-course rotation (one crop in 2.0 years):

Crop	Yield to seed ratio
wheat, winter	9.0
or summer	12.0
rye	9.5 (estimate)
barley (or grass for livestock)	12.0
chick peas	12.1
lentils	15.2
"pitos" (a vetch)	15.2

Second quality land (5,500 *fanegas*) produced every other year in a three-course rotation, then rested two years (i.e., one crop in 2.67 years):

wheat, winter	6.7
or summer	8.6
barley	8.0
rye	9.1

Third quality land (10,000 *fanegas*) produced every other year for ten years, then rested four or more years (i.e., one crop in 2.8 or more years):

wheat, winter	3.7
or summer	5.0
barley	5.3
rye	8.0

Although the yield ratios show a sophisticated use of first-quality land, overall land quality was poor. This meant that Ciudad Real probably produced about 22,000 fanegas of all kinds of grain each year in the mid-eighteenth century. This is a fair showing for the término, though it could hardly compare with producers such as Argamasilla de Alba and Manzanares.

The harvesting arrangements in and around Ciudad Real pointed out another disadvantage faced by the city's grain production. According to Manuel Colmeiro, La Mancha, along with the rest of central Spain, had to hire harvesters from the north in the seventeenth century, since the local people (so he believed) shunned an honest day's work.[16] La Mancha indeed had difficulty finding harvesters for its grain, but the reason had more to do with low population density than with laziness. Landowners in Ciudad Real often contracted for harvesters as early as May for the grain harvest, entrusting one or two men to arrange for the rest of the crew. The contract commonly included the wage agreement and enjoined the landowner to provide "bread, meat, wine, bone and other things that in Ciudad Real . . . are customarily given to the harvesters."[17] Harvest was in early August,[18] lasting about three days or until all the grain was reaped.

Once harvested, the grain passed to the threshing floors (*heras*) of the city. In the mid-eighteenth century only the first- and second-quality heras were used on a regular basis. Those of the third quality were not rented out for lack of customers.[19] Grain production may have fallen drastically in the eighteenth century, but it is more likely to assume that over the years damaged floors had simply been replaced by new ones.

Because of its location, Ciudad Real had little difficulty milling the grain. The Guadiana River powered nine flour mills (*molinos harineros*) within the city's término in the eighteenth century, six and one-half owned by wealthy householders or religious collectives of the city. Four other mills had once existed, perhaps as late as the seventeenth century, but by the eighteenth they had fallen into disuse. On an average, the eight mills produced close to 140 fanegas of grain in yearly revenue to their owners by the mid-eighteenth century.[20] There is some evidence that the mills had declined in value since the previous century. The mill named del Pedregosa produced 70 fanegas a year in rental from 1647 to 1657 and only 50 fanegas in 1751.[21] The mill named de la Higuera produced 145 fanegas yearly from 1690 to 1693, and an estimated 100 fanegas in 1751.[22] The apparent decline reflected a single five-year period, however, and may not be taken to represent a long-term trend. City residents continued to use local mills, and the small villages near Ciudad Real, such as La Cañada del Moral, also milled much of their grain at the molinos on the Guadiana.[23]

We know something of the crucial relationship between the grain harvests in Ciudad Real and the welfare of its citizens from the previous chapter. Given the uncertain harvests in the area, the municipal granary (pósito) often meant the difference between survival and famine in hard times, but there was an inherent contradiction between its dual role as a charity and a seed bank. When bread was scarce, the pósito's grain was sold to city bakers, to be made into subsidized bread.[24] This obviously jeopardized the next year's planting. Only in 1694 was a new pósito established solely as a seed bank, a donation of Don Alvaro Muñoz de Figueroa, an alderman on the city council as well as a familiar of the Inquisition and a member of the military order of Santiago. Don Alvaro had noted the distress caused to poor farmers in the city by years of bad harvests, droughts, locusts, and other disasters. To aid them, he set up a pósito with an original donation of 1,000 fanegas of grain, to be used only for seed. The secular authorities had no control over the grain or its distribution; it was administered by the deputy (*vicario*) of the Archbishop of Toledo, the prefect (*comendador*) of the convent of Descalced Mercedarians in Ciudad Real, and the founder or his heir. Due to the obvious need for the pósito's services, Don Alvaro added another 500 fanegas to his donation in October 1696; his niece and universal heir to the family *mayorazgo* (entailed estate) Doña María Catalina Muñoz y Torres added a further 312 fanegas in October 1725.[25]

All the donations were subject to the same restrictions. The grain was lent only to poor farmers of the city and its dependent villages for seed; if any was left over, farmers from Miguelturra, Alcolea, and El Pozuelo became eligible for loans. The maximum loan was 24 fanegas of grain distributed at sowing time and repayable at the following harvest with 4.2 percent interest.[26] In the case of default by a poor farmer, his debt would be shared by all the rest. The interest fees went to pay salaries to the hired administrator (*depositario*) and a notary, and nominal fees to the ecclesiastical patrons. Special care was taken to ensure that the capital stock of the granary would not be reduced. Money for needed repairs to the grain storehouse would come from suspended fees of the ecclesiastical patrons and an assessment among the borrowers. In a good year when no grain was lent, no salaries would be paid.[27]

Under the Bourbons, the secular authorities reabsorbed the direction of this charity, and in the nineteenth century the city, rather shortsightedly, abolished the pósito.[28] There is no doubt that the foundation had helped to avoid the ruin of modest farmers in Ciudad Real. When it was abolished, they were left to deal with unscrupulous money lenders when harvest failure threatened their survival.

VITICULTURE

"In all La Mancha there is very good wine," a seventeenth-century French traveler observed,[29] and his observation is still valid. The dry Valdepeñas red wines from north and east of Ciudad Real are often compared with French Beaujolais and Bordeaux. Areas of major wine production were numerous in sixteenth-century La Mancha, many of them clustered around Ciudad Real. Salomon's definition of first-rank producers (more than 1 million maravedís annually) included Miguelturra, Carrión de Calatrava, Daimiel, Villarubia de los Ojos, Membrilla, Manzanares, la Solana, Almodóvar del Campo, Villahermosa, and Campo de Criptana. Argamasilla de Alba was a producer of second rank (500,000 to 1 million maravedís annually); Villamayor del Campo and Villanueva de los Infantes belonged to the third rank (100,000 to 500,000 maravedís annually).[30] Tithe and tax records place Ciudad Real among the first-rank producers. In the early seventeenth century, the city's wine tithe indicated a yearly production worth well over 2 million maravedís. In the mid-sixteenth century wine was already so valuable as an export commodity that citizens of Ciudad Real were exempted from paying the *alcabalas* (sales tax) on its initial sale.[31]

In the mid-eighteenth century, the city devoted about 20 percent of its

término to vines and other noncereal culture, though the figure was probably somewhat less in the mid-sixteenth century. By 1751, each fanega of
first-quality vineyard, which contained about 1,000 vines, produced a
yearly average of 38 arrobas of wine. Each second-quality fanega yielded
24 arrobas and each third-quality fanega 14 arrobas.[32] If about 3,000
fanegas were devoted to vineyards (half of the noncereal land), the city
could have produced 42,000 arrobas of wine each year, even if all the
vineyards were third-quality.[33] Sancho Panza attested to the quality and
distinctive flavor of Ciudad Real's wines in his conversations with the
Squire of the Wood.

> "But, tell me, sir, on your Bible oath, is this wine from Ciudad
> Real?"
> "A rare judge!" answered the Squire of the Wood. "From no other
> place, that's a fact, and it's a good few years old too."
> "Trust me for that," said Sancho. "Don't suppose that I wasn't up
> to recognizing its quality. Isn't it good, Sir Squire, that I have such a
> fine and natural instinct for this wine-judging? You've only to give
> me a drop to smell and I can hit upon the place, the grape, the sa-
> vour, and the age; and the changes it's gone through, and every
> other point to do with wine."[34]

As in Valladolid, another famous wine district, most of the wine in La
Mancha was produced by small farmers. But whereas in Ciudad Real's
término an average vineyard changing hands in the seventeenth century
measured about 4 *aranzadas*, those in Valladolid were often no larger
than 0.5 aranzada.[35] (See Table 3.1). *Majuelos* had the highest average
unit price, probably because they contained many carefully nurtured
vines. Some of the older *viñas* and *parrales* shared the land with olives

Table 3.1. Viticulture land sales, 1600-1699.

Type of land and number of transactions	Average parcel size	Average price	First use of vellón	Sales of mortgaged parcels
Viña (vineyard) (105)	4.45 aranzadas	6,950 maravedís/ aranzada	1646	7
Majuelo (young vineyard) (51)	4.21 aranzadas or 1,730 vines	9,500 maravedís/ aranzada or 35 maravedís/ vine	1646	5
Parral (grape arbor) (54)	4.19 aranzadas	2,800 maravedís/ aranzada	1669	7

or other crops, separately priced, and a few had fallen into disuse, which lowered the unit price. The best viñas in the area drew a price of 10,000 maravedís per aranzada, but because of the wide range in price, the average was much lower.

A French traveler in the seventeenth century observed that "In this region they plant vines every five paces, and they work them with mules," and La Mancha already had earned the reputation of being a mule producer for the rest of Spain.[36] The use of mules probably helped the area meet the increased demand for wine in the sixteenth century. Mules were cheaper than oxen as well as better suited to the exacting work among the vines. On cereal lands, however, the advent of mules for plowing was considered a mixed blessing. Though mules could move faster than oxen, they were not strong enough for deep plowing, even if the frail Mediterranean plow had been suited to it. Some writers feared that the use of mules would decrease yields by failing to aerate the soil properly, and others predicted that widespread use of the frail and sterile mules would do great harm both to agriculture and to animal husbandry.[37] The debate was still going strong in the nineteenth century in Ciudad Real. Don Diego Medrano y Treviño, an erudite local citizen, reviewed the traditional arguments against the use of mules, but he concluded that as long as landholdings remained scattered and the peasantry poor, mules were the best work animals for Ciudad Real Province.[38]

OLIVES AND OTHER MINOR CROPS

In the sixteenth and seventeenth centuries, the areas around Guadalajara and the Tagus River basin contained all the important centers of olive culture in New Castile.[39] Nonetheless, olive groves (olivares) in Ciudad Real's término supplied part of the local need for oil, at least in good years. On a five-year average, each forty of the best trees produced 7.5 arrobas of oil yearly in the mid-eighteenth century. Forty of the second-quality trees yielded 5 arrobas and forty of the third-quality trees 2 arrobas. In Ciudad Real forty trees could usually grow on 1 aranzada. Based on this, Ciudad Real's unit oil production was less than half the average for the province of La Mancha in 1751.[40] The harvested olives were pressed in local oil mills, seven of them within the city walls and one outside in 1751. Five local nobles and one cleric from a noble family owned six of the total number; the remaining two belonged to convents in Ciudad Real. Though the revenue derived from their use was negligible, they did serve the local need for milling facilities and indirectly reinforced the control of the nobility and the church over the city's economic life.[41]

Other agricultural products were of far less importance. In the eighteenth century, some 550 fanegas of garden (*huerta*), watered laboriously by irrigation systems or by hand, produced some of the fruits and vegetables used by the city.[42] For the most part, however, the city relied upon imports from the Illescas area of Toledo Province and elsewhere, just as it had in the sixteenth century.[43] During the seventeenth century, some forty-five huertas changed hands, most of them in La Poblachuela to the southwest of Ciudad Real, others within the central city. The average size of a parcel was 6.9 aranzadas, or 4.9 if four very large parcels bought by a charitable institution are omitted, and most of the parcels were close to the latter figure. Huertas sold for a very good average price of 7,900 maravedís per aranzada, since most of them contained wells, an irrigation system, fences, a fieldhouse, or some other improvements.

A few fields were devoted exclusively to growing mixed grains for fodder. These *herrenales* appeared in only eighteen land sales in the seventeenth century, and few of them bothered to mention the size of the parcel. When they were measured, the herrenales were fairly small (about 2.5 fanegas) and had a value of about 2,700 maravedís per fanega, but the information is really too sparse to lend certainty to these figures.

Sumac (*zumaque*), a cash crop used in the curing of hides, was also grown in Ciudad Real, but its cultivation declined along with the hide industry. Only eight transactions of *zumacares* appeared in the land sales examined for the seventeenth century, with a parcel size range of 2-7 aranzadas. By the mid-eighteenth century, there were too few plants to bother collecting.[44]

LIVESTOCK

In the Habsburg period, La Mancha was considered a privileged zone for raising livestock, but that does not mean that the pasturelands were universally good or plentiful.[45] Because of unpredictable rainfall and blazing hot summers, the area could not support large numbers of animals for more than a few months of the year. For those few months—the fall and winter—the broad steppelike plains of La Mancha provided pasture for many of the sheep of Castile. During the spring and summer they foraged in the mountains, particularly in northwest Spain, which even today is the area of greatest livestock concentration. But the winters there were too cold, and the association of sheep owners (the Mesta) found fall and winter pasture for them in the milder climate of southern New Castile. The yearly migration of flocks along the established sheepwalks of the peninsula was a constant reminder that wool was the heart of Spain's export economy.[46]

The término of Ciudad Real lay between the central (Segovian) and eastern (La Mancha) sheepwalks, and passing herds paid a transit tax to the city. Their winter pastures lay further south, however, in the Valle de

Alcudia and in Murcia. Ciudad Real's término contained 6,000 fanegas of pasture in its total 30,000 fanegas, but this normally sufficed only for the work animals and smaller herds of its citizens.[47] They included most varieties of domestic beasts, with sheep and goats the most numerous, and a larger contingent of mules and asses than horses. The larger owners had to rent pasture outside the término for most of the year, an expense that lowered their income from livestock an average of one quarter for all types of animals. The best estimate of livestock owned by important citizens of Ciudad Real comes from the *Catastro* of 1751, summarized in Table 3.2. Since most of the animals were pastured outside the término of the city, only a rough estimate was possible, but even that was quite impressive. It is interesting to note that the two largest flocks of sheep, those of Don Alvaro Muñoz and Doña María Catalina de Torres, followed the ancient paths of the Mesta, and thereby provided a link between Ciudad Real and the larger world of the international wool trade. The much smaller flock of Doña Fabiana Sandoval was also migratory, but the document does not say where it found pasture.

The importance of livestock to the economy of Ciudad Real is clear both for the large owners with ties to the Mesta and for small farmers who owned livestock to work their fields and to supplement their incomes from agriculture. Tithes for sheep, cheese, and wool generally surpassed those for wine during the sixteenth and early seventeenth centuries, and they rose as wine values fell in the mid-seventeenth century.[48] It is far from clear, however, whether pastoral interests held back the development of agriculture in Ciudad Real. The identity of major livestock owners in the city lends some support to this hypothesis. Many of them were also major landowners and part of the ruling elite of the city.[49] Therefore, the people best suited to improve agriculture in Ciudad Real chose instead the surer returns of pastoralism. They even lowered their investments in land in the seventeenth century, as we will see in chapters 5 and 7. On the other hand, we can hardly blame them for acting in their own economic interests, and the difficulties of agriculture in Ciudad Real were not of their making. Land-use patterns identify Ciudad Real as a typical example of the Mediterranean rural economy. The lack of predictable rainfall and a low average soil quality held down the unit productivity of the land, and this was only partly compensated for by relatively large parcels for all types of cultivation. Climate and topography were especially disadvantageous for grain production, which occupied first place in the city's agriculture and in many ways determined the economic health of the city. Wine and olive oil were cash crops which offered a chance to link Ciudad Real to the larger market economy, but they could not substitute for local grain production unless a reliable market could assure the supply of grain from outside.

The basic dilemma of agriculture in Ciudad Real was thus the poverty

Table 3.2. Livestock owners and their herds: Ciudad Real, 1751.

Owner	Type of herd	Number[a]	Seasonal pasture[b]
Azañón, Juan de	sheep	170	Ciudad Real
Arenas y Pérez, Joseph	lambs (under two years)	400	Ciudad Real and elsewhere
Calcerrada, Julián and Antonio Dorado	sheep	200 500	Ciudad Real outside Ciudad Real
Delgado de Castro, Francisco	sheep	200	Ciudad Real
Crespi, Don Vicente	sheep	1,200	Ciudad Real
	mares	58	Ciudad Real, Yébenes
	mules and asses	60	Pozuelos, Ciudad Real
	cows and oxen	65	
Díaz de la Cruz, Don Pedro	sheep pigs	300 ?	Ciudad Real (w, f)
García, Don Joseph (*presbítero*)	sheep lambs	250 80	Ciudad Real Ciudad Real
Garrido, Dorotea and Joseph Muñoz, her son	sheep	200	Ciudad Real (w, f)
Haro, Don Diego de	sheep	250	Ciudad Real (w, s)
	rams	250	Villamayor (w), Ciudad Real (s)
	mares	60	Puebla de Don Rodrigo (w), Real Dehesa de Zacatena (s)
	mules and asses	60	Reino de Murcia (w), Ciudad Real (s, f)
Francisco el Monacho	sheep	140	
Muñoz, Don Alvaro	sheep	800	La Cañada (w, f), Argamasilla, Daimiel (w), Ciudad Real (f)
	rams	500	Malagón (w), Ciudad Real (f)
	mares	180	Pozuelo (w), Alcudia, Daimiel (s, f)
	mules and asses	170	Alcudia or Murcia (w), Pozuelo (f)
	cows bulls	200 100	Alcudia (w), Ciudad Real (f)
	goats	300	Malagón
	pigs	300	Alcudia (w, s), Piedrabuena (f)
	sheep with fine Leonese wool	15,000 or 16,000	montañas de León (s), Alcudia and elsewhere (w)
Muñoz, Don Diego	sheep mares	300 28	Ciudad Real outside Ciudad Real
Muñoz de Loaisa, Don Bernardino	sheep	300	Fernán Caballero
Prado, Juan de	sheep	80	
Rodrigo, Bernardo	sheep lambs	140 100	Ciudad Real Ciudad Real

Table 3.2 (cont.)

Owner	Type of herd	Number[a]	Seasonal pasture[b]
Romero, Tomás	sheep	350	
Sandoval, Doña Fabiana (widow of Don Juan Velarde)	sheep	800	Ciudad Real (w, f)
	rams	400	Cabezarados (w), Ciudad Real (f)
	mares	120	Ciudad Real (w, f)
	mules and asses	100	Ciudad Real (f), nearby villages
	fine sheep from Cuenca	2,000	migratory
Serrano, Joseph	sheep	200	Ciudad Real
Torres, Doña María Catalina de	sheep	400	Dehesa de Villafranca (w, f)
	rams	400	Pozuelo (w)
	mares	150	Alcolea (w, f)
	mules and asses	150	Alcudia or Murcia (w), Ciudad Real (f)
	cows and bulls	200	Almodóvar del Campo (w), Bolaños (f)
	sheep of fine Leonese stock	18,000 or 19,000	montañas de León (s), Alcudia and elsewhere (w)
Treviño, Don Diego	sheep	3,000	Ciudad Real
Treviño, Don Pedro	sheep	600	Ciudad Real (w, f), Miguelturra
	rams	700	Ciudad Real, Miguelturra (f)
	pigs	?	Maestranza de Calatrava
Treviño Calderón, Don Francisco	sheep	300	Ciudad Real
Valverde, Don Luis	sheep	350	Ciudad Real (s, f), Fernán Caballero, Ballesteros (w)
	rams	300	same
	mares	50	Ciudad Real (w), Campo de Calatrava (s, f)
	mules and asses	50	Ciudad Real (s, f), elsewhere (w)
Velarde, Don Juan	sheep	300	Ciudad Real
	mares	24	Ciudad Real (w, f)
Villaytre, the marqués of	sheep	300	Ciudad Real (w), Almagro (s)
Villaytre, the marquesa of	sheep	400	Ciudad Real, Almodóvar del Campo
	mares	30	

Source: AGS, *Respuestas generales*, lib. 468, question 20.

a. Minimum number of beasts 52,615.

b. w, winter; s, summer; f, fall; sp, spring.

of natural resources and a lack of efficient transport links and a reliable market outside the immediate environs of the city. The farmers of Ciudad Real had little incentive to experiment with new crops or methods of production in such a situation. Various sophisticated rotation schemes on the best land in 1751 show an awareness of the value of diversified cropping, but only within the framework of subsistence production. Income from livestock undoubtedly benefited some citizens of Ciudad Real and may have discouraged their investment in other parts of the local economy. It is not accurate, however, to blame the Mesta for agricultural stagnation in Ciudad Real. The major sheepwalks passed outside the término, and the city's continued right to tax herds when they did pass through its lands indicates that Ciudad Real held its own against Mesta privilege. In addition, about 36 percent of the city's ordinary income in 1751 came from pasture rental.[50] In sum, livestock raising was less the cause of uncertain agricultural incomes in Ciudad Real than their necessary complement.

INDUSTRY, COMMERCE, TRADE

IV

Industry, commerce, and trade occupied distinctly inferior places in the economy of Ciudad Real compared to agriculture. Yet each was vital to the functioning of the subsistence economy. Unless local agriculture could produce consistent surpluses, citizens could not afford to import basic manufactured goods from long distances. Therefore, a certain number of local craftsmen were needed to repair and replace agricultural equipment and to make simple consumer items. They, in turn, needed the income from a craft to protect their families against the vagaries of the harvest. If they could also produce articles in demand by outsiders, they might help the city to break out of the static patterns of subsistence production. Ciudad Real had some potential for industrial and commercial development during the early Habsburg period. That it did not develop this potential was due to many factors, some of them local and some related to the economic and political situation of Spain within Europe. Local commerce provided the lifeline for Ciudad Real and its neighboring communities, enabling them to purchase what they did not produce with what they did. Within strict limits, it was an efficient part of the area's subsistence economy, sustained (like industry) by its close links to agriculture.

The main source available for the occupational structure of Ciudad Real comes from the *Catastro de Ensenada* and its preliminary questionnaire, the *Respuestas Generales*.[1] The résumé of the *Catastro* listed some fifty occupations selected from the responses about wage earners and self-employed persons. The former group included artisans of all kinds, in addition to the agricultural workers discussed in the previous chapter. The self-employed persons included merchants and those in more minor commercial occupations, as well as the administrative and professional elite of the city.[2] Beyond that, no attempt was made to group individual occupations together by similarity of task. Even eliminating paupers and the disabled leaves most of the city's secular, nonnoble population in one undifferentiated group. I have grouped the diverse occupations under occupational categories such as agriculture, food-related occupations, and so on in Appendix B.[3] Most of the job titles were copied from the résumé of the *Catastro*, in which a single title often covered a wide variety of individual jobs. For example, *labrador* and *jornalero* included every type of agricultural laborer, and *administraciones* included a number of official functionaries. Judging from the more detailed, if less accurate, answers of the *Respuestas Generales*, a *guarnicionero* could be the maker of any type of leather saddle or harness fitting. Similarly, *herrero* described several different sorts of metal smiths; *carpintero*, craftsmen in wood; *albañil*, craftsmen in stone.[4]

ARTISANS AND LOCAL PRODUCTION

Most artisans specialized in a particular aspect of their crafts in Ciudad Real, giving the city a more versatile artisan population than even Appendix B indicates. In fact, the total of master craftsmen (*maestros*) and journeymen (*oficiales*) was much larger than we would expect for a city of 1,752 *vecinos* (householders).[5] It is probable that many of them were really farmer-artisans, involved in a craft only in the agricultural off-seasons. The rest of the time they farmed—either their own land or someone else's. For reasons that are not entirely clear, but perhaps having to do with a lower status for farmers, they identified themselves as artisans in the *Catastro*. The numerical importance of artisans and farmer-artisans in Ciudad Real was, in part, the natural result of the city's position as a trading center and the administrative head of a judicial district. But artisanry had also developed as an economic necessity, to augment the agricultural incomes of its citizens.

José Gentil da Silva, in his brilliant analysis of the Spanish economy, proposed that the agricultural income of a region in this period was inversely proportional to the importance of its industry, and he used figures from the *Relaciones topográficas* to illustrate his hypothesis. Around Ciudad Real, for example, agricultural income was low enough to suggest the need for supplementary occupations.[6] As we know from chapter 3, Ciudad Real was in one of the major grain-producing areas of Castile, though productivity was limited by poor soil and unpredictable rainfall. Large livestock owners could benefit from the extensive grazing land near the city, but the average peasant farmer had only a few small plots of farmland. In these circumstances, and given the wide year-to-year fluctuations of the harvest, many small farmers also learned a craft.

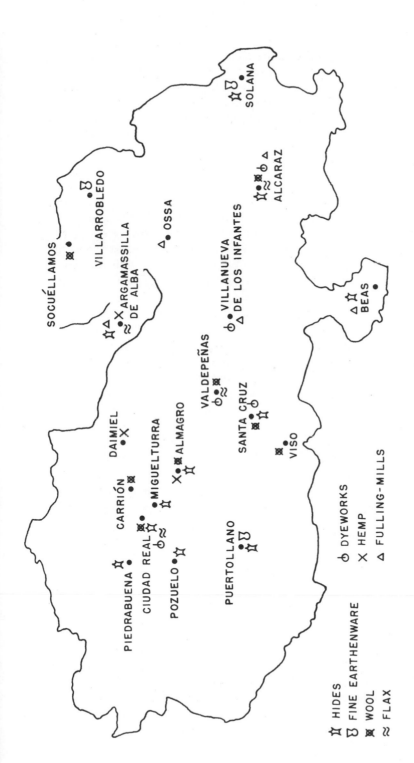

Figure 4.1. Industrial centers in the Ciudad Real area. (From María Dolores Marcos González, "Castilla la Nueva y Estremadura," pt. 6 of *La España del Antiguo Régimen*, ed. Miguel Artola, Salamanca, 1971, for the late eighteenth century.)

Another factor had impelled the citizens toward industry. Long and bitter feuds between the city and the order of Calatrava had disrupted both agriculture and livestock raising during the late Middle Ages. At one point a court decision awarded some of the land under Ciudad Real's jurisdiction to Calatrava,[7] and one local historian thought that this encouraged the population to rely more on industry.[8] Even after active feuding diminished, agricultural production was never high enough or sufficiently well distributed to eliminate the need for a craft to supplement the income of many farmers. With the sixteenth-century population rise, the need was even more urgent. Gentil da Silva estimates that by 1575 about one-third of the New Castilian population had to augment its farm income by artisanry to earn money for necessities.[9]

In all of New Castile, the Ciudad Real area had the highest proportion of wage laborers in the *Relaciones topográficas*, even with the city of Ciudad Real excluded.[10] Many of them were in the textile industry, though not as many as we might expect from the importance of sheep grazing in the area. But more important than the proximity of the wool was the ability of the area to compete for it on the international market. Demand for Spanish wool in the textile centers of northwest Europe pushed the price beyond the reach of Spanish industry. And, paradoxically, without royal protection few manufacturers could guarantee the wool supplies they needed. Although successive kings made efforts to encourage Spanish textiles, they had all but capitulated to the needs and wishes of the wool exporters of the Mesta and the merchant elite. To do otherwise would have alienated these powerful and wealthy groups. At least since the reign of the Reyes Católicos in the late fifteenth century, Spanish industry had made do with the leftovers. Thus, although there were small cloth industries in Membrilla, Almodóvar del Campo, and Puertollano,[11] as well as in Ciudad Real, they produced mainly coarse cloths for local consumption.[12]

Tradition has it that when Alfonso X founded Ciudad Real, he decreed the establishment of cloth manufacture in the city—for *bayetas* (baize) and *anascotes* (woolen twill).[13] For a time, the city may have tried to specialize in finer cloths. The Cortes complained in 1548 that Castilian weavers were not making enough cheap cloth for the home market and therefore prohibited the making of certain kinds of fine woolens. The weavers of Ciudad Real, along with those of several other cities, protested that they did not know how to make anything else and would have to suspend work. The protests were no doubt exaggerations, since Ciudad Real was known to produce some coarse cloths.[14] By the end of the century, there were two fulling mills (*batanes*) in the area, shared amicably by the citizens of Ciudad Real and the towns of Calatrava, and tax records suggest that textile manufacturing was flourishing.[15]

Textile and other workers of Ciudad Real were organized into numerous guilds that controlled production and played an active role in the corporate social and religious life of the city. Their official functions were regulated with the meticulous precision of brotherhoods everywhere. Even in such a small city, some specialized craftsmen concentrated their shops on a single street, such as the Calle de Cuchilleros (Cutlers' Street) and the Calle del Tinte (Dyers' Street). Inocente Hervás called Ciudad Real the industrial capital of La Mancha in the sixteenth century,[16] and local industry grew notably in the reigns of Charles I and Philip II, aided by the interest and support of the crown. The industries primarily concerned were textile and glove manufacturing, plus the subsidiary ones of wool and hide preparation. Philip II also ordered that an arms factory be opened in Ciudad Real in 1575, but there is no proof that it ever was put into production.[17]

Like textile manufacturing, the making of leather gloves had supposedly been encouraged by Alfonso X at the time of the city's foundation. The finely worked, perfumed gloves of Ciudad Real became famous, along with those of Ocaña and a few other centers, and they continued to supply the Spanish luxury market in the seventeenth century.[18] Four glovers in Ciudad Real participated in the land sales mentioned in the previous chapter, and one of them, master glover Antonio de Cárdenas, owned at least four pieces of grain land in the city's término.[19] This suggests both the relative prosperity of the city's glovers and the intimate connection between agriculture and industry among the city's residents.

By the late sixteenth century industrial growth was marked in Ciudad Real and its surrounding area, and a sizeable number of local inhabitants were salaried artisans. Some worked at their crafts full time, but others were farmers engaging in a craft for supplementary income. Population growth in the sixteenth century seems to have stimulated output in agriculture and industry at first,[20] though eventually it may have strained the local food supply, particularly after the arrival of the Moriscos from Granada. Industry then became a needed source of income for the city as a whole, as well as for individual citizens. In addition, there were trading links from Ciudad Real north to Madrid, west to Portugal, and southwest to the departure points for the New World. All of this made the Ciudad Real area potentially the most "progressive" industrial region in Castile by the late sixteenth century, according to José Gentil da Silva.[21] Unfortunately, he ignored several important obstacles to the industrial development of the region. Textile manufacturing was the only craft that could have employed large numbers of workers, but coarse local cloths could not find a market large enough to support expanded production unless they could be made cheaply and in quantity. This, in turn, would have required a uniform level of skill, a commitment to industry, efficient transport, and reliable marketing arrangements that were simply not available. Agriculture and artisanry were complementary pursuits in the region, both of them necessary to provide a surer subsistence than either one could have done alone. The involvement of Ciudad Real's artisans in land transactions illustrates this.[22] Short of massive investment and other incentives, the local farmer-artisans could not have been expected to change the only way of life that offered them a degree of security.

Commercial transport was another problem. Although it was adequate for the local economy, it was not suited to a large export operation, nor could it have been easily converted. The mules used for transporting trade goods were available mainly in the agricultural off-seasons; transport, too, was tied to agriculture and to the limited needs of the local economy. Full-time transport, the kind needed for an active export trade, would have been prohibitively expensive separated from its agricultural base.[23] Again, short of structural changes in the local economy, the Ciudad Real area could not produce its coarse textiles cheaply enough to capture a wider market.

The demand for fine Spanish cloth was already well covered by larger textile centers with sophisticated techniques of manufacturing and marketing. Segovia, for example, was the main textile manufacturing city in Habsburg Spain, with large capitalistic enterprises as well as smaller workshops. Altogether, Segovia produced about 13,000 pieces of cloth each year in the late sixteenth century.[24] It is unrealistic to suppose that the Ciudad Real area could have successfully challenged Segovia or other major producers of luxury cloths, and, by the late sixteenth century, there is evidence that the entire market for Spanish cloth had begun to contract.

In part this decline was related to demographic and agricultural pressures which limited the demand for manufactured goods within Spain. More serious was the failure of Spanish goods to compete in the international market, a failure often blamed upon increasing labor and raw-materials costs and the power of the guilds.[25] Even within Spain cheaper and better foreign products were allowed to flood the market, with the predictable consequence that many local industries were ruined. Woolen and linen manufactures in Toledo fell precipitously in the first quarter of the seventeenth century.[26] In 1655 there were reports of industrial ruin from all over Spain, including Toledo, Córdoba, Seville, Granada, and Valencia.[27] Some important craft guilds seem to have vanished, according to the contemporary observer Francisco Martínez de Mata. He blamed the incursions of foreign merchandise into the Spanish and Indies markets for this decline and said that even the famous gloves of Ocaña and elsewhere were being displaced by foreign products.[28]

Ciudad Real's glove industry did manage to survive, but figures for the alcabalas hint at overall production declines in the seventeenth century in the city's industry. The alcabalas for Ciudad Real and its partido were compounded during the reign of Charles I so that they no longer fluctuated along with actual sales.[29] Still, the relative weight of various parts of the tax indicates the importance of industry in the late sixteenth century.[30] Textiles (*paños*) were the most important manufactured products; hide and leather goods (*zapatería, salvajina*) and clay and wood products (*barro y madera*) also accounted for substantial parts of the taxes on manufactured goods. Since the figures were for transactions in the partido, we cannot be sure of the amount paid by citizens of Ciudad Real alone. By 1593-1597 they seem to have paid about 624,000 maravedís a year in alcabalas and *tercias*, and the whole partido paid just under 4.5 million maravedís.[31] By 1610 the city's assessment had fallen to 320,000 maravedís a year, and the partido's assessment was similarly reduced. In part this reflected a shifting of the tax burden from the traditional alcabalas to the new millones tax on foodstuffs. But that shift was itself due to the impoverishment of Castile's urban centers and their industries.

Ciudad Real's industry could not help but suffer from the sharp population declines of the early seventeenth century, including the loss of the Moriscos. Yet it is not clear how important a part the Moriscos had played in the economic life of the city, even if we reject Hervás's view that they all worked in agriculture.[32] After the forced relocation from Granada, Moriscos were at least a quarter of Ciudad Real's population.[33] That they were welcomed as new residents is a strong indication that the city's economy was still healthy in 1570; the corregidor specifically mentioned their value to agriculture, and it is clear that they moved into artisanry as well.[34] Indeed, many general studies associate the Moriscos with textiles and leatherwork almost exclusively.[35] Figures for the city's alcabalas between 1557-1561 and 1593-1597 show strong tax increases in cloth, shoemaking, firewood and charcoal, basketry, and vegetables— products that are often associated with Morisco workers. Even though the tax rates had nearly trebled in that period, the much larger increases for those particular products lend support to the idea that Morisco immigrants contributed greatly to the city's overall production.[36] When they were expelled between 1610 and 1614, this probably created dislocations in the economy, but we must be careful not to overestimate the long-term effects of the expulsion. Shortly after the arrival of the Granadines in Ciudad Real, the city's agriculture began to falter, along with that in the rest of Castile, even though industrial production held up until about 1600. It is evident that the Moriscos arrived—unfortunately for all concerned—just in time to aggravate an approaching Malthusian crisis. Still, they were able to fit within the local mix of farming and industry in Ciudad Real, and the abundance of land in the término meant that their presence, even in such large numbers, was not seen as a threat by the resident Old Christian population. When they were later expelled, they did not take irreplaceable skills with them, but they did take part of the tax base and the local market demand. In the short term, then, the expulsion probably affected local industry more than agriculture, but it is not likely that it did more than aggravate patterns that were already apparent because of the city's isolation and lack of efficient market links. It is even arguable that the expulsion was a blessing in disguise because it reduced population to match the contracted market for industrial products in Castile.[37]

By the end of Philip III's reign in 1621, textile manufacturing had practically disappeared from Ciudad Real, a disappearance hastened by unrestricted imports of cheap Portuguese cloth. The guilds of textile workers, which had been strong enough to oust the corregidor during the revolt of the comuneros in 1520, dwindled to nearly nothing.[38] Seventeenth-century monarchs could do little to reverse the downward trend, given the political and military situation in Europe. In 1682 Charles II rather belatedly tried to restore textile manufacturing by permitting nobles to own textile works without losing their nobility. His Bourbon successors used more active means to restore Spanish industry and commerce. With peace and generally more favorable economic conditions in the eighteenth century, their work began to have some effect.[39] In Ciudad Real the mid-eighteenth century shows some evidence of industrial recovery. Artisan guilds were well represented in the Catastro, and the large number of those in the building trades indicates that the city was enjoying a minor building boom.[40] Even so, industry would remain a distinctly lesser partner of agriculture in Ciudad Real.

COMMERCE AND TRADE

The roads traversing La Mancha have been there at least since Roman times, providing commercial links among the nucleated population centers and between them and the wider world. The main highways, however, tended to skirt the borders of the Manchegan plain or to pass north to south through Manzanares and Valdepeñas. Other roads, sometimes only sheep tracks, served the interior of the region. The secondary roads were notoriously bad in the Habsburg period, and they may have deteriorated thereafter.[41] A Frenchwoman traveling in 1690 provides our only glimpse of passenger transport in La Mancha, which was adequate if hardly luxurious. Passengers crossed the plain in large oval wagons called galeras. Each one had six wheels, an awning, and seats for forty travelers, and fully loaded it required twenty beasts to pull. Since there were few inns or hostels along the way, the galeras carried most provisions for their passengers, serving them as a kind of traveling hotel.[42]

Ciudad Real was connected to the Levant by a road from Alicante through La Solana and Membrilla, to the north and south by a road between Toledo and Córdoba, and to the west by a variety of lesser roads linked with the main highway between Madrid and Lisbon.[43] The north-south route between Toledo and Córdoba was the most traveled, but the western connection may have been more important commercially for Ciudad Real. It was along this road that the buyers from Extremadura and Portugal came to purchase agricultural and other products. In bad years Ciudad Real sometimes imported grain from her western neighbors.[44] The area supported several major fairs up to the end of the sixteenth century, including those of Luciana (September), Montiel (October), Daimiel (November), and Ciudad Real (April and August). In addition, Ciudad Real held a free market every Tuesday which was exempt from all sales tax. When the city petitioned the crown for aid in 1621, Philip IV limited his largesse to moving the market to Saturday.[45] Through these fairs and markets, Ciudad Real and the towns around it were able to supply most of their needs. For some products, a wider trade was necessary. The Manchegans bought fish and olive oil from Andalusia, fruit from Valencia, and iron from Vizcaya.[46] Even though the overall volume of trade probably shrank in the seventeenth century, local exchanges remained active and vital parts of the area's economy.

Bulky goods such as grain and wood often were transported in *carretas* (large carts) where the roads could accommodate them. Drawn by oxen or—more commonly in La Mancha—by mules, the carretas provided intraregional and interregional links between the various towns of the Castilian interior. Even large carting operations were seldom divorced completely from agriculture; the most active carting season remained the spring and late summer, when the animals were not required for work in the fields. Large carters in the *Catastro* were generally known as *traficantes*, or *tratantes*; smaller carters-for-hire were more commonly called *trajineros*, or *trajinantes*.[47] According to the *Respuestas Generales*, Ciudad Real had thirty-six carretas trajinantes, all owned by two persons. Each cart earned about 500 reales yearly during the summer carting season, or a total of 18,000 reales, based on a five-year average. The interesting thing is that both owners were noble, Doña María Catalina de Torres and Don Diego de Haro.[48] Doña María Catalina, who owned twenty carts, was the niece and universal heiress of Don Alvaro Muñoz y Torres, founder of the seed-grain pósito in 1694.[49] She also owned over 20,000 head of livestock and maintained the largest personal household in the city, with 167 servants. Although most of Doña María Catalina's income probably came from other sources, her twenty carts would rank with the more modest of the largest owners found by Ringrose.[50] Don Diego de Haro was the only professional carter listed for Ciudad Real, probably because he was primarily dependent upon carting for his livelihood. Based on his income figures, he owned sixteen of the city's thirty-six carts.

In addition, the city listed four minor carriers (cosarios), whose incomes ranged from 550 to 3,300 reales a year. According to Ringrose, cosarios were more numerous in Andalusia. Although they spent a good deal of their time in carting, they were not part of the privileged association of carters.[51] The Catastro did not state how many carts each cosario owned in Ciudad Real. Even if we assume that each owned only one, the holdings of Doña María Catalina de Torres and Don Diego de Haro would combine with them to give an average of 6.67 carts per owner in Ciudad Real. This was much higher than Ringrose found for smaller towns in La Mancha, higher, in fact, than the provincial averages for anywhere else but Soria and Cuenca.[52] This is not a surprising pattern for a large city in a sparsely populated region.

Local trade also relied on the cheaper but more cumbersome caravans of pack animals—usually mules and asses. In 1751, Ciudad Real listed four caravan owners ("trajinantes o arrieros con caballerías menores"), each of whom made an average of 1,300 reales a year, and one muleteer (arriero) who made 700. It is probable that these carriers were also involved in agriculture at least part of the year. With alternative sources of income for the carters and muleteers, transport costs could remain relatively stable, despite wide variations in the price of commodities. Even so, transportation costs might raise the price of goods by 20 percent, as Bennassar has shown for Valladolid.[53]

Within Ciudad Real merchants with wide divergences in income handled both local and long-distance merchandise. If we can believe the Respuestas Generales, the city had no wholesale merchants or brokers in 1751, though five persons "earned part of their money and wealth from [exchanging] the fruits that this region produces" with goods imported from outside.[54] Their average yearly income of 2,000 reales was much lower than that of the six major merchant shopkeepers (mercaderes tenderos). Dealing in "cloth, silk clothing, linens, spices, dry goods, and other merchandise," they earned an average income of 5,400 reales a year.[55] Four of the six, surprisingly, were nobles, clearly identified in the personal responses to the Catastro.[56] Together they earned about 18,500 reales a year, which was nearly 23 percent of the total income of all wholesale and retail merchants in the city.[57] Cristóbal de Serradilla, one of the two nonnobles, evidently represented a group of linen drapers, though the income of the enterprise was listed solely in his name.[58]

Two dozen other shops also served the city at the time of the Catastro, divided into three categories according to the annual income of the proprietor. The five men and one woman who ran first-rank shops each earned about 1,500 reales yearly, except for one who made 2,200. Six men owned second-rank shops that produced about 750 reales yearly. The nine women and three men who ran third-rank shops each made only 360 reales a year, or about the same as a journeyman artisan who worked 180 days at two reales a day.[59]

One of the largest merchants in Ciudad Real in the mid-seventeenth century was Alonso de Sevilla y Torres. Although no extensive study of credit was made for this book, numerous obligations to Alonso de Sevilla turned up in the crisis between 1647 and 1653.[60] They concerned a variety of items sold in his store, and one debt involved a bill of 7,000 reales, payable in two years. In 1652 and 1653, he was listed as a common councilman as well as a merchant, a sure indication of his importance.[61] Merchants did not have a high social status in Habsburg Spain or, for that matter, anywhere in Europe except in the Netherlands. The classic route to their upward mobility lay in buying their way into a more prestigious way of life, often by way of state service or lower bureaucratic employment.

This makes the strong participation of nobles in the commercial life of Ciudad Real in 1751 somewhat unexpected. Spanish law specifically forbade noble involvement in ordinary commercial ventures. Owning land and livestock were acceptable noble occupations, as was owning a textile manufactory after 1682. But traditionally, nobles were expected to shun all forms of trade or risk losing their special status as nobles. Obviously, this did not apply in Ciudad Real in 1751, any more than it had in Seville or Cádiz when the local nobility had an opportunity to profit from the vulgar exchange of goods.[62] Popular ideas of the Spanish nobility notwithstanding, they did not always shun productive commercial opportunities.

Just how long the nobles of Ciudad Real had been engaged in business is debatable, and again we are hampered by the lack of an earlier counterpart to the informative *Catastro*. The four noble merchants mentioned in the *Catastro* were newcomers to Ciudad Real, three of them from Burgos Province and one from Alava.[63] It is possible that their families had become noble only after acquiring wealth from trade, in the classic pattern of upward mobility. If so, they had departed from the pattern by remaining merchants, rather than commencing to live nobly as farmers and herders. There is some evidence that other nobles in Ciudad Real were involved in trade before the eighteenth century. In 1640 Francisca Treviño Carrillo Maldonado, daughter of Gonzalo Treviño Carrillo and Elvira Maldonado, sold her shop to Don Cristóbal Treviño Carrillo, her cousin and judge (*alcalde*) of the Santa Hermandad Vieja of Ciudad

Real.[64] At least the buyer, and probably the seller as well, was a noble and a member of one of the city's most distinguished families. There is no question that the major carter in Ciudad Real in 1751, Doña María Catalina de Torres, came from one of the city's finest and wealthiest families.

One hypothesis is that the nobility of Ciudad Real moved into trade during the seventeenth century as income from the land began to falter. Castilian nobles were already in control of the great wool export trade through their prominence as sheep owners in the Mesta. In commercial centers such as Ciudad Real, local trade would be another logical source of income for them. If all this is true—and the evidence suggests that it is —Ciudad Real's nobles were more like the merchant-aristocrats of eastern Europe[65] than the ideal noble caricatured by Cervantes's Don Quixote.

CREDIT AND DEBT

The trading arrangements in Ciudad Real round out the picture of its economy. Simple cash or barter sales probably accounted for much of the sales volume, but there are few records of these transactions for the historian. Fortunately, even the simplest of economies needs a certain amount of credit to give flexibility to the system and to assure its contin-uation in times when either money or goods is scarce. One form of credit was the *mohatra*, whereby a farmer in effect sold a future harvest in re-turn for merchandise.[66] In Ciudad Real the most common form of credit encountered for the Habsburg period dealt with simple purchases of food or other items. In examining the notarial records (*protocolos notariales*) of Ciudad Real, I came across several hundred letters of debt for grain. Some were loans by the city's pósito during hard times,[67] and the repay-ment terms were quite flexible. Others prescribed exact dates for pay-ment in full, with heavy penalties if the payment was delayed.[68] Without exception, the nominal sales price for grain in the documents was the official legal maximum (*tasa*), but we must assume that the real price exceeded the tasa in many cases.[69] Large quantities of wine were also bought on credit terms, often by wine merchants. In one case, no pay-ment at all was made until two months after the sale, when the merchant could begin to make money from his new stock.[70] In a similar manner, large quantities of olive oil bought on delayed payment terms were obvi-ously for resale.[71]

By far the largest number of simple credit sales involved animals and animal products. Work animals—mules and occasionally horses—ap-peared most often, and their terms of sale were generally delayed several years to allow the buyer time to make a profit with his new animals. The price of a working mule varied widely. The most expensive sold for

1,500 reales in 1646, to be paid off at the rate of 12 reales a day, beginning at a date in the future.[72] More ordinary animals sold for anywhere between 300 and 1,000 reales. Horses had a lower bottom price, and the most valuable ones were destined for show and not for work.[73] Sheep sales also contained long-term payment clauses. Wool-bearing animals sold for 16 reales in 1602.[74] Meat animals brought a higher price and had much shorter terms of sale.[75] Obligations for animal products such as wool, hides, and salt pork appear with frequency in the records. Their credit terms were much shorter than those for live animals.

Next to extended payment terms for the sale of merchandise, the *censo* was the most widespread credit instrument in early modern Castile. In general terms the censo was an annual percentage payment for a larger sum, but it could arise from a variety of situations. In the absence of public banks,[76] private contracts served a necessary role in alleviating short-term distress, financing expansion in agriculture and industry, and arranging long-term payments on fixed obligations. One type of censo seems to have developed in the mid-fourteenth century when creditors who had lost hope of full repayment for a short-term debt converted it to a fixed annual payment.[77] In Castile such debt conversions were usually constituted as irredeemable (*censos perpetuos*) or for the term of several lifetimes. In the sixteenth century the censo became a true instrument of credit, rather than a salvaging operation for lost capital. A growing population, the rise in prices, and general prosperity encouraged many people to expand their production, particularly in agriculture. They borrowed funds by selling a censo, or secured mortgage loan, on their property, often to local creditors. Increasingly, these new censos were redeemable (*censos al quitar*) at a fixed term, while the perpetual censos almost passed out of use by 1533-1535.[78] As long as prosperity lasted, the creditor had a good chance to recover his money for further investment. In Ciudad Real the large tax payments on the sales of censos and land in 1557-1561 indicate a lively market for capital in the local economy.[79] For mortgage censos the government steadily lowered maximum interest rates during the early sixteenth century, usually following a reduction in the market rate. In 1534 the legal maximum for new censos was set at 14,000 *al millar* (7.14 percent), but this rate could vary widely for other types of censos. The legal rate was maintained thereafter to help debtors, despite the changing economic situation of the seventeenth century.[80]

Other types of censos were not simple mortgage loans at all. Noble landowners might contract a censo as a means to arrange extended payment terms for dowries, bequests, or simple debt. In many of these cases, however, the censo mortgaged part of the income on landed capital, not the land itself. Thus, censos could be contracted even on entailed estates. Another interesting type of censo functioned like a quitrent or simple lease; for a fixed annual payment, the holder of the land in question could use the land, or even sell his lease to it, as if he were the legal owner.[81]

For the question of debt and hard times, it is the secured mortgage censo that interests us. Until 1550-1560, debtors could pay interest or even redeem their censos with little trouble, because of agricultural prosperity and rising prices. Seizures of mortgaged goods—especially parcels of land—for nonpayment were very rare; creditors even avoided them, preferring the interest income.[82] The end of agricultural and demographic good times hurt debtors badly. In the disastrous harvest cycles of the seventeenth century, the indebted peasant often found himself on the edge of ruin. When he could not pay his debts or his censo interest payments, he might have to forfeit his land and join the ranks of the landless day laborers.[83] Other classes of debtors were similarly hurt by the seventeenth-century economic malaise.

Many of the creditors for all groups of debtors were members of the ecclesiastical establishment and wealthy residents of the large towns and cities of Castile. They, too, were affected by the end of the sixteenth-century boom. Loans to farmers became risky business and some of them turned instead to government bonds (*juros*) or to short-term, high-interest loans to the upper nobility. For others, the land itself became a more attractive investment, not necessarily for income, but for enhanced social prestige.[84]

No systematic study of censos was made for this book, but many of them cropped up in the course of the search for land sales. Most censo holders came from the same two social groups mentioned by Felipe Ruiz: the ecclesiastical establishment and urban professionals and bureaucrats, or their widows. One group of eight censo holders in Ciudad Real included five religious collectives, one doctor, one perpetual alderman (*regidor perpetuo*), and a man whose wife was a Poblete, one of the oldest families in Ciudad Real.[85]

Industry, commerce, and trade in Ciudad Real were partners of agriculture in a localized subsistence framework. As a system, it functioned well enough in a stable situation largely governed by agriculture. When the land produced a harvest within predictable limits, there was sufficient seasonal transport to exchange goods between neighboring communities, enough money to purchase manufactured goods produced by local artisans, and enough money for debtors to meet the payments on short- and long-term debts. The difficulty came when the balance between population, resources, and distribution was upset. For example, during the sixteenth century, a rising population strained local food production and encouraged the expansion of arable land. This, however, limited the pasture available for the livestock that tilled the land and hauled trade goods during the agricultural off-seasons. In artisanry, a rising population stimulated demand and induced farmer-artisans to rely more heavily upon the income from their crafts, since pressure upon the land meant that some of them could not afford to farm enough land to feed their families. Within strict limits, population growth seems to have stimulated growth in the local subsistence economy, and this should have produced a marketable surplus in either agriculture or industry, a surplus that could have stimulated improved commercial links between Ciudad Real and its markets. Unfortunately the difficulties for improving and increasing industrial production were as formidable as those for improving agriculture. Local craftsmen needed powerful inducements to change their traditional reliance on both agriculture and industry. Without proven demand for their products, or royal support for new industries, the artisans and farmer-artisans of Ciudad Real could not concentrate on industrial production without condemning their families to an even more uncertain livelihood. And, just when Ciudad Real had reached a point favorable to more industrial development—in the late sixteenth century—the entire market for manufactured goods, and especially Spanish manufactured goods, was shrinking. In fact, the limits of expansion within the subsistence economy had been reached, not only in Ciudad Real or in Spain, but in the European economy and its satellites. Rather than continuing its expansion, the whole system contracted. Declining or stagnating population, lower agricultural production due to unfavorable climate and other causes, less demand for manufactured products (and therefore less need for commercial links)—all characterized the early seventeenth century in Ciudad Real, in much of Spain, and in at least part of the rest of Europe. The areas that were able to break out of the subsistence framework by a greater concentration on industrial production and exchange, notably England, emerged from the period of contraction strengthened. In Spain, however, the economy's ability to adjust to the new situation was hampered partly by topographical and historical disadvantages of Spanish production, partly by a royal policy that favored raw materials exporters and guilds over the needs of native manufacturers. The Spanish economy became a supplier of raw materials and certain agricultural products for the more advanced countries of northwest Europe. Internally it continued as a collection of localized subsistence economies linked by an adequate but limited commercial network. When the European population began to rise in the last half of the eighteenth century, other countries could absorb the increase and continue to grow. In Spain, population growth instead strained the delicate Malthusian balance of population, production, and transportation, producing what David Ringrose has called a "bottleneck" in the subsistence economy.[86] But although inadequate transport was a key element in this bottleneck, improved transport alone would not change things. A whole new system of production and distribution was needed to transform the subsistence economy into one allowing growth, a system that would employ the human and material resources of the Spanish interior with greater efficiency. Diego Medrano y Treviño saw this quite clearly for Ciudad Real in 1843.[87] The city and province of Ciudad Real had been locked into a static system of production and distribution in the seventeenth century. The condition of many people even deteriorated in the late eighteenth and nineteenth centuries,[88] especially with population growth after 1750. There was nothing immutable in the agricultural and industrial depression of the area, but to change it required simultaneous changes in agriculture, industry, and transportation. In the Habsburg period, without appropriate market stimulation and transport links, this did not occur. Instead, those with money in Ciudad Real adjusted their investments to the contracted economy rather than trying to change it. And the government was both unwilling and unable to help, because of its involvement in foreign wars.

CHANGING PATTERNS
OF LANDOWNERSHIP IN THE
SEVENTEENTH CENTURY

V

In Ciudad Real the power of seigneurs was weak in comparison with other areas in Castile. It is worth repeating that many farmers in the término of Ciudad Real were owners of at least part of the land they farmed. Others were farmer-artisans with added insurance against inflation and hard times. The lands of Calatrava surrounding Ciudad Real were classic areas of seigneurial jurisdiction, but the city itself was a royal enclave containing many free peasant proprietors as well as dependent landless laborers. We can therefore find most levels of society represented in land transactions in the city during the seventeenth century, the most interesting period in which to trace the reversion to a subsistence economy. Appendix C describes the sources used to examine landownership changes and how they were selected, defined, arranged, and analyzed. The land sales provided two clusters of information, one on the buyers and sellers and the other on the land. The first part of this analysis will deal with the interaction of social groups and land categories in the aggregate. Clergy and institutions, nobles, and nonnobles (the three social groups chosen) show very different patterns of involvement with various land categories and with landownership in general. The second part of this analysis will move closer to the people involved, focusing particularly on the occupations among nobles and nonnobles who participated in land transactions. Changing landownership patterns in Ciudad Real provide important evidence of the ways local residents adjusted to the contracted market for basic foodstuffs in the seventeenth century. They also contribute to our knowledge about the assumed increase in the concentration of landownership in that period.

Most of the buyers and sellers of common grain land (*tierra*) in Ciudad Real were from the city, and nearly all of the outsiders and outside land were from its dependent villages. There is no evidence that speculators had the slightest interest in the transactions. The tables in Appendix C show that clergy and institutions, as well as nobles, were disproportionately represented among the buyers and sellers of tierra, compared to their numbers in the total population.[1] In other words, tierra was already concentrated to a certain extent in the hands of the first two groups, especially the nobles. Of the twenty-nine largest transactions, four buyers and four sellers were clergy or institutions, ten buyers and twelve sellers were noble. Overall, nobles sold more tierra than they bought over the course of the seventeenth century. The figures for clergy and institutions were about evenly balanced, whereas the figures for nonnobles show them buying more than they sold. Thus, in nearly three-quarters of the transactions, there was a clear movement away from a concentration of ownership in noble hands.

The other category of grain land—the quiñones—had a rather different pattern. As in the tierra sales, most of the buyers, sellers, and pieces of land were from Ciudad Real or its surrounding villages. And again, the first two social groups were disproportionately represented among both buyers and sellers. But the gap was much narrower than for the tierra sales. The same pattern of noble disinvestment in land occurred in the quiñones, but gains were made by clergy and institutions as well as by nonnobles. The less extreme distribution of the quiñon parcels is natural, given the definition of the land category. The quiñon was more accessible to small owners than the larger parcels of tierra, especially in a region where tierra parcels were large. Quiñones may have helped owners to overcome the fragmentation of parcels in Ciudad Real's término, a problem shared by most other cities in Spain. By pooling resources with neighbors the owners could consolidate the tasks of sowing and reaping and still be free to dispose of their shares at will.

The three categories of viticulture land—viñas, majuelos, and parrales—had the most egalitarian distribution. Around Ciudad Real, viticulture seems to have been the preserve of small farmers throughout the period under study. This was also the case around Valladolid, although the parcels there were much smaller. The painstaking work of caring for vines did not lend itself to absentee landlords, or even to very large holdings. Of the three largest viñas transacted, two were only 10 aranzadas each and the third was 34 aranzadas. Predictably, a religious order bought one of the 10-aranzada pieces, the second was sold by a noble, and the largest piece was bought by an important escribano (scrivener). Nearly all of the other sales involved smaller parcels and more ordinary people. On balance over the century, clerical and institutional holdings stayed about the same, noble holdings declined, and those of nonnobles increased. Most interesting is that the viticulture land sold included more parcels from outside the término of Ciudad Real than any other land category, about 25 percent overall. With few exceptions, these lands were in the término of Miguelturra, Ciudad Real's nearest neighbor to the east. The rest came from other wine-producing areas close to Ciudad Real. There were also a large number of outside buyers and sellers. Over the course of the century they bought more land than they sold by a factor of 2 to 1, in many cases buying land outside Ciudad Real that had previously been owned by city residents. A plausible explanation for this is that city residents in the seventeenth century were pulling back from previous investments outside the término that dated from the sixteenth-century boom. In part this may have been an attempt to consolidate landholdings closer to home, but for some it was undoubtedly a movement out of land investment altogether.

There were 101 sales primarily involving olive trees in the seventeenth century, and many more with olive trees as an incidental part of the sale. Nearly all of the land, buyers, and sellers connected with olivares were from Ciudad Real, in contrast to the situation with vineyard sales. Olivares were usually sold by the number and size of the trees, rarely by land surface area. The range went from as few as 26 trees to as many as 400, but most sale packages were not far from the average of 132.

All of the large olivar transactions concerned clergy, institutions, nobles, or highly placed nonnobles. Overall, however, the buyers and sellers of olivares showed a social stratification somewhat less extreme than those in the tierra sales. Nobles declined in landholding over the course of the century, clerical and institutional holdings rose somewhat, and nonnoble holdings rose considerably. The unequal distribution of olivares thereby lessened over the century, although it remained clearly defined.

Clergy and institutions played a much larger role in huerta transactions than in any other, buying over half of the parcels involved. A single religious institution bought the four largest parcels and another smaller one. The forty-five huerta transactions also showed nonnobles divesting themselves of nearly 50 percent more land than they bought, contrary to their behavior with the other categories of land. One possible explanation is that huertas were often city lots for building sites rather than for serious horticulture. With wells, trees, and improvements, however, such lots classified as huertas. They were very attractive as investments or as building sites, and even in the depressed seventeenth century, religious institutions were prospering in Ciudad Real.[2]

A correlation existed between the amount of land transacted and the social group of its buyer and seller. The largest transactions in each category of land almost invariably concerned a noble, a cleric, or an institution. A correlation also existed between social group and land category.

The land categories with the most concentrated ownership involved a disproportionate number of clerics, nobles, and institutions. Considering all the categories of land, ownership became less concentrated in noble hands in seventeenth-century Ciudad Real. Clerical and institutional ownership stayed about the same, and nonnoble ownership increased. Zumacares and huertas were exceptions to this pattern, but they were not important enough to affect the total picture.

The shift in secular landownership from nobles to nonnobles is even more striking when we consider the individuals involved.[3] Overall, 76 percent of them participated in only one transaction, 14 percent in two, 4 percent in three, and 2 percent in four. In other words, 90 percent were involved in one or two transactions each, and 96 percent in from one to four transactions each. As Table C.4 in Appendix C shows, there was a pattern to the participation of nonnobles, clergy and institutions, and nobles in different numbers of transactions, though it did not vary directly as the number of transactions increased.

In the cases where occupational information was available, participants in one transaction showed the broadest range of occupations among both nobles and nonnobles. All those nobles identified by occupation fell into the occupational category of administration, professions, services, and health, defined in Appendix B. Besides twelve aldermen, there were two administrators of the salt tax, one physician, one royal tax accountant, one barrister, and one municipal judge. There were also twenty-five widows (all but six of them selling land rather than buying it), and representatives of the military orders of Montesa, Calatrava, Santiago, and San Juan.

The nonnobles involved in one transaction included representatives from each of the occupational categories defined in Appendix B. As in the noble group, the largest number of representatives was from the administration category, with notaries of various kinds the most numerous. After a considerable gap, agriculture followed administration in the number of participants, with farmers (labradores) accounting for nearly half of them. The only other noteworthy categories represented were apparel manufacturing and commerce, but the rest each accounted for a few buyers and sellers. In addition, there were forty-nine widows (thirty-seven selling land), and two university degree holders. Many noble and nonnoble widows sold land, suggesting that they were in financial difficulty, perhaps burdened with debt after the deaths of their husbands. In the short term, the land sales by widows represented a disbursal of accumulated capital, even though they increased the volume of sales and enabled others to add to their holdings.

With two transactions, the administration and agriculture categories had nearly the same number of participants, but farmers were more numerous than any other occupation among nonnoble buyers and sellers. Apparel and commerce were the only other categories worthy of note. Among the nobles, only the administration category was represented.

The break in the number of participants came with three transactions. All occupational categories declined in participants and the minor artisans were absent altogether. As we might expect, administration was the most numerous occupational category for the nonnobles and the only one for the nobles. Agriculture was a poor second in the nonnoble group and apparel was third. Even if we combine the artisan categories, their total was not equal to the administration figure; for two transactions, it was at least equivalent. Beyond three transactions, we are no longer dealing with occupational categories, but rather with noteworthy individuals who happened to have a particular occupation. The most numerous participants in four transactions were in administration or agriculture; the only artisans were a shoemaker, a silversmith, and a cord maker. The three nobles involved were all aldermen. Oddly enough, there were no nobles participating in five transactions, but the nonnobles included a tanner, a baker, a merchant, a farmer, and a notary. There was a shoemaker on the lists for six, seven, eight, and nine transactions; a tanner for nine; and a farrier for seven. The other participants in numerous transactions were either common councilmen, notaries, or merchants.

Among the more numerous participants, we can follow the careers of several individuals. Gaspar Dueñas y Mora progressed from being chief postman in 1669, to administrator and founder of a pious foundation (1689), to one of a fixed number of solicitors (1698).[4] Felipe Muñoz Delgado was one of a fixed number of scriveners in 1683 and a royal tax accountant by 1687.[5] Juan Treviño de Loaisa y Masa held a variety of public charges, from perpetual alderman (1689) and lieutenant of the king's representative (1691) to chief magistrate of Ciudad Real (1691).[6] Cristóbal de Ureña progressed through seven transactions, holding the posts of notary public (1651), depositor of the municipal granary (1680), and administrator of a pious foundation (1689).[7] Several other notaries managed to move up in the ranks of Ciudad Real's bureaucracy in a similar fashion. The most interesting career evidenced in the land sales was that of Juan de Rojas, the only individual who participated in seventeen transactions. Beginning as a merchant in 1628, he had become alderman and common councilman by the 1670s.[8]

Overall, frequent participants in the transactions concentrated more often on grain land than any other categories. This is not unexpected, however, given the large proportion of grain land in Ciudad Real's término. More interesting are individual specializations in one type of land, especially among those who participated in four or more transactions.

Two typical examples were the gardener who sold three garden plots in La Poblachuela[9] and the glover who bought and sold grain land exclusively.[10] Don Juan de Aguilera Ladrón de Guevara, a perpetual alderman of Ciudad Real and a member of one of its oldest families, bought thirty-one pieces of land in Alcolea, including sixteen grain parcels and thirteen garlic fields.[11] Another set of neatly bunched transactions was Felipe Muñoz Delgado's purchase of two olive groves and an oil press.[12] There are numerous examples of seemingly organized plans of land acquisition and disquisition which involve one type of land exclusively. In the case of purchases, there was often the notation that the new parcel "aligns the land of the said buyer" indicating that the buyer was consolidating as well as expanding his holdings. A larger number of multiple transactions dealt with several kinds of land, even though concentrating in one. Sometimes the distribution was more or less evenly divided between grain and vine lands, as in the purchases of Luis Muñoz[13] and the blacksmith Pedro de la Pina,[14] or between grain and olive lands, as in the sales of Alfonso Sánchez Cordobés.[15] The pious foundation established by Don Pedro del Saz Correa was the only large purchaser that concentrated in huertas as well as grain lands.[16] And Juan Cordobés, a master shoemaker, was the only person who concentrated in zumacares.[17]

Dealing only with those persons who named an occupation, city people controlled the land around Ciudad Real.[18] Persons in administration, commerce, and various crafts accounted for nearly all of the individuals with specified occupations. Those in agriculture accounted for a much smaller share. Of the participants in one transaction, for example, there were thirty persons in agriculture and seventy-three in administrative occupations alone. Furthermore, administration was the only occupational group among the nobles and the largest single occupational group for nonnobles. This indicates that urban investment in the land around Ciudad Real was carried out, above all, by the ruling elite of the city. Among the many nobles in this group were names belonging to the oldest and most distinguished families in Ciudad Real. However, the nobility of Ciudad Real declined in importance as landowners during the seventeenth century. Their successors in many cases, and the real beneficiaries of the shift toward nonnoble landownership, were the nonnoble members of the administration group. They outnumbered the nobles nearly 3 to 1 in the transactions, and a list of their occupations places them firmly in the ruling elite of Ciudad Real.

Another important urban group in the land transactions was the artisans. Entirely nonnoble, the artisan categories together accounted for nearly as many participants as administration. It is clear that artisans played an active part in the land transactions of the seventeenth century, buying almost twice as often as they sold. Among them, there were implied differences in individual wealth. The shoemaker who bought six pieces of land[19] and the six shoemakers who each sold one piece of land[20] were probably on different economic levels. However, even the latter could not have been at the bottom of the economic heap, if only because they owned land to sell. We cannot pretend to have a broad cross section of the artisan population in the land sales, or to know how many were full-time artisans, rather than part-time artisans and part-time farmers. Nonetheless, a significant number of those calling themselves artisans were sufficiently prosperous to transact land during the seventeenth century.

Even such tenuous evidence of prosperity in Ciudad Real contrasts with the view commonly held of La Mancha. Eighteenth-century travelers in the Manchegan countryside saw an endless tragedy of meager crops and exploitation of the common people.[21] According to Jean Sarrailh, rural poverty was the rule rather than the exception in eighteenth-century La Mancha, as well as in Extremadura and other parts of central Spain.[22] But the case of a city was necesssarily different. In Ciudad Real there were opportunities for craft employment at least part of the year for farmers; for those who were primarily artisans, farming provided the insurance against hard times. Artisan involvement in land transactions thus testifies to the diversified nature of Ciudad Real's economy as well as to the relative well-being of the city's artisan community.

Very few participants in the land sales called themselves farmers, and overall, less than half listed an occupation at all. It is reasonable to assume that at least some of the unidentified persons were farmers, perhaps even most of them. Without further information, no sure statements can be made about small proprietors in Ciudad Real, but the many complaints about the decline of agriculture in the city suggests that they shared in the plight common to the Castilian peasantry.

The standard hypothesis has it that peasant proprietors were slowly being squeezed from their lands by circumstances and that the land was becoming concentrated in fewer hands, usually those of nobles, clergy and the church, and urban bureaucrats. Until the sixteenth century, the small farmers of New Castile held a position in many ways superior to their counterparts in the rest of Spain. In part, this resulted from royal favors such as liberal town charters, land grants, and protection against their enemies, such as the order of Calatrava near Ciudad Real. In part, it resulted from the general prosperity of the countryside as Castile recovered from the Black Death. But the inflation of the sixteenth century eventually caused harm to the small proprietors of Castile. Their resources for keeping up with inflation were minimal, unless their farms were entirely self-sufficient. Otherwise, they were subject to a number of pressures due to rising prices. For those peasants who rented at least part of the land they farmed, one-third to one-half of the harvest might go to the landlord as rent by the late sixteenth century.[23] The famous arbitrista Cellorigo, writing in 1600, called the high cost of renting land the most active cause of peasant misery.[24] A bad harvest, a desire to expand his holdings or convert to a higher-priced crop, or the need for goods he did not produce could drive a peasant into debt at inflated prices. For small sums, he might secure the loan with a lien on the coming harvest.[25] For larger sums, he might sell a censo secured by a lien on his land or other possessions. He was then responsible for a yearly interest payment (*ré-dito*) to the buyer of his censo, at a rate specified by law in money or in kind. If he failed to keep up the payments, and this appears to have been more common after the end of the sixteenth century, the creditor might take over his land. More commonly, the debtor unable to pay the interest due would sell the encumbered land before it was taken over, since that would ensure him at least some compensation; in either case, however, he lost the land.

In the large cities and towns of Castile, the bureaucratic elite often invested in land in the surrounding countryside, taking advantage of the financial distress of the former owners. In areas such as Ciudad Real and Cuenca, out of the way and perhaps less affected by inflation, the peasant proprietor may have had a better chance of survival,[26] as might the local nobles, free from the ruinous expenses of the large cities. Although there was clear evidence of noble disinvestment in land in and around Ciudad Real, individual noble families, like the church, continued to own a disproportionate amount of land. The land sales merely show that a new group of bureaucratic landowners was added to their ranks.

It is less clear whether landownership was being concentrated in fewer hands. Numerous individuals were involved with the transactions of several different parcels of land, but this was not unusual, given the general fragmentation of landholdings in Castile. There is a hint of more concentration of ownership in the participants in only one transaction. Of their total numbers, 57.4 percent were sellers and only 42.6 percent were buyers. This suggests that some persons ventured into the land market only to sell their land and that their places were taken by larger owners, or at least by those more active in the land market. The evidence for this is far from conclusive; it would take a detailed study of inheritance patterns and a complete cadastral survey to prove or disprove the accepted hypothesis of increasing concentration of landownership for Ciudad Real. It is certainly plausible, however, that in times of economic distress marginal cultivators would fall by the wayside.

What do seventeenth-century land sales tell us about the evolution of agriculture in Ciudad Real? First, the total volume of sales seems to have been much heavier in the last two quarters of the century than in the first two. This may indicate a quickening of economic activity in the city after 1650, despite the troubles of the late Habsburg period. This pattern would agree quite well with demographic changes in the city. On the other hand, the volume of sales may have been influenced by the choice of data. Since I was interested in the crisis periods discussed in chapter 2, I chose notarial records with particular care to cover those periods fully. This might have skewed the majority of sales toward the second half-century. Even assuming that Table 5.1 reflects reality, the pattern over time for various land categories is ambiguous. The timing of majuelo sales might be taken to mean that viticulture was expanding again in the last quarter of the seventeenth century, following a slump in the second and third quarters.[27] Tithe records support such an interpretation, as does the evidence of population recovery, since vines require much more labor than other kinds of cultivation. On the other hand, the majuelos might have replaced, rather than augmented, existing vineyards. We will need to know more about total agricultural production before we can judge the accuracy of the timing shown by land sales, but some points are none-theless clear.

Second, the sales show little or no evidence of a speculative land market in Ciudad Real. There were few documented cases of the same piece of land changing hands more than once in the course of the century. When this did happen, the price was invariably the same as in the original sale.[28] The active market for land and censos in the mid-sixteenth cen-

Table 5.1. Land sales by quarter-century.

Category of land	Total sales	1600-1624 (%)	1625-1649 (%)	1650-1674 (%)	1675-1699 (%)
Tierra	265	24	15	33	28
Quiñón	136	19	17	26	38
Viña	105	46	21	29	4
Majuelo	51	4	10	16	70
Parral	54	17	22	46	15
Olivar	101	8	20	34	38
Huerta	45	9	15	38	38
Herrenal[a]	18	17	28	39	17
Zumacar	8	38	38	12	12
Average[a]	—	21	21	30	29

a. Discrepancy over 100% from rounding off.

tury, as shown in the tax on sales of land and censos, did not continue into the seventeenth century. Where territorial expansion by large land-owners did persist, it was at a much slower pace.[29]

Third, the land sales do not indicate a move to exploit the land more rationally, either for crops or for pasture. The few attempts to consoli-date individual holdings in Ciudad Real were quite modest, and the new bureaucratic landowners, for the most part, bought only the cheapest pieces of land.[30] Short of modern methods of irrigation and fertilization, their parcels could only be seen as profitable investments if they were to be converted to pasture. There is no evidence that this happened, and in the absence of an enclosure movement, it would have been impossible to convert a few scattered parcels of land to pasture anyway. The propor-tions of arable land and pasture shown in the Catastro differed little from those during the Habsburg period.[31]

Instead of buying arable land to convert to pasture, the major live-stock owners in Ciudad Real preferred to move their flocks along the routes of Castilian transhumance or to purchase formerly common pas-ture from the crown. By grants or sales, encroachment on the traditional baldías, or royal lands used for common pasture, had been going on for centuries,[32] but some towns were able to withstand the pressure better than others. Ciudad Real lost some of its best pasture but retained the rest. One choice parcel along the Guadiana River was in private hands from at least the mid-seventeenth century, as part of the entail founded by Don Luis Bermúdez Mesía de la Cerda.[33] A second area of 500 fane-gas, also on the banks of the Guadiana, passed into private hands in 1712. A third was granted to the marqués of Peñafuente at about the same time and was held by his son-in-law Don Vicente Crespi y Mendoza at the time of the Catastro de Ensenada. Ciudad Real, like other cities in Castile, fought for the return of common pasture that had fallen into private hands. Unfortunately, the costs of the continuing lawsuits even-tually forced the city to abandon them, leaving private persons in control of several thousand fanegas of the city's best pasture.[34] When the popula-tion was low this did not do much harm to the general citizenry. In fact, the city even rented out additional pasture to provide revenue for meet-ing the royal tax bill and other municipal expenses.[35]

Why was land a desirable investment for the bureaucrats of Ciudad Real in the seventeenth century, just as it was for their counterparts in Valladolid and Madrid? The obvious alternatives of seigneurial exploita-tion and agrarian capitalism provide no satisfactory explanation. Plenti-ful land and relatively few farmers made rack-renting, the standard tool of seigneurial exploitation, impractical, though rental income of a mod-est sort was no doubt some incentive. Capitalist development of the land was also beside the point, in the absence of strong market demand to encourage increased productivity. The Madrid market had little effect on Ciudad Real, possibly because the natural disadvantages of soil and climate made production too uncertain in most years to justify much investment. Though some wine traveled to Madrid from La Mancha, grain was better supplied by the plains of Old Castile.[36] In short, the most attractive return from the land in Ciudad Real was probably prestige. Landownership was a socially acceptable outlet for capital, and an important attribute for the socially mobile. It was also a secure investment in bad times. It is hardly surprising that the new bureaucratic landowners in Ciudad Real behaved much like the traditional ones, if these were the reasons they had become landowners.[37] But without anyone to foment agricultural change, the pattern of subsistence production lasted until very recently, disappearing only with the rapid growth of the mid-twentieth century.[38] That agriculture took so long to change was no one's fault; there was no strong incentive to change. But through the Habsburg era and beyond, the persistence of the old pattern meant that many citizens could not be assured of survival from one year to the next. Most of them lived just above the subsistence level in good years and fell below it when bad harvests or increased taxes upset the delicate balance between needs and disposable income.

ROYAL TAXATION

VI

We have seen how structural weaknesses in Ciudad Real's economy placed natural limits on its growth in the early modern period. We
should not forget, however, that the city's economic life was also subject
to government intervention. Taxation was the most obvious form of this
intervention, forcing local producers into the market, extracting their
surplus production, and partially redistributing it to the holders of government bonds. Taxation was particularly heavy in the Habsburg period,
yet even earlier, royal decisions had adversely affected the city's economy. Alfonso XI tended to favor Calatrava during the fourteenth century, leaving the city without political or economic support against its
great rival. A century later the Inquisition generated some local income
in its two years in Ciudad Real, but it also harassed many prominent
converso residents and ruined them financially. When the crown moved
the Inquisition to Toledo and the royal court of justice to Granada, it
symbolized the end of royal favor for Ciudad Real. At the same time the
crown's absorption of the military orders strengthened the alliance of
crown and nobility, which often worked against urban centers such as
Ciudad Real.

Throughout the Habsburg period and beyond, the city had no claim to
the crown's favor other than its loyalty, and even that was tarnished in
the ill-fated revolt of the comuneros against Charles I. Successive monarchs viewed the city primarily as a source of taxes to pay for their inces-
sant wars, ignoring the pleas of local citizens that the tax burden was becoming unbearable. Still, Ciudad Real, like the rest of Castile, remained
loyal to the crown through the extremely hard times of the seventeenth
century. It is interesting to speculate about why the Spanish monarchy
had such docile subjects in Castile, when its peripheral holdings erupted

in a series of revolts and when other countries experienced chronic civil unrest in the same period. There is no simple explanation, but scholars working on areas where revolts did occur provide clues to the Castilian situation.

In all of the successful uprisings—the Netherlands and Portuguese rebellions against the Spanish monarchy, and the English Civil War—elite participation seems to have been crucial. It was also prominent in serious rebellions that did not succeed: the Catalan revolt and the French Fronde. Roland Mousnier has shown that local French nobles often acted as catalysts—when they did not actively participate—in many revolts sparked by hard times and fiscal exactions in seventeenth-century France.[1] By inference, then, we can postulate that a lack of elite unrest in Castile explains the lack of serious revolts under the Habsburg monarchs. In fact, it is entirely plausible that the nobility, far from being alienated from the crown, was its main support in the provinces, thus forestalling, or at least not encouraging, popular unrest. Since the late Middle Ages, successive Castilian kings and queens had coaxed the nobility away from rebellion by giving it effective control over the internal economy and local politics of Castile. The favored status of the Mesta, the laws of Toro (1505) regarding primogeniture, and other favors bound the Castilian nobility to the crown, even though the nobles had lost much of their power in national politics.[2] When the price rise of the sixteenth century and the expenses of their social station drove many nobles into debt, entail prevented their ruin, but it also discouraged the further extension of credit to them. The crown then stepped in with offices, pensions, and dowries for hard-pressed families. It even administered some noble estates for a time, on the presumption that the head of the family could not properly do so.[3] All of this bound the Castilian nobility to the crown in an elaborate form of debt peonage, which ensured their own loyalty and made them potential agents against popular unrest. In Ciudad Real, the local nobility controlled the city government as well as their own estates, and this made them highly unlikely to champion any sort of local opposition to the crown.

The Cortes, or parliament, of Castile was similarly neutralized as a voice of opposition. Only eighteen cities were represented in the Cortes in the Habsburg period, each city's two deputies (*procuradores*) presumably speaking for a wide hinterland as well as for their hometowns. (Toledo, for example, ostensibly represented Ciudad Real and the Campo de Calatrava.) The first two estates had ceased meeting. After the end of the urban-based comunero revolt, the chastened Cortes lost much of its force as the loyal opposition. Since supply preceded redress, the often-quoted complaints of the deputies had little meaning. In addition, deputies received a percentage of all taxes they approved, which was hardly an inducement to fiscal responsibility. After 1665 the deputies no longer even met as a body, preferring to be polled by mail.[4]

Ciudad Real, then, had no intermediary force to protect it from the demands of a powerful crown, and just as the sixteenth-century boom came to an end, royal taxation suddenly caught up with inflation and stayed abreast of prices thereafter. Falling on a city that lost over 41 percent of its households between 1591 and 1625 and that had no protector against royal demands, royal taxation weakened the city's already faltering economy and hampered its ability to recover from the periodic harvest failures and epidemics of the seventeenth century.

I will consider only royal taxation, but we should not forget that the heaviest single tax on the agricultural population was the ecclesiastical tithe, or *diezmo*. As a fixed levy on agricultural production—usually about one-tenth—it kept pace with prices and production. Until the late sixteenth century, diezmos were higher than all royal taxes combined, and Noël Salomon has seen them as a major drain on rural incomes.[5] Still, the power of the church and a long tradition sanctioned the diezmos. Royal taxation, on the other hand, was an unwelcome novelty, varying with the needs of the crown more than with the incomes of ordinary taxpayers.

It is known that total royal revenue increased over ninefold between 1494 and 1598. At the same time, however, a fourfold price increase, a doubling of the Castilian population, and the massive infusion of revenue from the Indies meant that the average nominal and real taxes were actually declining until about 1575.[6] The most important personal tax was the *servicio*, originally an extraordinary levy voted by the medieval Cortes in times of need and payable by personal assessment of the commoners of Castile. During the reign of Charles I (1516-1556), the *servicios ordinarios* were regularly imposed, and even the "plague of the *servicios extraordinarios* came to be endemic."[7] By the end of the reign, both servicios were more or less stable at 150 million maravedís a year. They stayed at this level throughout the reign of Philip II, although at times additional servicios would be added for special needs, such as the king's four marriages.

Much more important were the medieval imposts on transactions, the alcabalas. They had probably developed from seigneurial or municipal imposts, and the crown had gradually taken them over since the thirteenth century. By the Habsburg period, the alcabalas were considered to be worth 10 percent of everything sold or exchanged, without exemption. In practice, certain products, regions, institutions, and groups of persons were exempt, and perhaps 5 percent of all alcabalas remained in private hands. The alcabalas nonetheless were the mainstay of royal finance until the late sixteenth century, providing one-third or more of all revenue from Castile. Furthermore, they set a valuable legal precedent for the crown by falling upon all citizens who bought and sold in the marketplace. From the late fifteenth century, some alcabalas were compounded (*encabezado*) into fixed sums instead of fluctuating with the value of transactions. The practice was generalized by Charles I in 1536 and continued under his successors. By this time also, the alcabalas had fallen in absolute value because of exemptions and fraud; overall, they may have been worth as little as 2-3 percent of sales in the early sixteenth century.[8]

During the reign of Philip II (1556-1598) the relative burden of taxation was at first no more onerous than it had been under his father. Though taxes continued to rise, population, prices, and wages kept pace. Then the situation changed. Economic growth in Castile reached its natural limits just as Philip's foreign commitments led him to demand more revenue. Many areas then found themselves in an uncomfortable position between rising taxation and stagnating production. The servicios stayed at the same general level, but the alcabalas were trebled in 1575 and lowered only slightly in 1578.[9] Since the alcabalas fell most heavily upon the cities represented in the Cortes, the deputies held firm against further increases. Instead they approved a new tax on consumer goods, the *millones*, in 1588. A first grant of eight million *ducados*, payable in six years, was designed to restore the navy and add to royal income after the defeat of the Great Armada. Despite continued opposition, both inside and outside government, the millones were extended in 1596 and became a regular feature of Castilian taxation thereafter.[10]

The reign of Philip III (1598-1621) gave the common taxpayer some relief. At peace with Europe, the government lowered the alcabalas, but the king and his ministers missed the chance for real fiscal reform when they allowed the millones to continue. A basic grant of two million ducados a year began in 1601, paid by an excise duty (*sisa*) on essential consumer items such as wine, oil, meat, and vinegar. The tax was paid by the vendor, who passed it on to the consumer by holding back part of the merchandise sold. Through a papal dispensation, the clergy contributed a lump sum in lieu of actual sisas, but they never ceased to complain about having to contribute at all. The nobility also acknowledged the universality of the tax but tried continually to foist it off on the common people.

If the economic policy of Philip III was shortsighted, the policy of Philip IV (1621-1665) was disastrous. As much for modern analysts as for contemporary observers, it was "an impenetrable forest, a dense jungle, in which whoever pretends to explore all its windings will only succeed in getting lost."[11] The author of these words, Antonio Domínguez Ortiz, had in mind the total economic policy of the government, including many ingenious examples of currency manipulation. For taxes alone, suffice it to say that their main weight fell on basic consumer items—meat, wine, oil, fish, soap, paper, and other goods. Philip IV and his councillors made periodic attempts to reform the structure of royal finance, but each time strong opposition forced the abandonment of reform plans. Instead, the servicios and alcabalas continued at their stable rates, and the millones grant was raised to four million ducados a year in 1632 with additional duties on salt, soap, tallow candles, fresh and salted fish, paper, tobacco, sugar, ice and snow, and other items. Approved by the Cortes for six-year periods, this basic levy was known as the "24 millones" for its total value in ducados.[12]

As the Thirty Years' War in Europe increasingly involved Spain, even this was not enough. Several new imposts were added to the millones, and an additional 4 percent to the alcabalas, one each in 1639, 1642, 1656, and 1663. This levy, the *unos por ciento,* was collected as a separate tax and fluctuated greatly in total value for the remainder of the century.[13] Also, after 1637 all official documents had to be written on stamped paper (*papel sellado*), ostensibly to guarantee their authenticity, but actually to generate revenue for the crown. At first there were four classes of paper, designed for use with specific types of documents. As a general rule, the monetary value of a transaction determined the class of stamped paper it required.

Quality	Cost per folded sheet (pliego)	Amount stamped on front of each fold
1	8 reales, or 272 maravedís	136 maravedís
2	2 reales, or 68 maravedís	34 maravedís
3	1 real, or 34 maravedís	17 maravedís
4	20 maravedís	10 maravedís

In 1640 another class of paper appeared for the transactions of the poor and for the performance of official duties (*despachos de oficios*) in which the maker had no pecuniary interests.[14]

At the same time, a dizzying array of fiscal expedients tried to shift some of the burden to the elite of Castile: the king and his ministers sold offices and titles to the status-conscious and at the same time undermined the tax-exempt position of the nobility by forced loans and forced sales of government bonds; they tried to reclaim some of the alcabalas still in private hands; they tampered with the currency. All of this drove the aristocracy close to rebellion and nearly broke the tacit pact between monarchy and upper nobility in Castile, a pact that had preserved social peace for over a century. Frightened by several small revolts and by the alienation of the aristocracy, Philip IV and his ministers fell back on ordinary revenues and on loans at exorbitant interest. The highest taxes during Philip IV's reign came in the decade 1650-1660, in the aftermath of a ruinous cycle of bad harvests, famine, and epidemic disease. Ironically, even with increased taxes the crown gained little liquidity. Fraud, accumulating arrears, high collection expenses, and interest payments to creditors meant that, although taxpayers contributed more than twelve million ducados a year in millones alone, the crown received only about one-quarter of it.[15]

It is not surprising that many areas in Castile fell short of their assigned quotas during the last half of the reign. To make up the deficit, the crown instituted a separate assessment of the millones arrears (*quiebras de millones*) and collected these and other taxes by stringent and inequitable means.

During the reign of the last Habsburg, Charles II (1665-1700), the ramshackle fiscal machine creaked on, but several important partial reforms made it work more efficiently. Tax collection and collectors were more closely regulated. The duke of Medinaceli, best remembered for his drastic devaluation of copper coinage (vellón) in 1680, also considered numerous proposals for tax reform. The magnitude of the task forced him to fall back on selective reductions of the millones and the alcabalas in 1683. The count of Oropesa, who succeeded Medinaceli in 1685, and the marqués of los Vélez, superintendent of the Council of Finance from 1687, also favored overall tax reform but settled for piecemeal remedies. Arrears of the millones and alcabalas up to the spring of 1686 were excused by a royal decree in February 1688.[16] A general reorganization of judicial districts in 1691 finally laid the groundwork for tax reform, but it could not be carried out until the late eighteenth century, when Spain's European hegemony, like the Spanish Habsburgs, had passed into history.

In Ciudad Real, the ecclesiastical tithe was also the heaviest single tax until the late sixteenth century, higher than the sum of all royal taxes. According to Noël Salomon's figures, fifty-five towns near Ciudad Real paid average yearly diezmos of 579 maravedís and 8.5 fanegas of bread grain for each householder, somewhat higher than the average for all of New Castile.[17] The grain alone would be worth over 2,200 maravedís at 1574-1578 prices, assuming that the payment was half wheat and half barley.[18] Based on some fragmentary diezmo records and on the *Catastro* answered in 1751 in Ciudad Real, we can estimate that residents of the city paid average yearly diezmos of 2,000-3,000 maravedís throughout this period.[19]

Figure 6.1 summarizes the extant information for royal taxation in

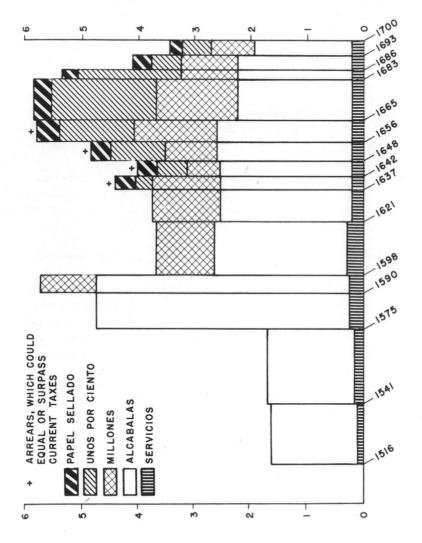

Figure 6.1. Estimated yearly royal taxes in Ciudad Real (in millions of maravedís).

Ciudad Real. Early in the reign of Charles I, the servicios ordinarios and extraordinarios rose only slightly, from 109,000 maravedís in 1527 to 114,600 maravedís in 1539-1541. Since the population also rose in that period, the average per householder remained steady at about 95 maravedís. A new assessment in 1541 raised the average to 145 maravedís, slightly lower than that for all of Toledo's collection area, of which Ciudad Real was a part.[20]

Alcabalas were the main royal tax in Ciudad Real, as they were elsewhere in Castile. In 1534 the partido paid 1.48 million maravedís a year in alcabalas and tercias (the crown's share of the ecclesiastical tithe).[21] Much of this total was probably paid by nonresidents doing business in the city, but we will nonetheless consider the alcabalas a charge on Ciudad Real, since that is the way they were assessed and collected. It is clear that the burden of royal taxation was light during the early sixteenth century, compared with the tithe and with the rising population.

The early years of Philip II's reign showed little deviation from this pattern. Servicios hardly changed until the middle of the reign; then they rose to 225,000-250,000 maravedís a year, perhaps as early as 1567, definitely by 1582-1584. They were paid in part by an assessment among the common taxpayers and in part by income from the rental of city lands.[22] Much more important were the alcabalas, through which the king hoped to increase royal revenue and to spread taxes more evenly among his subjects. The assessment for 1557-1561 is a case in point (Table 6.1). In a clear and very interesting account, each part of Ciudad Real's alcabalas was listed with the old rate of assessment and an estimate of its value raised to 10 percent. The old rates ranged from 1.7 percent to 10 percent of sales value, but the most lucrative parts were all assessed at low rates. Sales of animals on the hoof, meat, and private credit arrangements (censos) paid only 1.7 percent in alcabalas, and grain sales paid 3 percent, although together they were far and away the most valuable transactions in the partido. The compounded assessment raised most parts of the tax to a uniform 10 percent rate; meat and animal sales seem to have retained some exemption. In addition, the city's own products (wine, gloves, grain, and cloth) and its residents were free of most alcabalas and all personal assessment (repartimiento). There is evidence, however, that the boom of the early sixteenth century had slowed by 1557-1561. The yearly alcabalas, even when most of its parts were raised to 10 percent, were still lower than they had been in 1534.

By the end of the century Ciudad Real's alcabalas had trebled, along with those in the rest of Castile. The partido paid an average of 4.47 million maravedís a year between 1593 and 1597.[23] Some of the increase was undoubtedly absorbed by the rise in population and the volume of transactions. Ciudad Real had gained 700 new households in the Morisco relo-

Table 6.1. Alcabalas and tercias: Ciudad Real and its partido, 1557-1561 and 1593-1597 (in thousands of maravedis).

Item	1557-1561[a]		1593-1597[b]
	Total yearly value	Yearly value with exemptions	Total yearly value
Tercias	304.9	304.9	590.8
Carnecerías (meat markets)	442.6	430.6	874.1
Peso (things sold by weight)	245.9	226.9	301.5
Paños (cloth)[c]	35.0	35.0	223.8
Vino y vinagre (wine and vinagre)[c]	0	0	271.8
Lana y queso (wool and cheese)[c]	5.5	5.5	213.5
Pescado fresco y seco (fresh and dried fish)	161.9	123.4	234.7
Leña y carbón (firewood and charcoal)[c]	24.7	21.7	156.9
Pan en grano y harina (breadstuffs in grain and flour)	65.7	59.7	181.5
Esparto (basketry)	5.6	2.6	68.2
Fruta verde y seca (fresh and dried fruit)	130.0	97.5	269.7
Heredades (sales of property, including censos)	407.2	395.2	117.8
Hortaliza (vegetables)[c]	6.1	3.1	90.2
Barro y madera (clay and wood articles)	36.5	24.3	95.0
Bestias (animals)[c]	7.1	0	88.8
Aves y caza (game, fowl, eggs)[c]	6.0	0	25.1
Salvajina (skins of wild animals)[c]	6.1	0.2	27.3
Sal (salt)	11.8	9.8	9.2
Almonedas (public auctions)	20.0	—	—

Table 6.1 (cont.)

Item	1557-1561[a]		1593-1597[b]
	Total yearly value	Yearly value with exemptions	Total yearly value
Especiería (groceries)	37.6	—	—
Zapatería (shoemaking)[c]	19.0	11.0	102.3

a. AGS, CG, leg. 2304.
b. AGS, Expedientes de Hacienda (Ciudad Real), leg. 81.
c. Dramatic increases.

cation of 1570-1571,[24] which added nearly 30 percent to the taxable population. The Moriscos could also have contributed to the notable rise in alcabalas for cloth, firewood and charcoal, basketry, vegetables, and shoemaking. Other alcabalas rose more modestly, and that for heredades fell dramatically, suggesting a sharp decline in the partido's land and credit market before 1600. This would be consistent with the agricultural crisis so well analyzed by Fernand Braudel.[25] Taken overall, it is not likely that rises in population, prices, and the volume of transactions absorbed the whole rise in Ciudad Real's alcabalas. Instead, their real per capita weight increased as the government sought ways to pay for Philip II's costly wars.

An additional charge came with the first repartimiento of millones in 1590. Ciudad Real was assessed 808,179 maravedís yearly, or 4,849,074 maravedís for the six years of the levy.[26] On the basis of a new population count in 1591, Ciudad Real's quota jumped to over 1 million maravedís a year, or just under 500 maravedís for each householder.[27] Using Alvaro Castillo's criteria for the relationship between millones and wealth, Ciudad Real was a moderately wealthy city at the end of the sixteenth century,[28] though not nearly as wealthy as Toledo.

After the record assessments of the 1590s, those of Philip III's reign dropped to more moderate levels. Servicios did rise slightly in the early years of the reign, but the real change came in the alcabalas, which were lowered to just over 2.25 million maravedís a year.[29] They would stay at this level until the end of the seventeenth century, though individual years could vary in the amount actually collected and in the time required to collect it. Added to this was the *martiniega*, a medieval tax acknowledging the overlordship of the king, and 300 fanegas in bread grains for the royal tercias of the diezmo.

Already in 1617 the alcabalas of Ciudad Real were mortgaged for more than their total cash value, and in addition several crown debts from Madrid had been temporarily charged on the alcabalas of Ciudad Real. Most of these latter concerned assignees of the General Agreement of 14 May 1608, by which Philip III settled with his creditors after suspending payments in 1607. Another part of the alienated funds included interest payments on government bonds (juros) at a rate higher than 5 percent interest, most of them dating from the sixteenth century when such rates were common. In the account for 1617 most juros were adjusted to a uniform 5 percent (20,000 al millar), and by 1621 all juros were legally set at that figure. In the final account for 1617, dated 5 May 1625, the crown had managed to collect 3.01 million maravedís from the partido, a sum far above the basic assessment.[30]

Various accounts for 1619-1621 show that city residents alone paid yearly alcabalas of 335,000 maravedís and that all of it went to pay collection expenses for the partido.[31] In a sworn statement Andrés de Alarcón, the royal tax commissioner, explained that he had even charged his suit of clothes for Philip III's funeral to the alcabalas revenue, "because of the small salary of [his] commission, not having more than 500 maravedís" a day to live on.[32]

Even lowered, the alcabalas remained the most important royal tax in Ciudad Real, contrary to the situation elsewhere in Castile, where they declined in value relative to the millones. The difference was due to the structure of Ciudad Real's partido, which contained only the city and a few inconsequential villages. Elsewhere the millones shifted consumer taxes from urban centers to the hinterland. In Ciudad Real there was no hinterland to speak of and any tax assigned to the partido was effectively paid by the city. Unfortunately we lack records for the millones until 1637, but based on earlier and later records they can be estimated at between 1 and 1.5 million maravedís a year. If this estimate is correct, total royal taxes by 1621 were 34 percent lower than they had been in the final years of Philip II's reign. In addition, prices fell about 7 percent in 1601-1610 and then stabilized until 1621,[33] but unless Ciudad Real paid no millones at all, the reign of Philip III must be seen as a calamitous time for the city. In 1610 the king expelled 2,000-3,000 residents as part of the general expulsion of the Moriscos.[34] Harvest failures and disease also took their toll, so that by 1621 the number of householders stood 41 percent below its 1591 level. Since fertility often drops in crisis times, the total population may have fallen even farther. Ciudad Real felt the loss of its Moriscos more acutely than other areas did, but there is little doubt that all Castile emerged from the reign of Philip III weakened in population and productive capability.[35]

Royal taxes in the reign of Philip IV reflected the worsening financial base of Castile and the increasing needs of the crown for ready money.

For many reasons, among them the complexity and wealth of documentation, I have split the reign into several characteristic periods. In the first, from 1621 to 1637, the burden of taxation scarcely changed from the previous reign. Traditional servicios were worth a yearly total of 286,700 maravedís, including expenses; identical accounts from 1621 to 1629 show that most of the tax went to pay foreign creditors of the king.[36] The alcabalas, whereas they too stayed at their previous level, were heavily mortgaged to the holders of government bonds, some of them from the area around Ciudad Real. In the 1620s, however, Philip IV often confiscated income due to internal juro holders in order to free money for financiers such as Juan Lucas Palavesin.[37] Prices in the same period may have helped the residents of Ciudad Real meet their obligations. From 1621 to 1630 commodity prices in Castile rose about 20 percent, fueled by war expenses and a heavy coinage of vellón. A 50 percent devaluation of vellón in August 1628 slowed the rise in the 1630s without actually halting it.[38]

In the next period, roughly from 1637 to 1648, the crown began a long struggle to increase—or at least to maintain—its income despite all-out war abroad and slipping revenues, rising prices, and rebellion at home. Prices in Castile were only 0.82 percent higher in 1640 than in 1631, but military expenses, the depreciation of vellón, harvest failures, and epidemics drove prices up again in 1641-42 and from 1646 to 1650.[39] It is doubtful, however, that inflation still made taxes easier to pay, and the partido of Ciudad Real had increasing difficulty beginning in the late 1630s. Although the basic servicios levy remained the same, the crown allowed the partido a rebate of 180,000 maravedís in each three-year assessment period "in view of its necessity and lack of inhabitants."[40] The amount actually due, then, was 226,700 maravedís a year. Compared to other taxes the servicios were unimportant, but at least they were paid regularly and fully, and before 1644 they were nearly free from permanent indebtedness.

For the alcabalas, payment lagged far behind the due dates, though the assessment held stable. The final account for the 1642-1644 alcabalas was not made until late in 1649, and that for 1650 did not appear until 1664. Still, war expenses had to be met, and in the early 1640s alcabalas revenue from Ciudad Real was diverted from juro holders to the financiers Duarte Brandon Suárez and Alexander Palavesin.[41] The permanent juros on all taxes, in fact, were often preempted, and after 1637 the crown habitually took one-half of each year's juro income in a new tax called the *media anata*.[42] Though Ciudad Real continued to pay about 2.6 million maravedís a year for the alcabalas, less of that sum remained in Spain to service the crown's long-term debt, and more of it passed to foreign financiers for short- and middle-term debt.

The Cortes proved more willing to increase the millones than the servicios or alcabalas, particularly under the pressure of foreign wars. In 1637 Castile was asked to make a supreme effort. Ciudad Real and its *tesorería* (the partido plus forty-one towns belonging to the order of Calatrava) paid 23.9 million maravedís in millones that year. All of it went to Elisio Imbrea, Francisco María Piquinote, Duarte Fernández, Manuel de Paz, and Jorge de Paz Silveira—Italian and Portuguese financiers. Altogether the tesorería was ordered to pay them 37 million maravedís for services to the king in Barcelona, Genoa, and Flanders, the crucial "Spanish Road" of money and troops.[43] The remainder would be paid from the millones of May 1638. Of the 23.9 million paid in 1637, over half came from the basic levy on foodstuffs; some came from a voluntary subscription of the citizens, and the rest came from statutory additions to the millones, such as the "8,000 soldados" levied in 1638 to pay the salaries of 8,000 soldiers employed against the French.[44]

Between 1638 and 1644, yearly millones assessments for the tesorería stabilized at 14-15 million maravedís, of which Ciudad Real paid 8-10 percent (1-1.5 million).[45] The irony is that, while the millones appeared to be increasing, the amount collected was just holding stable in Ciudad Real, when it came in at all. Payments due in 1643-1647 were delayed an average of fifteen years.[46] When old parts of the tax fell short, the crown simply added new ones, desperately trying to maintain the level of revenue. There was even a separate assessment of the arrears—the *quiebras de millones*—that began in 1637. The quiebras aimed to collect from Castile 2 million ducados every fifteen months, although the amount paid was generally less than 1 million. Unlike the rest of the millones, the quiebras had no fixed resources; instead, each taxation area raised the levy however it could, either by direct personal assessment, additional sales taxes, or local revenue. Though the quiebras were much smaller than the regular millones, they were more resented by taxpayers for their haphazard and arbitrary administration.[47]

A perfect example of new taxes to supplement old ones was the addition to the alcabalas known as the unos por ciento. For the first 1 percent levied from 1639 to 1642, Ciudad Real's tesorería was assessed 3.8 million maravedís a year, due in three equal installments. The city alone owed 280,000, or about 7.3 percent, of the total. Most of the other forty-one towns in the tesorería owed considerably less, but four of them (Valdepeñas, Almagro, Manzanares, and Daimiel) owed more than Ciudad Real. Many towns immediately fell into arrears, most notably Almagro and Daimiel. The former had paid nothing of its 1640 assessment four years later, and those for 1641 and 1642 were also delayed. Although Almagro and Daimiel were not among the towns begging for tax relief listed by Domínguez Ortiz, their difficulties are clearly evident from the tax returns. Numerous smaller towns were similarly in arrears, though the city of Ciudad Real seems to have paid its full assessment in the same period.[48]

A second uno por ciento began in 1642, asking another 3.6 million maravedís a year from the tesorería, 280,000 of it from Ciudad Real. The documents that have been preserved show an erratic pace of collection, and few of them are final accounts. Of the total due for the first uno por ciento in 1644, less than two-thirds had been collected by the end of 1648. Since the account was declared closed, the crown apparently wrote off the remainder as a bad debt. There is a similar situation in two final accounts for 1645-1647, dated 11 August 1656. In one of them the tesorería supposedly paid 7.1 million maravedís a year for both unos. The other account, reflecting reality rather than wishful thinking, indicated that the area had actually paid only 2.3 million maravedis, or less than one-third of the assessment.[49]

To make up the deficit the crown instituted numerous smaller taxes and special assessments in this crucial period. After 1636 records for all taxes and other official documents had to appear on the stamped paper sold by the government. Since it increased the already high cost of doing business, papel sellado was a great annoyance in administrative centers such as Ciudad Real. Except for two brief periods when the cost was arbitrarily doubled, the city paid roughly 318,000 maravedís a year for papel sellado from 1643 to 1716.[50] Added to this were other minor levies, forced loans, and forced sales of government bonds.[51] Although each one alone was not large, their cumulative effect added perceptibly to the total demands of the crown in Ciudad Real. From 1637 to 1648, however, the crown gained little ground in its attempt to increase royal income for wartime expenses. Despite the additions of new imposts, total revenue from current taxes sagged after 1642, and only the vigorous collection of arrears from Ciudad Real's diminished population pulled it back up again. In 1641-42 and again after 1646, the crown's purchasing power was further eroded by inflation, in part created by irresponsible monetary policies.

In the final period of Philip IV's reign, from 1648 to 1665, the crown was more successful in extracting revenue from Ciudad Real, despite natural catastrophes such as the 1647-1652 series of harvest failures and epidemics. Just as the crisis arrived, the crown began a concerted effort to collect all back taxes for the continuing war with France and the Catalan and Portuguese rebellions at home. From September 1648 to February 1651 Ciudad Real was forced to pay 2.7 million maravedís in unos por ciento, most of it in arrears (*restos*).[52] Immediately afterward there was apparently an audit of Ciudad Real's tax returns, which lasted from 4 October 1651 to 22 April 1654.[53] Though the commissioners of the audit found no evidence of fraud, they were able to collect (perhaps extort would be a better word) an enormous amount of money from the partido: 341,000 maravedís in back servicios;[54] 1.3 million in current and past-due unos por ciento;[55] and about 2 million in quiebras de millones, collected from November 1650 to April 1654. The total quiebras paid by the tesorería was nearly 22 million maravedís, which included taxes from as early as 1640.[56] If local residents deliberately avoided tax demands, they can hardly be blamed. The area had suffered every misfortune, and Ciudad Real escaped famine in 1647 only because of the prompt action of local officials in purchasing grain from Extremadura. Still, with close supervision, the crown was able to perform the fiscal equivalent of squeezing blood from a stone.

Regardless of the partido's difficulties, royal tax assessments continued to rise, perhaps because Ciudad Real was thought to be more prosperous than its neighbors, perhaps because it was easier to extract money from Ciudad Real than from towns controlled by the order of Calatrava. From 1648 onward, each part of the unos due from Ciudad Real was raised to 450,000 maravedís,[57] whereas the assessment for the whole tesorería fell by about two-thirds. The imposition of a third uno por ciento in 1656 and a fourth in 1661 raised the partido's total assessment to 1.8 million maravedís a year.[58] Collections, however, proved more difficult than assessment. Nothing at all of the first uno of 1654 had been paid by late 1666, and only part of the unos for 1655 and 1656 had been paid by 1669.[59]

Unfortunately for tax officials, they were held responsible for the arrears. Jacinto Fernández of Ciudad Real was ruined by his posts as treasurer of the unos por ciento and depositary of the millones and other taxes in the late 1640s and 1650s. In 1659 he was given two weeks to present some accounts that had fallen due ten years earlier. Eventually the debt was excused, because Fernández was "so poor and needy that he has to beg alms in order to eat in the prison where he is currently [confined] for other debts to the royal treasury."[60]

Throughout the tesorería of Ciudad Real late payments were chronic, and though total revenue had fallen drastically, the claims upon it had not. Juro holders on the first uno por ciento of the tesorería still claimed 3.3 million maravedís a year, though revenue had fallen to less than 1 million in 1655. To overcome this dilemma, six of the twenty-three juro holders were paid in full from the revenue; the others received nothing. Another six turned up on the list for the same tax for 1664, and five more were paid from the second uno por ciento that year, which suggests that payments were rotated from year to year among the claimants. Of the six favored in 1655-56, only one had the remotest connection with the tesorería of Ciudad Real—Don Alvaro de Bazán, the marqués of Santa Cruz.[61] The rest represented a cash flow out of the area.

Records of the servicios show a similar erosion of the rights of juro holders.[62] In 1642-1644 most of the revenue from the servicios went to pay Italian and Portuguese financiers of the crown: Maceo Macey, Fernando Tinoco, Jorge de Paz Silveira, and Juan Lucas Manzolo. Together they received over 75 percent of the total for the three-year period. But a new element was added thereafter in the form of permanent claims on the revenue. The licentiate Don Antonio de Torres Treviño, a native of Ciudad Real and a former commissioner of the Inquisition in Potosí, Peru, bought a government bond paying 92,572 maravedís a year from the servicios revenue of Ciudad Real; he also purchased another juro in the name of a trust fund for a friend's children.[63]

During the next collection period the permanent juros rose to nearly two-thirds of the total revenue, reducing the amount still free to pay the crown's bankers. There is evidence that the city had some difficulty paying the full amount it owed; at the end of 1650 over 17 percent of the total due from 1645-1647 was still outstanding.[64] In response the crown shifted payments away from juro owners, as Table 6.2 demonstrates. Half the income of most juros was already withheld for the media anata. In 1659-1662 owners of third-priority juros lost an additional 20 percent, and owners of fourth-priority juros lost everything. Even then, in Ciudad Real "it seems that [the exempted juros] would not fit in said year [1660]."[65] Similarly, four years later Philip IV confiscated 80 percent of juro income from the unos por ciento to finance one more desperate offensive against the Portuguese rebels.[66]

The last eighteen years of Philip IV's reign hardly qualify as a time of prosperity, yet the crown was successful in maintaining tax revenue from Ciudad Real. Even though prices showed little change from 1650 to 1662, by the end of the reign the nominal tax burden in Ciudad Real was about 50 percent higher than it had been at the beginning, or just about equal to inflation in the same period.[67] We should not infer from this that taxes were less burdensome to the economy than contemporaries said they were. An arbitrary and inequitable system does not improve simply because it gets no worse. We should also remember that before Philip IV's reign some of Ciudad Real's tax money remained in the area as redistributed wealth from the common taxpayers to the elite holders of government bonds. During his reign, local wealth was more often siphoned off to pay for foreign wars. Thus the only group in the city with potential to invest was deprived of its income.

After the chaos of Philip IV's final years, the reign of his successor looked something like order. Taxation in Ciudad Real remained high at first, but so did prices until the devaluation of 1680.[68] The yearly millones levy for 1665 to 1671 was 1.46 million maravedís, a sum consonant with earlier levies. The astonishing thing is that the entire six-year total

Table 6.2. Juros on servicios ordinarios and extraordinarios of Ciudad Real.

Juro holder	Yearly value in maravedís			
	1644	1647	1654-1656	1660-1662
Foundations established by Antonio de Torres Treviño	92,572	92,572	28,542	30,857
Trust fund set up for the children of Juan López de Brianda	34,714	34,714	17,357	11,571
Foundations established by Don Antonio de Galiana	—	33,863	18,812	11,287
Don Francisco Fernández de Andía, viscount of Santa Clara. Mortgaged to king, who then gave its income to Don Juan Jiménez de Arista, householder of Madrid, probably in 1654	—	—	6,007[a]	6,007

Source: 1644, AGS, *CMC 3ª*, leg. 2642; 1647, leg. 2109; 1654-1656, leg. 1531; 1660-1662, leg. 511.
a. Reduced from 16,819.

had been paid by November 1673.[69] The unos por ciento also came in regularly, and more of their income was used to pay local juro holders in Ciudad Real.[70]

More efficient tax collection may have contributed to Ciudad Real's more timely tax payments after 1665,[71] but it is also probable that the city was recovering economically by the last decades of the seventeenth century, despite dramatic setbacks. The devaluation of 1680 created severe, but temporary, distress, and it was followed by one of the worst crises of the century. Tax collection was sluggish during these years,[72] but thereafter assessments drifted downward in keeping with the new value of money, and payments came in regularly. The unos were cut in half in 1686 (and called the *medios unos por ciento* or the *dos por ciento*.)[73] The alcabalas were officially set at 1.69 million maravedís a year at the end of the reign,[74] and there were also decreases in the millones in 1683-1686 and again in 1693-1701.[75]

The early eighteenth century was also punctuated by several periods of economic distress. These were reflected in tax assessments as well as in population movements. In 1735 the crown lowered the traditional servicios by one-third for a term of six years, because of the poor harvests and the epidemic afflicting Ciudad Real. This was the same remedy that had been applied in 1621, and for the same reasons. In 1735 the crown was evidently convinced that the city's population had fallen to 647 households, including nobles and paupers. Such a low figure is not creditable, even in so difficult a period as the 1730s, but tax relief was undoubtedly welcome in any case.[76] By the time of the *Catastro* in 1751 Ciudad Real paid an average of 4.6 million maravedís in royal taxes, and its population had almost recovered to its late-sixteenth-century peak. Some of the tax money returned to city residents in the form of juro interest payments. In addition, secular income in 1751 included 51,848 reales (1,762,832 maravedís) in salaries for offices "alienated from the royal crown." This represented a redistribution of wealth to the elite of the city; though the money did not come directly from taxes, it was equivalent to 38 percent of the city's total royal taxes in 1751.[77]

Because estimates of total production are notoriously imprecise in this period, it is difficult to quantify the effects of royal taxation in Ciudad Real.[78] We can, however, compare general trends of taxation, population, and prices. From an almost negligible amount in the early sixteenth century, royal taxation grew suddenly and dramatically from 1575 to 1600, just as population and prices slowed their expansion. Lower taxes from 1600 to about 1637 and stable prices from 1600 to 1625 did not compensate Ciudad Real for a 41 percent drop in households, recurrent bad harvests, and industrial decay. A renewed drive for tax revenue in the reign of Philip IV coincided not only with moderate inflation but also with a period of lowered population and production and general economic distress. Not until the reign of Charles II were there signs of recovery, demonstrated by an end to the chronic delays in tax payments.

It is clear that taxation policies and the confiscation of private wealth contributed to the severity and persistence of economic distress in Ciudad Real, and probably in all Castile. This was partly a matter of timing. By responding to European politics, fiscal policy changes often showed a perverse disregard for economic reality in Castile. The result was that royal taxation was low during the inflation and population growth of the early sixteenth century, and high during the economic distress of the seventeenth century; private wealth was largely untouched when the economy was growing, but it was frequently confiscated when stagnation and decline had set in. Given the perceived needs of defending Spain's European possessions, it is doubtful that the Habsburg monarchs had much choice. What is interesting here is that their fiscal policy was self-defeating.

All levels of society in Ciudad Real were adversely affected by royal taxation in ways that are obscured by a simple comparison between price levels and aggregate taxation. Common taxpayers paid personal taxes and the bulk of the regressive excises on foodstuffs and other necessities. Nobles were exempt from personal taxes, but in Ciudad Real they paid sizeable amounts in transactions taxes (expecially the unos por ciento) and were legally subject to the millones. Those who owned government bonds saw their interest income diminished by royal confiscations, and wealthy citizens were also obliged to contribute in the form of loans to the royal fisc and in forced purchases of government bonds from it. The tax records of Ciudad Real show that during the Habsburg period local revenues increasingly flowed outward to pay foreign bankers of the crown, rather than staying in the area as redistributed income to holders of government bonds. Thus, although population began a slow recovery after a low point in the 1620s, the city's economy could not follow suit until the last decades of the seventeenth century.

THE URBAN ELITE

VII

A very narrow upper stratum of society directed the political fortunes of Ciudad Real. For the most part, they belonged to the hereditary nobility of the city, but increasingly, wealthy and influential commoners joined them in the administrative elite, and even in the nobility itself. Together with the church, they also controlled much, perhaps even most, of the city's wealth. How Ciudad Real's leading families organized political power in the city, and how the entire upper stratum managed its wealth, are crucial to an understanding of the city's economic evolution between 1500 and 1750.

THE CHURCH

The clergy and its institutions were wealthy and powerful in Ciudad Real. Native sons and daughters left lavish endowments to existing foundations and established several new ones in the course of the early modern period. As we might expect, many of the donors belonged to the first families of the city, as did a number of the more prestigious clerics.[1] As individuals, the clergy and religious of Ciudad Real were as varied in wealth and position as their secular counterparts. We see them, however, less as individuals and more as a collective entity of considerable strength and numbers. At all levels of Spanish society, people lived in an ambience of faith and its outward forms, making the church an important part of daily life. The church also exercised power as a depository of large amounts of land and other wealth and as a source of sometimes indiscriminate charity. Because of its economic and spiritual power, the church became an obvious target for social critics such as the arbitristas. Besides the large legacies they inherited, religious institutions often invested in censos, juros, and land. As a rule, religious institutions owned more credit paper than land, though individual clerics did control large amounts of land in certain areas, including Ciudad Real.[2] This was in addition to the official church patrimony and the income from diezmos and several smaller levies on agricultural production. Even a brief examination of the ecclesiastical establishment in Ciudad Real will illustrate why the church was attacked by those interested in social and economic reform.

First of all, the number of clergy and religious was growing in the late sixteenth and seventeenth centuries, diminishing the potential work force further than it already was by demographic decline.[3] When a noble entered the religious life, he or she often brought personal wealth into the cloister, exempt from taxation. A printed petition for entry into the Dominican convent called Santa María de Gracia in Ciudad Real listed one nun's dowry at 800 ducats in 1677, which argues for the wealth of the convents and their inhabitants.[4] Clerical vocations claimed a noticeable part of the total population, wealthy and otherwise. Gerónimo de Uztáriz calculated that ecclesiastics accounted for about one-thirtieth (3.33 percent) of the Spanish population in 1712, if one included the servants and relatives in their households.[5] Possibly the total was even higher. Bennassar estimated that there were about 1,500 religious (3.75 percent of the population) in Valladolid in 1591, not including their households.[6] At the same time in Ciudad Real, clergy and religious were about 1.7 percent of the population. By 1751 this had risen to 2.97 percent, or 5.34 percent including their households. Altogether there were sixty-six clerics with 153 dependents and 168 monks and nuns with thirty-four servants.[7]

Ciudad Real contained the three parish churches already mentioned, in addition to several monasteries. Despite the city's economic difficulties during the Habsburg period, pious donations continued apace to these institutions and to set up new foundations. Some donors were wealthy residents of the city, but others were native sons and daughters who had made their fortunes in the New World. In the late sixteenth century Don Antonio Galiana Bermúdez, a noble of the military order of Montesa, and his wife, Doña Isabel Treviño, endowed two new convents of Descalced Carmelites for monks and nuns. After a legal battle over the terms of Galiana's will, work on the monks' convent started in 1611, and they took possession in 1619. The nuns' convent ran into even more trouble; despite an additional gift by Don Juan de Benavente, their building was not ready until the reign of Charles II.[8] At the time of the *Catastro*, both convents were apparently doing well, each with about 20 permanent residents.[9]

The main benefactor of the Observant Franciscans was Don Luis del Marmol, secretary of Charles I and notary of the Chancillería of Granada. Founded in 1527, the convent had about 20 resident monks in 1751.[10] A later foundation, that of the Descalced Mercedarians, had a good deal of trouble getting started and staying afloat financially. The original donation came from Don Andrés Lozano, a native of Ciudad Real who became a ship's captain and merchant involved in the Indies trade. In his will and codicil of January 1610, Lozano spread his resources among the convent, his surviving sisters who still lived in Ciudad Real, and various friends, creditors, and informal dependents in the New World and the Old.[11] He seemed more concerned with providing prayers for the repose of his soul than with providing a viable financial base for the monastery. The will allowed only 3,000 ducados to buy an appropriate house for the monks in Ciudad Real and to construct a chapel within it. Another 1,000 was to complete the decoration, and 500 a year was to support the monks. Considering that the retable alone of Nuestra Señora del Prado cost 10,500 ducados, Don Andres's gift was not likely to be sufficient.[12]

Not surprisingly, other charitable foundations in Ciudad Real opposed the new convent, fearful that the monks and their operation would drain needed support away from them. To make peace, the new order promised to live on its own endowment, and, thanks to declining house values, the monks were able to purchase a fine old house in 1621—somewhat in disrepair—for only 800 reales.[13] Still, there was not enough money to build an appropriate church for the order until Don Alvaro Muñoz de Figueroa and his wife, Doña María de Torres, provided funds in 1673.[14] Don Alvaro was also the donor of the seed-grain pósito of Ciudad Real in 1694 and one of the city's most important benefactors.

Other natives chose to endow specific charities or chaplaincies in their home parishes. The most impressive set of gifts came in 1643 from Don Diego López Treviño, a deputy of the Inquisition in Peru, and the licentiate Don Antonio de Torres Treviño, a cleric who was also employed by the Inquisition. Altogether, the two men left an endowment that generated 22,400 ducados annually: 3,000 for a convent of monks, Hospitalers of San Juan de Dios; 14,400 for 12 chaplaincies in the parish of San Pedro; 3,600 to provide dowries for 18 poor noblewomen; 600 for 6 university scholarships; 500 for a local school of primary letters; and 300 for a local grammar teacher.[15] The foundation of Hospitalers ran up against strong opposition from the clergy of San Pedro, but eventually they won their case and began caring for sick men who were either poor or members of the order of San Juan de Dios. The same monks took over the job of teaching grammar when the endowed chair was suspended in 1821, but they seem to have done it poorly.[16]

The parish of Nuestra Señora del Prado was particularly favored with donations during the Habsburg period. Of about sixty large chaplaincies that Padre Jara described in his book, twenty-one were founded in the seventeenth century, plus nineteen more established by the will and codicils of Don Pedro del Saz Correa in 1672-73. Some of the finest offerings came from natives of Ciudad Real who had become rich in the Indies. Even far from home, they called upon Nuestra Señora del Prado when they were in danger and thanked her for their good fortune.[17] Juan de Villaseca, a native of Ciudad Real who became secretary to the viceroy of Mexico, donated 10,500 ducados for an elaborate retable, which was carved and gilded between 1612 and 1617.[18] Closer to home, Don Felipe Muñiz, a *contador* (receiver; accountant) of the royal Council of Finance, donated funds for a storage room for the image's costumes. Other donors, such as the alderman Juan Bautista Vélez, left their entire estates to the church of Nuestra Señora del Prado. Because of their generosity, the church building and decorations were completed in the late sixteenth and early seventeenth centuries.[19]

In addition, numerous small shrines found patrons in the seventeenth century, a time, as we know, of economic difficulty for the city. It is probable that people of means put their money into pious works at least in part for lack of alternative uses for it. If these donations made the religious life of the city extraordinarily rich, they also represented a sterile use of capital that furthered the accumulation of property in the hands of the church.

Some donations caused more immediate trouble for the city, as we have seen with the difficulties surrounding the founding of the convents of Descalced Mercedarians and Carmelites. Many other pious gifts were not specific enough to avoid long, bitter, and costly battles which sometimes consumed the entire estate of the donor. In addition, the seventeenth and eighteenth centuries saw a series of acrimonious feuds between the parishes, convents, and *cofradías* (religious brotherhoods) of Ciudad Real, usually involving the rights and privileges of each. In one such case, the clergy of Nuestra Señora del Prado objected to the Corpus Christi procession's halting in order to celebrate a mass at San Pedro. The rival church claimed that the San Pedro mass was against the intentions of Pope Urban IV, who had instituted the holy festival. They eventually carried their case to the Roman curia, which decided against San Pedro.[20]

The high clergy of Ciudad Real occasionally tried to exert its power in opposition to the civil authorities. The *vicario eclesiástico*, who represented the archbishop of Toledo in Ciudad Real and the Campo de Calatrava, was the most powerful cleric in the city, but on at least one official occasion he presumed too much. Ciudad Real commonly held bullfights on August 15 and 16 to earn money for civic repairs and to honor the Virgin. The vicario boldly seated himself on a balcony of the main square to watch, enthroned in an elaborate chair with crimson velvet cushions. The king's representative ordered him to change the seat, since it was suited only for royalty, but the vicario ignored him. This dispute between the civil and ecclesiastical authority in Ciudad Real was eventually settled by the high court in Granada in 1660, against the vicario's claims.[21]

The cleric involved was the licentiate Estéban Caballero de la Serna, one of the few priests for whom there is plentiful information in the land sales of Ciudad Real. He was an ordinary priest (clerigo presbítero) in 1624, but by 1642 he had become vicario of Ciudad Real and the Campo de Calatrava. Two years later he added the title of general inspector (visitador general) of the ecclesiastical affairs of the district. In 1659 he still held all the earlier posts, in addition to holding a benefice in the church of San Pedro in Ciudad Real. Undoubtedly, he was one of the most powerful figures in the religious life of the region.[22]

Charles II granted the vicarios of Ciudad Real greater authority over the towns in the Campo de Calatrava, and one vicario in the mid-eighteenth century made dubious use of this authority. When the Count of Arandía arrived to begin inquiries for the Catastro de Ensenada, the vicario Don Josephe Marín de la Cueva, abetted by the clergy in several towns, persistently obstructed his efforts. This so upset Arandía that he took to his bed for a week, apparently from nervous exhaustion. Only the direct intervention of the archbishop of Toledo allowed Arandía to get on with his work.[23] Each of these incidents, small in themselves, illustrates both the power and the pretensions of the highest-ranking church official in Ciudad Real.

Perhaps what the vicario had wanted to avoid was a disclosure of the church's wealth. In the city of Ciudad Real, ecclesiastical income in 1751 easily surpassed that of the laity. Excluding land rents, the beneficed clergy made 266,165 reales a year, according to the general responses to the Catastro, and patrimonial income added another 6,662 reales. Over half of the total income apart from land rents came from traditional imposts on the citizenry—tithes and other exactions. Another 20 percent was income from government bonds. Lay incomes, again excluding land rents, came to 231,529 reales, 22 percent of that in posts alienated from the crown—a sizeable transfer payment back to the city's elite.[24]

On the other hand, the church was a major source of employment in Ciudad Real. In the mid-eighteenth century, tithe collectors, notaries, and other appointees cost the ecclesiastical establishment nearly 37,000 reales each year in salaries, if all the posts were held by laymen. Administrators of the many pious foundations earned another 6,940 reales, but this came from the income of the foundations concerned.[25] Unquestionably, the church had increased in wealth and power between 1500 and

1750, largely through donations of land and other bequests from wealthy citizens.

NOBILITY

As a body, the nobles of Ciudad Real enjoyed the same privileges as the nobles of Toledo, which left them free of all ordinary taxation. Their number during the seventeenth century is uncertain. In the late sixteenth century (1575-1580), about 2.5 percent of the householders of the area claimed nobility (*hidalguía*), but many of these cases were under litigation.[26] Though everyone seems to agree that the number of nobles rose during the following century, there is little evidence for this in Ciudad Real.[27] In the *Catastro* of 1751 about 2.3 percent of the city's householders was noble,[28] but the ratio of nobles to commoners varied widely from town to town. For example, San Benito near Ciudad Real boasted six nobles in a total of forty-one householders in the mid-sixteenth century.[29] Overall, then, Gentil da Silva's estimate of one noble for every twelve commoners (8.3 percent) in the Ciudad Real area is plausible, though it does not reflect the situation in the city alone.[30]

The only systematic discussion of the city's nobility is found in a manuscript preserved in the provincial archive of Ciudad Real. The author, Josephe Díaz Jurado, was the parish priest of San Pedro in the early eighteenth century. His work as we know it consists of three incomplete chapters written shortly before the *Catastro*. The third chapter deals with the most important families in the city, tracing their lineage as far back as possible. Prominent family names in the seventeenth century included Treviño, Aguilera, Velarde, Bermúdez, Muñoz, Loaisa, and Cueva. Others—Forcallo, Ledesma, Cárdenas, and Barona—were newcomers, but they quickly consolidated their positions by distinguished marriage alliances.[31]

The "very illustrious, very ancient" family of Treviño headed any list of Ciudad Real's nobility. According to Díaz Jurado they were originally from the Basque province of Alava and participated in many of the early battles of the Reconquest. When Ciudad Real was founded in the mid-thirteenth century, a Trevino was among its first nobles. By the seventeenth century, the family was related by marriage to every other important family in the city and exercised considerable power in the municipal government.[32] The Aguileras had received their nobility in the thirteenth century and settled in Ciudad Real from Andalusia in the late fourteenth. They, too, married well and wisely; Coca, Muñoz, Messía, Céspedes, and Treviño were some of their early matches. In the mid-seventeenth century, Don Juan de Aguilera Ladrón de Guevara was head of the family and a perpetual alderman of Ciudad Real. He appeared frequently in the notarial records, both in land transactions and in his official capacity as alderman. In 1679 he bought an enormous amount of land in Alcolea, consisting of thirty-three different parcels.[33] His children by two marriages held positions of power in the area as clerics, soldiers, knights of the military orders, and wives in other noble families.[34]

Don Juan's first wife, Inez de Treviño, gave him three sons who served with distinction in the campaigns of Philip IV. His second wife, Juana Treviño y Bermúdez, was the sister of Don Cristóbal Treviño y Bermúdez, holder of the Bermúdez family *mayorazgo* (entailed estate), founded by Don Antonio Galiana y Bermúdez and usually called the mayorazgo de Galiana. The children of this marriage included three boys, who all became members of the military order of Saint John of Malta, and four girls.[35] The descendants of one of the boys married quite well, to the marquesa of Peñafuente, maid of honor to the queen. Their daughter, Doña Manuela León de Aguilera y Enríquez, married Don Vicente Crespi y Mendoza (brother of the count of Orgaz), who became a resident of Ciudad Real and appeared in the rolls of the *Catastro*. It is possible that the Aguileras remained prominent in Ciudad Real when other families fell under a cloud at the time of the War of the Spanish Succession. I have been unable to find out which families supported the cause of the Austrian archduke in this conflict. From the Aguileras' continued good fortune, there is every reason to suppose that they were loyal to the French successor to Charles II.

The Velardes followed a similar pattern, though their nobility dated only from the reign of Philip II.[36] At least four of the family's members figured prominently in the land transactions of the seventeenth century: Don Antonio Velarde Cevallos, his brother Don Juan Velarde Cevallos, and the latter's sons, Don Cristóbal and Don Luis Velarde de Céspedes.[37] With the exception of Don Antonio, they were selling land, not buying it. The Bermúdez family also sold considerable amounts of land in the seventeenth century, but their lineage and prestige were unassailable. The Bermúdez claimed descent from no less a person than the Cid himself! They had settled in Ciudad Real at the time of the Reyes Católicos and rapidly consolidated their position by marriage and official posts. One branch of the family had died out by the time of the *Catastro*, but another had married into the Velarde y Céspedes, who, along with the Muñoz y Torres, were the most prominent noble families mentioned in the *Catastro*. Don Luis Bermúdez Messía de la Cerda was preeminent among the aldermen of Ciudad Real in the mid-seventeenth century. In addition he owned at least five other municipal offices and the right to name several subordinate officials. According to Díaz Jurado, he held the entailed estate of Villaquirán and jurisdiction over the pasture area called Santa María de Guadiana.[38]

The Muñoz family had allied itself by marriage to the Loaisas shortly after arriving in Ciudad Real in 1435. At first, their descendants kept the name Muñoz de Loaisa regardless of subsequent marriages with other families.[39] By the seventeenth century, other branches of the family were equally prominent, and in 1751 the Muñoz y Torres, for example, boasted the richest man in Ciudad Real—Don Alvaro Muñoz y Torres.[40] Also among the wealthiest citizens in 1751 was Doña María Catalina de Torres, whom we have already met in several contexts. Related to the great Muñoz family, she was also the widow of Don Diego Muñoz Gutiérrez de Montalvo, a knight of the order of Calatrava, and the universal heiress of her uncle Don Alvaro Muñoz y Figueroa, founder of the seed-grain pósito. Doña María Catalina was a central figure in the intellectual life of Ciudad Real, serving as hostess for gatherings (*tertulias*) of the city's intelligentsia. Her daughter, Juana Muñoz y Torres, further enhanced the family's prestige by marrying the head of the Velarde family.[41]

The Cuevas, supposedly an old noble family from Andalusia, came to Ciudad Real rather late. In the Habsburg period they seem to have held only one aldermanic office, and the notarial records show them selling land with some frequency in the course of the seventeenth century.[42] One reason may have been the sheer size of the family in the mid-seventeenth century. Don Antonio de la Cueva married Doña María Bermúdez in 1668, and together they had twenty-four children, the largest family encountered in the documentation. Fifteen of them died before reaching adulthood, slightly more than the average attrition rate in that century. The subsequent lives of the survivors illustrate quite clearly the limited choices open to the offspring of Spanish nobility. All five surviving daughters entered convents in Ciudad Real, two as Dominicans and three as Franciscans. Only one of the surviving sons married and stayed in Ciudad Real as the heir to the family fortune. Of the others, one died a bachelor in a neighboring town, one died unmarried as a captain of cavalry, and the last emigrated to the Indies and was not heard from again.[43]

Peter Boyd-Bowman, who has studied emigration to the Indies, found that 69 of the emigrants he traced in the sixteenth century came from the province of Ciudad Real. Of a total of nearly 5,500 emigrants, this figure is not high.[44] However, natives of Ciudad Real who did venture abroad often distinguished themselves. García Jofre de Loaisa, a knight commander of the order of Saint John, was in charge of one of the earliest attempts to pursue Spanish claims to the Portuguese Moluccas. When he died in 1526, a year after the expedition began, he was replaced by his lieutenant, Sebastián del Cano.[45] Local historians mention several other eminent natives who gained their fame in the Indies. Juan Alfonso de Estrada was a discoverer and early governor;[46] his son, Juan de Estrada, entered a preaching order and served in Mexico, translating many native works into Castilian in the mid-sixteenth century. Fray Antonio de Ciudad Real, another local friar, worked as a theologian in Yucatán, New Spain.[47]

We already know of several native sons who made fortunes in the New World and sent at least part of their treasure home to enrich Ciudad Real. Juan de Villaseca, the donor of the retable in Nuestra Señora del Prado; Andrés Lozano, founder of the convent of Descalced Mercedarians; and the two most generous founders of charitable organizations, Don Diego López Treviño and Don Antonio de Torres Treviño. All made their money in the New World or in trade between the New World and Spain.[48] Even in the depressed 1640s and 1650s, emigration to the Indies continued strong.[49] For many a young man without an inheritance, the Indies still provided a chance to make a fortune of his own.

Ciudad Real produced at least one very colorful figure for the Indies: Don Juan Velarde Treviño, a knight of Calatrava and the son of Doña Andrea Treviño and the licentiate Juan Velarde, a justice of the Audiencia in Granada under Philip II. Before going abroad, Juan Velarde Treviño was the governor of Almagro and participated in a distinguished delegation from Ciudad Real to the king in 1640.[50] In 1646 Velarde became the nineteenth corregidor of Potosi, the brawling mining town in Peru. Evaluations of his conduct in office are often contradictory, even within the one chronicle that we have. In attempting to quiet the endemic factional violence in town, he hanged ninety-six persons, and he made other enemies who were able to retaliate. The most dangerous was undoubtedly Don Francisco Nestares Marín, president of the local Audiencia. Velarde was driven from office in 1650 in a campaign spearheaded by Nestares, accused of everything from counterfeiting to fraudulently claiming to be a rich man's heir. The official inquiry into his tenure in office (called a *residencia*) lasted several years, and though Velarde was cleared of most of the charges, he still died in disgrace just as the case was coming to a close.[51]

Velarde's experience was exceptional, of course; there were enough others who came home rich to excite the imagination, and the envy, of their fellow citizens. Delgado Merchán cites several drives as the incentives for New World emigration: hunger, a desire for Quixotic adventures, an affinity for exploration, and most of all greed, stimulated by the knowledge of fortunes that neighbors had made in the New World. Emigration to the Indies and the pattern of disinvestment in land by Ciudad Real's nobility were two sides of the same coin. As economic opportunities contracted in the city, local investments contracted as well, and some enterprising members of the local elite sought their fortunes elsewhere.

Those nobles who stayed in Spain, particularly if they fell heir to landed estates, remained the social and economic arbiters of the country. If the evidence is equivocal in Ciudad Real, elsewhere it is clearer that the nobility was increasing its hold on the land during the Habsburg period. In addition, under Charles I and the later Habsburgs, the crown showed an accelerating tendency to sell jurisdictional rights, which went almost exclusively to nobles.[52] A favorite source of revenue was the vast holdings of the military orders, which had come under habitual royal control early in the reign of the Reyes Católicos. In the Campo de Calatrava near Ciudad Real, Charles I sold at least five towns outright between 1539 and 1553. His successors continued the practice, which reached maximum intensity under Felipe IV in the seventeenth century. At the time of the *Relaciones topográficas*, however, there were only nine towns (3,581 vecinos) reported that were controlled by private seigneurs in the Ciudad Real area; forty-five (18,506 vecinos) were still ruled by the military orders and fifteen (1,418 vecinos), by the crown. Though these numbers included only those towns that submitted relaciones, it is clear that the military orders remained in control of most of the area as late as 1575.[53]

Despite their landholdings, the Castilian nobility were largely urbanized by the seventeenth century. Their exalted social position and the lack of a strong urban patriciate had quite naturally left the cities open to noble control in the late Middle Ages. The situation was regularized after the Reyes Católicos, and often half the municipal offices in a given town were legally set aside for nobles. From the brief sketch of Ciudad Real's noble families it is obvious that few of them had ties to the nationally powerful high aristocracy. Instead, most would fit in the lower three ranks of the five categories of nobles described by Domínguez Ortiz: (1) grandees and those with important titles (duke, count, marquis, viscount); (2) nobles with high-ranking official posts; (3) nobles of the military orders; (4) those of wealth and distinguished lineage; and (5) poor and simple nobles.[54] Though they lacked national prominence, local nobles managed to dominate Ciudad Real as effectively as their more powerful counterparts dominated the largest cities of Castile.

John Lynch wrote, "The greatest cities of Castile—Toledo, Avila, Ciudad Real, Seville—were dominated by aristocratic families who spread out a network of influence throughout the land . . . In some of the principal towns of Castile—Valladolid, Avila, Toledo, Alcalá de Henares, Plasencia, Ciudad Real, Trujillo, Córdoba, Seville, Madrid itself—the nobility had a legal monopoly of municipal offices, which they often exercised through deputies or rented out for money."[55] Valladolid had been controlled by the same ten families since the Middle Ages.[56] In Ciudad Real as well, "the nobles of most worthy and ancient lineage" monopolized the administrative posts in the city.[57] The nobles had a useful meeting ground to parcel out offices in the cofradías to which they belonged.

There were two in Ciudad Real that were largely noble: the Cofradía of Señor Santiago, supposedly founded by Alfonso XI, and the Slaves of Nuestra Señora del Prado, founded in 1577, possibly as a counterpoise to the brotherhood in the rival parish.[58]

The *Catastro* contains a complete listing of municipal offices and other posts alienated from the crown in Ciudad Real. Altogether there were twenty-two persons listed whose names carried the noble appellation "Don." They controlled all but one of the aldermanic offices and several others. Twenty nonnobles controlled the lesser posts. Many of these men held other positions of power in the city and its surroundings, demonstrating the inbred character of the elite. Don Josephe Velarde was the corregidor of Ciudad Real in 1751, the governor (*alcaide*) of the pasture Santa María de Guadiana, and the owner of several notarial posts and minor judicial offices. Jacinto García Prieto, Francisco Peñuela, and Juan Díaz de la Cruz also owned notarial posts, for both local government and royal tax collection. Other municipal officials administered charitable or religious foundations in addition to their official charges: Julián de Calcerrada, Juan Manuel Barona, Antonio Ruiz Delgado, and Don Ignacio Palacios. And several were major livestock owners: Juan Díaz de la Cruz, Julián de Calcerrada, Don Diego Muñoz, Don Pedro Díaz de la Cruz, Don Juan de Azañón, and above all, Don Alvaro Muñoz y Torres, the wealthiest man in the city.[59]

Several partial lists of officials in the sixteenth and seventeenth centuries contain many of the same family names. In 1537 the city's aldermen included two Bermúdez, a Poblete, a Galiana, and a Martibáñez.[60] In 1609 a group of seven aldermen included three Treviños and a Bermúdez. Another mention of municipal officials at about the same time added another Bermúdez, a Loaisa, and a Poblete.[61] A delegation to Philip IV in 1640, carefully selected for its prestige and lineage, contained Don Juan de Aguilera Ladrón de Guevara, Don Alvaro Muñoz de Loaisa, Don Martín de Martibáñez, Don Juan Velarde Treviño, and Don Francisco Bermúdez de Avila.[62] The Treviño family was especially important as guardian of the statue of Nuestra Señora del Prado, the city's patroness. It was a rare gathering of prestigious ciudadrealeños that did not include at least one Treviño.

The neighborhood around the church of San Pedro in the oldest part of the city was long the preferred address for Ciudad Real's first citizens. Besides Treviño, illustrious family names in San Pedro included Velasco and Velarde, Torres and Poblete, Céspedes, Pulgar, Loaisa, Aguilera, Guevara, and Coca, as well as several others. In time some of them died out and newcomers or collateral heirs took over the old family fortunes. Some, through misfortune or mismanagement, dissipated their wealth and faded into obscurity. For whatever reason, the Pobletes and the

Cocas were no longer visible in the seventeenth century; the Calderón de la Barca family did not become visible until the early eighteenth century.[63] Though the personnel changed, the corporate entity of Ciudad Real's nobility retained the power, the economic base, and the sense that they—as individuals and as a body—were better than the rest of humanity.

If this was generally true on a local level, it was less so on a national level. Since the late fifteenth century, the nobility of Castile had lacked a political forum. Power continued to drift away from them and toward a stronger crown. Even the most precious of noble privileges, exemption from taxation, became little more than an empty form in the Habsburg period. Castilian nobles were forced to contribute heavily to the support of the state, particularly during the seventeenth century. The fiction of their tax-exempt status was maintained because they did not pay the personal taxes of common subjects; rather they paid in the form of forced loans, gifts, official commissions, and the compulsory purchase of government bonds.[64]

Economically, too, many Castilian nobles were in serious difficulties before the end of the sixteenth century. Because of the need to maintain their style of life in the face of rapidly rising prices, many nobles went heavily into debt. In discussing the effects of economic disasters on the nobility of Castile, Noël Salomon asserts that it had so lost its collective economic base as to cease being a true class, even though the psychological base remained.[65] Poor nobles who worked for a living and those newly impoverished by debt belied the noble ideal of idleness and luxury.

Though Salomon is undoubtedly correct that many prominent noble families became impoverished in the Habsburg period, the fortunes of individuals should not be confused with the fortunes of the group. The nobility was never a closed caste in Spain but instead was constantly being renewed by the addition of talented and wealthy newcomers. If the newcomers were less effective at changing the noble outlook than new nobles in England, for example, it was because the noble ideal was stronger in Spain, forged by a longer tradition as a military caste, and later reinforced by the lack of something better to do. The line between taxpaying commoners and the nobility was still crucial in early modern Spain, even if differences in wealth had blurred traditional social distinctions such as a person's manner of dress and style of life. The seventeenth century witnessed a lively debate all over Europe about the definition of true nobility. In Spain, the mania to prove one's family noble or one's blood pure assumed the proportions of a major social disease.[66]

Cervantes's *Adventures of Don Quixote* is full of the uneasiness of a traditional society trying to adjust to a new world in which wealth was increasingly the arbiter of social behavior. In Dorothea's tale, she described her parents as "people of humble birth, but so rich that if their rank were equal to their fortune they could have nothing more to desire . . . In short they are farmers [but] people whose wealth and fine way of life are gradually earning them the name of gentlefolk, or even nobles." Another farmer's daughter, the fair Quiteria, appeared for her marriage to Camacho dressed "like a fine palace lady!" and the wedding feast itself was beyond the means of many noblemen.[67]

In a society where "riches [could] solder a great many cracks," a poor nobleman was a double embarrassment. When Don Quixote asked what people were saying about his exploits, Sancho replied that he was not only laughed at for becoming a knight errant, but for daring to do so without the wealth that knights ought to have. " 'Then first of all,' said he, 'let me say that the common people take your worship for a very great madman, and they think I'm a great simpleton too. The gentlemen say that you're not content with being a country gentleman, but must turn yourself into a Don and launch forth into knighthood, with no more than a paltry vineyard and two acres of land, and hardly a rag to your back. The knights say that they don't like the petty gentry to set up in competition with them, especially squires who black their own shoes, and mend their black knitted stockings with green silk.' "[68] There is ample evidence that poor nobles continued to be an embarrassment. Of the nobles listed in the *Catastro* for Ciudad Real, there was at least one small farmer, two servants who cared for livestock, and two day-laborers! Legally, at least, wealth did not define the Castilian nobility, and these men could retain their social status despite lowly occupations.[69] It was easier for an enterprising and wealthy commoner to move up the social scale than it was for an impoverished noble to slip down. Patents of nobility were for sale during the reigns of the later Habsburgs, although their purchasers were widely disdained. And in Ciudad Real a merchant such as Juan de Rojas could become a common councilman in the late seventeenth century. It is possible that two of the nobles who were merchants in the city at the time of the *Catastro* had enhanced their social status by marrying into the city's finest families, even though they arrived in the city claiming to be from noble families in Burgos.[70]

Another classic avenue of social advancement was a university degree, which often opened the way for a post in royal service.[71] Even on a local level the bureaucracy was one of the most popular vehicles for social advancement. The municipal officials in Ciudad Real were part of the city's administrative elite, whether or not they were nobles. The prestige of the offices rather than the nominal salaries they paid made even a minor notarial post a coveted occupation. It was the administrative elite of Ciudad Real, especially the nonnobles, who played such a prominent role in land transactions during the seventeenth century, along with a few persons in large-scale trade and commerce. By moving into landownership, they were approaching the traditional preserve of the privileged estates in Spanish society—the church and the nobility. In other ways as well, newcomers to the upper ranks of Ciudad Real's society easily adopted the value system of the old elite. We have already noted that there was little to distinguish new landowners from old in their management of the land. Also in the preference for credit paper as a source of income, the elite of Ciudad Real can be viewed as a single, unified group.

For many reasons, Spanish agriculture became less financially attractive during the seventeenth century. Many urban dwellers who had previously invested in land found that censos and juros gave a better return for their investment. Juros, often bearing high interest, were to the money-hungry government what censos were to its private counterpart; that is, both censos and juros were much-needed sources of credit. The crown offered or forced the sale of juros to its citizens for a cash payment, assigning future tax revenues to pay the yearly interest fees. Periodically, the juros came under attack as a highly dangerous fiscal expedient, but the government was in no position to redeem them. In fact, Philip IV converted all government debts into juros in 1663, mortgaging taxes far into the future. In a period of economic stagnation, the burden of juro fees could not be lightened, except by drastic measures. Philip IV taxed, reduced, and suspended payment on juros intermittently throughout his reign, and his successor did the same. Unlike censo owners, juro owners had no legal recourse when the government defaulted on the interest payments.[72] For example, when a 20 percent discount on juros held on the alcabalas was ordered in 1660, the treasurer in each partido simply prepared a list of the new payment schedule.[73]

For those willing to take the risk, juros were a tempting investment. They were especially popular with religious collectives, which usually had other sources of income. Bennassar found that over half of the juros he examined in Valladolid belonged to religious collectives and institutions. There were enough private persons on the lists, however, to show the preponderance of Valladolid's greatest families among them.[74] There was a similar pattern for the forty-one juros on Ciudad Real's alcabalas in 1620-1622 (Appendix D, Table D.3).[75] Sixteen of them were held by religious or charitable institutions, accounting for nearly 38 percent of the total juro payments. Some of the money went for the upkeep of hospitals and convents, some for charity, and some for clerics employed to pray for the soul of a benefactor. Several of the largest institutional juro owners were religious collectives in the city of Toledo, representing a loss of money from Ciudad Real.

Of the twenty-five individual owners, nine at least were recognizably from the most prominent families in the city, including the names Treviño, Bermúdez, Poblete, and others. Particularly interesting was the presence of important financiers and groups of financiers of the crown. Livia Balbi held the largest single juro on the city's alcabalas. She was a member of the Genoese family that had been financing the Spanish Habsburgs since the sixteenth century, and the wife of a Palavesín (as the family name was known to the Spaniards), one of the other Genoese families that financed the international adventures of Philip IV.[76] One important group of juro holders had been caught in the crown's suspension of debt repayments in 1607. By a General Agreement of May 1608 they were assigned juros to placate them and to enable them to recover at least part of the money they had loaned.[77] Their juros, as well as several others held by individual owners, represented money flowing out of Ciudad Real, and in some cases, even out of the country. Altogether, less than half of the juro payments on the alcabalas went to individuals and institutions in the city itself,[78] and the situation worsened during the reign of Philip IV.

There were similar problems with the juros on the servicios ordinarios and extraordinarios. Investment income claimed by residents of Ciudad Real was increasingly siphoned off to pay more pressing debts.[79] The cost of such maneuvers by the government was, however, exceedingly high: the discrediting of juros as an investment and an erosion of public confidence in the good faith of the government. Investor confidence was shaken even more by the frenzied monetary juggling of Philip IV and his ministers during the last half of his reign.[80]

Juro interest payments seem to have been paid more regularly in the relatively peaceful reign of Charles II, but their actual value was considerably reduced. A partial list of juros on all of Ciudad Real's taxes in 1689-90 showed reductions for private owners as high as 65 percent from the face value of the juros. One held by the city of Ciudad Real had been reduced by 82 percent.[81] Religious institutions dominated the list, with eighteen out of twenty-six entries. Although the proportions might be quite different in a complete list, they suggest that religious institutions, and the pious foundations they controlled, were increasing their share of the income from credit paper in the city. According to the estimates of the *Catastro*, in 1751 ecclesiastical income easily surpassed secular income in Ciudad Real, and 20 percent of it came from juros.

The institutionalized church and individual clergymen were immensely powerful in Ciudad Real during the seventeenth century. There is also evidence that the power and wealth of the church was growing. Wealthy laypersons and clerics donated large legacies to religious institutions in the city. Some of these were charitable foundations and performed needed social services. But a considerable number of the legacies were unproductive socially and economically. Donors established chaplaincies and even entire convents to pray for the repose of their souls. The individuals appointed to the chaplaincies earned an income from them, but the wealth itself was unproductive, in most senses of the term. The power of the Catholic faith and the anxiety of persons facing death explain only part of this mania for pious foundations. Had there been ways for wealthy individuals to use their money productively, it is logical to assume they would have done so. In the absence of better investments,' however, they left their money to the church. There was another consideration, too. The confiscatory taxation policies of the Habsburg kings affected everyone in secular society, even the nobility. The church, on the other hand, and its charitable institutions, were generally spared from heavy taxation. Wealthy laypersons often gave their fortunes to the church during their lifetimes, reserving an income from the foundations they set up, rather like a modern tax-sheltered annuity. There are several instances of this in the juro records of Ciudad Real, most notably in the foundations of the licentiate Antonio de Torres Treviño.[82] By the nineteenth century, the concentration of all kinds of wealth in ecclesiastical hands was a national scandal, and it was often blamed for the economic difficulties of Ciudad Real Province.[83]

Another powerful group in the city was the nobility, both for its wealth and for its ability to arbitrate local politics, taste, and social behavior. As individuals and as family members, the nobles of Ciudad Real preserved their position by desirable marriages and a life-style that was commensurate with their status. Although primogeniture was standard in Spain, second and subsequent children retained noble status, unlike the situation in England. But position without wealth could be an embarrassment, and more than one noble second son (segundón) emigrated to the Indies to make his own fortune. A few of the emigrants from Ciudad Real returned home wealthy to establish their own distinguished families. Some set up prayer funds, convents, and other pious foundations in the churches and monasteries of Ciudad Real, and donated substantial amounts for the decoration of these same institutions. In fact, the seventeenth century was a major period of ecclesiastical construction in the city, despite the generally depressed economic picture.

The nobility of Ciudad Real continued to direct the political fortunes of the city, largely by controlling most of the municipal offices, though individual commoners could buy their way into the lower ranks of the city's bureaucracy, and perhaps even aspire to nobility. Once accepted into the elite, they apparently behaved no differently from its older members. To live nobly, to engage only in those occupations considered suitable for the nobility, was their social ideal. The widespread mania for hidalguía is usually connected to the disdain for work that supposedly characterized Spanish society. And Pierre Vilar, in a brilliant article, wrote of the sense of unreality at all levels of society in the early years of the seventeenth century; many refused to believe that the greatness of Spain had passed and continued to rely on archaic economic and social forms.[84]

There is no doubt that such attitudes existed, nor is there much doubt that they deepened the difficulties of the Spanish economy. Whether they caused these difficulties is another question. In previous chapters, I discuss the impediments to change in agricultural production that led to the stagnation of agriculture. I also discuss the even stronger impediments to industrial development. Neither agriculture nor industry, then, were attractive investments for people with money, though landownership remained desirable for social climbers. Where then did the wealthy invest their money? Some of them became involved with the export of fine wool to the textile factories of northwestern Europe and elsewhere. Many wealthy Spaniards, located advantageously in the port towns of Cádiz, Seville, and Bilbao, invested in the international trade to the Indies and to Europe. Though some were successful, Spaniards had less experience at this risky and highly skilled business than other nationalities, especially Italians.[85] For most of the Castilian elite, particularly for the nobility in isolated provincial centers such as Ciudad Real, these opportunities did not even exist. Instead, the secular elite of Ciudad Real responded to the contracting Castilian economy of the seventeenth century within a local context. They bought public offices to preserve their hold on the political, social, and economic life of the city; they donated large sums to the church; they gave their daughters attractive dowries; and they invested in those things that promised a fair return on their money. In Ciudad Real, this meant the commercial and transport facilities of the local economy and credit paper of all sorts. As we know from previous chapters, Ciudad Real's nobles and religious institutions owned the oil presses and flour mills used by city residents, and nobles were active in commerce and transportation. Both private and public credit paper were attractive investments before the mid-seventeenth century, and ecclesiastical institutions, individual clerics, nobles, pious foundations, and wealthy commoners all invested heavily in government bonds during the early Habsburg period. At best juros not only provided income for their owners, but their purchase, like the purchase of royal offices, also insured that some local tax revenue would stay in the city as transfer payments to the elite. The peculiar nature of the juros, unfortunately, reduced their value as investments. As Alvaro Castillo has pointed out, juros were personal contracts between the king and each investor more than they were impersonal government bonds.[86] This made juro owners subject to royal confiscations of their income, just as they were subject to other forms of indirect taxation by the impecunious crown.

It is doubtful that the Castilian nobility and other members of the elite would ever have been forces for change like their counterparts in England. The institutional structures in Castile made change very difficult at the best of times, and perhaps impossible under the pressure of nearly constant war. Nonetheless, it is difficult to maintain that the Castilian nobility had a lack of entrepreneurial ability and an exaggerated disdain for work. That simply was not true in Ciudad Real. Within the limits imposed upon them by the crown and by the vicissitudes of the market economy, they behaved quite rationally and with a keen eye for profits in the local milieu.

CONCLUSION

VIII

Ciudad Real shared in the major developments of late medieval and early modern Castile: the Reconquest of land from the Moslems, the growth of a centralized monarchy and religious orthodoxy, the discovery and exploitation of the New World, and the Habsburgs' dynastic and religious wars to preserve their inheritance in Europe and abroad. More often than not the city was a tool of the crown (or even its victim) in these great movements, rather than a full and willing partner. Nonetheless, its destiny was inextricably linked with that of its sovereigns, and city residents served the crown loyally—with one notable exception— through all the period of Spain's rise and fall as a European power. Founded to counter the power of the aristocratic military order of Calatrava during the Reconquest, the town received royal support for its rights to water, firewood, and pasture in the lands of Calatrava. Successive monarchs did not, however, sanction illegal incursions into those lands and often stepped in to mediate legal and military struggles between Villa Real and Calatrava. A royal decision in 1339 effectively barred the town's expansion into neighboring lands and impelled the citizens toward a diversified economy of agriculture, industry, and trade. In return for its loyalty the town was made a city in 1420 and briefly housed both the Inquisition and the royal court of appeals in the late 1400s. The Inquisition ruined Ciudad Real's remaining group of converted Jews before moving on to Toledo, and the departure of both institutions left the city with only modest resources to support itself.

Those resources were put to the test during the Habsburg centuries by a combination of internal economic developments and royal policies. Ciudad Real experienced growth, stagnation, crisis, and readjustment between 1500 and 1750, though the timetable varies depending upon whether we look at population trends, agriculture, industry and commerce, or investment patterns. The number of inhabitants in the city was already growing when the parish registers began in the early sixteenth century, and population continued to grow steadily until 1570, when it spurted upward with the relocation of over 3,000 Moriscos from Granada. With a rising population, agriculture was a good investment, and there was a lively market for land and various types of private credit in the mid-sixteenth century. There was also a local market for the city's cheap manufactured goods and a wider market for a few luxury items such as fine gloves and wine. The Moriscos who arrived in 1570 had skills similar to those of the Old Christian population already in residence, and they seem to have played diverse roles in the city's economy. That so many new residents could be absorbed by Ciudad Real indicates that the sixteenth-century boom continued at least to 1570.

What no one knew, of course, was that it could not last much longer. Population growth was already shifting the delicate balance between needs and available resources, and in Ciudad Real the arrival of the Moriscos aggravated the situation. From the late 1570s the region experienced a succession of inadequate harvests that caused widespread distress. Concurrently the government of Philip II trebled the tax on transactions and added an enormous levy on foodstuffs and other basic consumer items. This was not an arbitrary decision. The Netherlands revolt had turned into a major test of the crown's strength, England was openly at war with Spain in Europe and in the Americas, and the king also felt obliged to support various factions in the French Wars of Religion. For all of these needs, the uncertain flow of treasure from America was far from sufficient, and the royal fisc wanted the assurance of a steady flow of tax revenue from Castile. Still, for Ciudad Real and for Castile in general, the massive tax increase could not have come at a worse time. Industry in Ciudad Real seems to have held up longer than agriculture, but the cumulative effects of agricultural distress and higher taxes on all production reduced the money available for manufactured goods and began to have serious effects on industry by about 1600. Harvest crises continued as well, and the one in 1604-1605 was particularly severe in Ciudad Real.

In 1610 the Moriscos of Castile were expelled, including 2,000-3,000 from Ciudad Real. At one blow, the city lost between one-fourth and one-third of its total population, as if it had been visited by a terrible plague. In the short term this must have been a shock to the city's economy, though it is quite true that agriculture and industry were in difficulty much earlier. In the long term the effects of the expulsion are even less clear. The departure of the Moriscos reduced the taxable population drastically, but taxes were also reduced in the same period. Paradoxically the expulsion lowered the population just when it needed to be lowered to match the contracted opportunities in agriculture and industry. The city council complained that Ciudad Real suffered from a lack of inhabitants and general poverty in 1621, and they were right, but the Morisco expulsion was not the major cause of the distress.

In many ways, 1621-1625 marks the nadir of the city's economy in the early modern period. Thereafter population began to recover, though very slowly and unsteadily. Harvest failures and epidemics arrived near mid-century, and similar periods of distress occurred thereafter. In the middle third of the seventeenth century, Spain's involvement in European wars reached a peak, and so did royal taxation. Inflation reduced the real burden of taxes, but in Ciudad Real a lowered population and an economy that was far from buoyant made this period as difficult as the late sixteenth century. Not until the last third of the seventeenth century did the city's economy begin to recover along with its population, despite a prolonged economic crisis from 1677 to 1690. By the time of the government inquiry of 1751, Ciudad Real's population had nearly regained its late sixteenth-century level, and city residents were engaged in an impressive diversity of occupations. They were once again at the hub of local commerce and seemed to be experiencing something of a boom in building construction. Agriculture had scarcely changed from previous centuries, and it is difficult to know how effectively agriculture and herding were balanced. It is clear, however, that wealthy residents were major livestock owners with links to the Mesta and to the lucrative business of wool exporting. Also noteworthy is that nobles were heavily involved in local trade and commerce. This pattern of noble investment and the city's slow recovery through the seventeenth century were parallel developments, shaped in the difficult decades after 1621-1625.

Ciudad Real could not rely on international trade to revive its economy in the seventeenth century. It was too far from the coasts and its products were mostly bulky agricultural commodities and cheap manufactured goods that could not bear the high costs of long-distance land transport. In any case the market for agricultural and manufactured goods had shrunk along with population, and it was supplied in many areas by foreign imports. Ciudad Real's agriculture and industry therefore turned inward, and ordinary people in both sectors relied on a local market for the few things they could not produce themselves.

The local elite had a wider range of choices, including emigration to the Indies, but few found agriculture and industry attractive investments. Those with money to invest often turned their gaze away from local production, even when they continued to reside in Ciudad Real. Many local nobles sold part of their land during the seventeenth century and increased their investments in government bonds, among other things.

These can be seen as sterile uses of capital, but they promised a good monetary return and fulfilled the noble's moral obligation to help his sovereign. Dowries and charitable gifts provided less tangible returns, but they too were rational investments at a time when local agriculture and industry stagnated. Nobles did invest in the few profitable parts of the local economy—commerce, trade, and livestock raising—and they continued to dominate local government by their control of public offices.

The few nonnobles who shared in the political control of the city followed a similar investment pattern, with one interesting difference. As a group they bought more land than they sold over the course of the seventeenth century, despite its reduced value as a purely financial investment. Landownership was a sign of social prestige in Habsburg Spain, as it has been in most traditional societies, and the nonnoble elite of Ciudad Real acquired land to enhance their status rather than for capitalist exploitation. (There would have been little point to that, anyway, without the existence of reliable transportation links to market the surplus.) It would seem that only the nobility, secure in status, could afford to engage in the full range of economic opportunities that the economy of Ciudad Real had to offer. Those who aspired to nobility stayed with traditionally high-status investments: land, livestock, government bonds, dowries, and charitable donations.

In this way members of the secular elite of Ciudad Real preserved their incomes and their local political power during the seventeenth century and beyond, but they chose investments that did nothing to develop the local economy. Instead they simply adjusted to the realities of subsistence production. By 1751 Ciudad Real had a few economic links to the wider world—most notably the sale of wool and the payment of taxes. Otherwise the city and its surrounding area functioned as a nearly independent unit. Population grew slowly, but the economy did not change. La Mancha came to be viewed by the cosmopolitan residents of Madrid and other great cities as a stagnant backwater inhabited by lazy and ignorant bumpkins. What such critics ignored was that, given the restrictions created by soil, climate, topography, and history, the citizens of Ciudad Real had made an entirely rational set of choices. Their regional economy functioned well most of the time, though without perceptible changes in the patterns of subsistence production and consumption. When the growth of the early sixteenth century stalled, they had reverted to a system that ensured their survival—a partnership between agriculture and industry within a regional market network. They broke out of subsistence production only when dependable markets and efficient transportation links could ensure their survival equally well.

APPENDIXES
NOTES
INDEX

PARISH REGISTERS

The parish registers of Ciudad Real have much in common with others in the early modern period in Spain. Where they exist, records are lengthy, continuous, and fairly reliable. Unfortunately they lack explanatory information such as age and cause of death (for burials) and age and town of origin (for marriages). All the vital records in western Europe were sporadically kept until 1563, when the Council of Trent ordered local parishes to keep a record of baptisms. The registry of burials was not decreed until 1614, but many records in Spain began earlier.

There were three parishes in the city of Ciudad Real: Santiago, San Pedro, and Nuestra Señora del Prado, all of roughly equal size. Santiago, in the northeast of the city, was the oldest, dating from the thirteenth century. Part of the old Jewish quarter (*aljama*) lay within the parish; the rest continued into San Pedro. Santiago and its records were severely damaged in the civil war of 1936-1939; though the church has been partially restored, the early parish registers were completely lost. San Pedro in the southeast of the city was newer than Santiago—dating from the fourteenth and fifteenth centuries—and much more prosperous. Many leading citizens lived in the parish of San Pedro, though by the Habsburg period its rival Nuestra Señora del Prado was attracting their patronage. San Pedro's registers of baptisms began in 1517; marriage registers began in 1597; burial registers did not begin until 1708. The church of Nuestra Señora del Prado honoring the city's patroness presided over the western and northwestern parts of the city. Begun in 1531, the church is mostly in the Gothic style, like the simpler and more elegant San Pedro. It consists of a single colossal nave, one of the largest in Spain, made of brick and hewn stone. The Moorish quarter (*morería*) lay close to the church in the southern part of the parish district (*colación*). There are parish records for baptisms from 1536 to 1627 and from late 1663 onward. Marriage records exist continuously from 1564, and burial records exist from 1585 to 1602 and from 1649 onward. The few death records extant for the sixteenth century are not reliable, because they include only those who provided for prayers to be said for the repose of their souls.

In all of these registers, there is no evidence that the priest allowed much time between the event and its registration; most entries seem to have been made immediately. Other preliminary tests also indicated that the records are fairly reliable. For instance, the male sex ratios of both parishes' baptismal records show a close approximation to the biological norm. A normal population in which all live births are recorded would have a ratio at birth of 105 males to 100 females (described as a male sex ratio of 105). In the sixteenth and seventeenth centuries, the male sex ratio in San Pedro was 103 and that in Nuestra Señora del Prado was 107. Marriage registers are the only ones in which the ecclesiastical and the demographic information coincide. Baptisms and burials have less meaning for the demographic historian than do births (or conceptions) and deaths. Nonetheless, the ecclesiastical record is usually all that exists, and it is quite adequate if we keep its limitations in mind. I have made the following assumptions: (1) That recorded baptisms equaled births in time and in number. This underestimates births, but it is better to use the figures as they stand rather than applying an arbitrary correction factor. (2) That legitimate births accounted for the vast majority of all births and were much more likely to be recorded than illegitimate ones. Therefore all births are considered legitimate. (3) That burials equaled deaths in time and in number. In the tables that follow, the yearly totals of vital events stop in 1699. Table 5 and graphs for the eighteenth century have recently been published in Jerónimo López-Salazar Pérez, "Evolución demográfica de la Mancha en el siglo XVIII," *Hispania* 36 (1976):233-299.

Table A.1. Yearly baptisms: San Pedro (1517-1536, 1560-1566, 1583-1699).

Year	Number	Year	Number	Year	Number	Year	Number
1517	47	1589	92	1626	52	1663	65
1518	67	1590	88	1627	43	1664	65
1519	79	1591	76	1628	43	1665	64
1520	81	1592	75	1629	50	1666	61
1521	54	1593	80	1630	57	1667	60
1522	2	1594	85	1631	49	1668	47
1523	17	1595	75	1632	61	1669	60
1524	21	1596	75	1633	58	1670	43
1525	44	1597	70	1634	50	1671	64
1526	55	1598	70	1635	63	1672	60
1527	79	1599	84	1636	67	1673	68
1528	62	1600	87	1637	49	1674	67
1529	57	1601	101	1638	55	1675	72
1530	69	1602	99	1639	55	1676	67
1531	51	1603	88	1640	49	1677	74
1532	62	1604	91	1641	48	1678	57
1533	76	1605	66	1642	55	1679	70
1534	70	1606	89	1643	64	1680	58
1535	59	1607	84	1644	52	1681	60
1536	85	1608	88	1645	71	1682	82
		1609	58	1646	60	1683	93
		1610	77	1647	64	1684	60
1560	11[a]	1611	61	1648	49	1685	19
1561	70	1612	61	1649	52	1686	65
1562	57	1613	60	1650	69	1687	59
1563	38	1614	54	1651	60	1688	71
1564	62	1615	42	1652	58	1689	67
1565	15	1616	49	1653	60	1690	76
1566	82	1617	50	1654	67	1691	69
		1618	45	1655	71	1692	60
		1619	43	1656	60	1693	76
1583	55	1620	46	1657	72	1694	66
1584	57	1621	42	1658	64	1695	60
1585	66	1622	43	1659	61	1696	85
1586	88	1623	45	1660	59	1697	67
1587	108	1624	63	1661	69	1698	77
1588	104	1625	35	1662	65	1699	68

a. Probably incomplete.

Table A.2. Yearly baptisms: Nuestra Señora del Prado (1536-1627, 1663-1699).

Year	Number	Year	Number	Year	Number	Year	Number
1536	82	1569	90	1602	91	1668	69
1537	70	1570	128	1603	79	1669	78
1538	82	1571	87	1604	84	1670	65
1539	80	1572	108	1605	74	1671	74
1540	104	1573	96	1606	55	1672	77
1541	84	1574	81	1607	61	1673	61
1542	86	1575	89	1608	45	1674	74
1543	76	1576	66	1609	51	1675	73
1544	34	1577	31	1610	21	1676	78
1545	47	1578	78	1611	38	1677	70
1546	51	1579	39	1612	33	1678	76
1547	58	1580	81	1613	32	1679	92
1548	73	1581	70	1614	37	1680	70
1549	71	1582	76	1615	35	1681	59
1550	61	1583	92	1616	33	1682	72
1551	69	1584	87	1617	45	1683	73
1552	105	1585	68	1618	31	1684	55
1553	86	1586	80	1619	31	1685	41
1554	89	1587	95	1620	25	1686	67
1555	78	1588	97	1621	60	1687	73
1556	79	1589	22[a]	1622	49	1688	75
1557	32	1590	78	1623	45	1689	84
1558	50	1591	75	1624	54	1690	66
1559	47	1592	78	1625	51	1691	91
1560	67	1593	86	1626	45	1692	85
1561	82	1594	81	1627	43	1693	84
1562	85	1595	109			1694	72
1563	80	1596	106			1695	73
1564	84	1597	106	1663	22	1696	86
1565	75	1598	94	1664	76	1697	90
1566	100	1599	78	1665	97	1698	84
1567	74	1600	94	1666	79	1699	75
1568	87	1601	73	1667	63		

a. Probably incomplete.

Table A.3. Yearly marriages: San Pedro (1597-1699).

Year	Total	Year	Total	Year	Total	Year	Total
1597	21	1623	8	1649	19	1675	31
1598	34	1624	15	1650	25	1676	11
1599	31	1625	20	1651	19	1677	6
1600	25	1626	13	1652	15	1678	25
1601	24	1627	20	1653	17	1679	25
1602	22	1628	24	1654	26	1680	12
1603	33	1629	11	1655	21	1681	19
1604	32	1630	19	1656	14	1682	23
1605	21	1631	18	1657	10	1683	23
1606	33	1632	14	1658	17	1684	12
1607	44	1633	14	1659	23	1685	17
1608	22	1634	9	1660	26	1686	18
1609	31	1635	19	1661	21	1687	21
1610	17	1636	15	1662	9	1688	36
1611	13	1637	15	1663	13	1689	19
1612	8	1638	15	1664	19	1690	24
1613	12	1639	14	1665	14	1691	16
1614	15	1640	12	1666	18	1692	12
1615	20	1641	17	1667	17	1693	16
1616	19	1642	18	1668	22	1694	12
1617	11	1643	22	1669	6	1695	26
1618	4	1644	25	1670	21	1696	26
1619	13	1645	22	1671	19	1697	26
1620	13	1646	12	1672	19	1698	17
1621	13	1647	23	1673	23	1699	11
1622	19	1648	19	1674	18		

Table A.4. Yearly marriages: Nuestra Senora del Prado (1564-1699).

Year	Total	Year	Total	Year	Total	Year	Total
1564	26	1598	9	1632	9	1666	8
1565	20	1599	23	1633	16	1667	19
1566	17	1600	30	1634	13	1668	23
1567	11	1601	25	1635	16	1669	20
1568	—	1602	21	1636	15	1670	27
1569	—	1603	17	1637	15	1671	19
1570	3	1604	21	1638	12	1672	18
1571	19	1605	16	1639	14	1673	26
1572	16	1606	11	1640	14	1674	18
1573	17	1607	22	1641	22	1675	19
1574	11	1608	11	1642	15	1676	23
1575	6	1609	17	1643	18	1677	27
1576	13	1610	16	1644	13	1678	27
1577	10	1611	20	1645	13	1679	22
1578	—	1612	17	1646	17	1680	16
1579	—	1613	7	1647	15	1681	15
1580	5	1614	—	1648	7	1682	22
1581	4	1615	14	1649	20	1683	35
1582	8	1616	16	1650	18	1684	20
1583	10	1617	7	1651	26	1685	21
1584	4	1618	10	1652	26	1686	32
1585	12	1619	17	1653	17	1687	24
1586	20	1620	13	1654	29	1688	26
1587	10	1621	22	1655	22	1689	24
1588	15	1622	20	1656	14	1690	23
1589	20	1623	7	1657	14	1691	28
1590	15	1624	20	1658	18	1692	19
1591	17	1625	8	1659	18	1693	12
1592	15	1626	6	1660	20	1694	18
1593	7	1627	14	1661	22	1695	23
1594	—	1628	20	1662	27	1696	28
1595	7	1629	20	1663	22	1697	20
1596	21	1630	18	1664	17	1698	28
1597	20	1631	24	1665	20	1699	18

Table A.5. Yearly burials: Nuestra Señora del Prado (1597-1602, 1649-1699).

Year	Total	Year	Total	Year	Total	Year	Total
1597	20	1656	42	1671	50	1686	54
1598	26	1657	33	1672	17	1687	52
1599	1[a]	1658	52	1673	42	1688	32
1600	30	1659	76	1674	23	1689	38
1601	14	1660	87	1675	39	1690	28
1602	18	1661	71	1676	44	1691	46
1649	50[b]	1662	61	1677	43	1692	39
1650	66	1663	35	1678	72	1693	44
1651	54	1664	57	1679	32	1694	36
1652	51	1665	52	1680	36	1695	55
1653	99	1666	57	1681	58	1696	54
1654	38	1667	125	1682	68	1697	53
1655	37	1668	77	1683	65	1698	59
		1669	50	1684	283	1699	73
		1670	33	1685	116		

a. Probably incomplete.
b. August-December only.

NONNOBLES BY OCCUPATION (1751)

APPENDIX B

Category and occupation[a]	Number vecinos	Salary in reales per person/day or per person/yr.
1. Agriculture, livestock, fishing		
labrador (farmer)	202	3/day
sons, brother, foremen doing the same work	250	2/day
jornalero (day laborer)	603	3/day
	4	1/day
cazador (hunter)	?	6,230/yr. for all
2. Administration, professions, services, health		
abogado (advocate; lawyer)	5	3,960/yr.
médico (physician)	3	4,033/yr.
cirujano (surgeon)	4	1,925/yr.
boticario (druggist)	4	4,125/yr.
barbero (barber-surgeon)	19	2/day
sacristán (sacristan)	8	1,112/yr.
escribano real (royal scrivener)	5	2,870/yr.
notario (notary)	5	3,968/yr.
preceptor de gramática (grammar teacher)	2	1,650/yr.
maestro de primeras letras (primary school teacher)	5	528/yr.
empleados en rentas provinciales (provincial tax officials)	?	26,190/yr. for all
correo (mailman)	?	6,600/yr. for all
administración (public officials)	?	20,230/yr. for all
justicia (judicial officials)	?	9,520/yr. for all
empleados en generales (minor posts)	?	12,651/yr. for all
arrendador de ramos reales (royal tax farmer)	1	1,100/yr.
aguador (water-carrier)	5	288/yr.

Category and occupation	Number vecinos	Salary in reales per person/day or per person/yr.
3. Food-related		
molinero (miller)	12	2/day
confitero (confectioner)		
maestro (master)	2	4/day
chocolatero (chocolate maker)		
master	6	5/day
pastelero (pastry cook)	2	4/day
panadero (baker)	26	4/day
carnicero (butcher)	4	1,012/yr.
4. Textiles		
tejedor (weaver)		
master	8	4/day
oficial (journeyman)	3	2/day
cardador (carder)		
master	13	4/day
tintorero (dyer)		
master	1	4/day
batanero (fuller)		
master	3	4/day
aprensador (presser)		
master	1	2/day
journeyman	2	2/day
5. Hides and leather		
zurrador (currier)		
master	2	6/day
journeyman	6	3/day
curtidor (tanner)		
master	2	4/day
journeyman	1	1/day
guarnicionero (harness maker)		
master	8	4/day
6. Apparel making and repair		
sastre (tailor)		
master	11	4/day
journeyman	16	3/day
zapatero (shoemaker)		
master	14	4/day
journeyman	52	2/day
sombrerero (hatter)		
master	4	4/day
peluquero (wig maker)	1	3/day
7. Household goods (non-metal)		
alfarero (potter)		
master	1	4/day

Category and occupation	Number vecinos	Salary in reales per person/day or per person/yr.
tejero (tile maker)		
master	2	2/day
espartero (basket maker)	7	3/day
cerero (chandler)		
master	3	3/day
cordelero (rope maker)		
master	5	4/day
polvorista (gunpowder maker)		
master	7	2/day
8. Metallurgy		
platero (silversmith), master	2	4/day
herrero y cerrajero (smith and locksmith)		
master	10	4/day
journeyman	12	2/day
herrador (farrier), journeyman	6	3/day
calderero (coppersmith, etc.)		
master	4	4/day
journeyman	4	3/day
9. Building, quarries, public works		
carpintero (carpenter)		
master	19	6/day
journeyman	17	2/day
albañil (mason)		
master	10	6/day
journeyman	7	3/day
pintor y dorador (painter and gilder), master	1	6/day
10. Commerce, trade, transport		
comerciante o mercader de tienda abierta (shopkeeper)	35-40	80,620/yr. for all
mesonero (innkeeper)	1	4,500/yr.
large- and small-scale transporters	10-15	29,650/yr. for all

Sources: AHN, *Hacienda: Catastro*, libs. 7465-68; AGS, *RG*, lib. 468, questions 17, 29-32; Pérez Valera, *Ciudad Real en el siglo XVIII*, pp. 32-36. The general occupational categories were adapted from Louis Henry, *Manuel de démographie historique* (Paris, 1967).

a. We can estimate very roughly that, in modern terms, 68 percent of the householders worked in the primary sector of the economy (category 1), earning 42 percent of the total income; 20 percent worked in the secondary sector (categories 3-9), earning 23 percent of the total income; and 11 percent worked in the tertiary sector (categories 2 and 10), earning 35 percent of the total income.

LAND SALE DATA FOR THE SEVENTEENTH CENTURY SOURCES AND METHODS OF ANALYSIS

APPENDIX C

The land sale data used in this study come from the city's large collection of notarial papers (*protocolos notariales*) contained in the provincial archive, which has very good holdings for the seventeenth century. The collection is well cataloged, according to the name of the notary, and most of it is in a usable condition. By some preliminary screening, notaries with very brief or badly deteriorated papers were rejected, as were those who dealt exclusively with church patrimony or royal business. The nine notaries chosen had a large volume of private secular transactions over a long time span. The volume and diversity of their work offered the best chance to gather a representative selection of land transactions over the century. Altogether, the records of these notaries produced bills of sale (*cartas de venta*) for about 800 transactions. Unlike the *Catastro* (1751), the documents cannot define landownership at any given time. Instead, they illustrate changes over time in the seventeenth century without duplicating work already in progress. Until her untimely death in the summer of 1976, Isabel Pérez Valera was working on the individual responses to the *Catastro*, contained in the provincial archive of Ciudad Real. Her son, Jerónimo López-Salazar, is continuing her work, and the French scholar Jean-Pierre Amalric has been working for many years on an analysis of the general responses contained in the archive of Simancas.

Since most of the documents used in this study were bills of sale, they followed a similar legal formula regardless of when or by whom they were written. By the seventeenth century hurried versions of the official courtly style of handwriting (*cortesana*) had led to the flowing script known as *procesal* or to eccentric adaptations of cortesana. Don Quixote had harsh words for the lawyers' clerks who "use a legal hand that Satan

himself will not understand" (*Don Quixote*, pt. 1, chap. 25, p. 208). Fortunately, the most extreme of these styles did not penetrate to isolated
places such as Ciudad Real. At worst protocolos were illegible only because of the personalized style of the notary. For each land transaction I
noted the identity of buyer and seller; the type of land involved; its location, size, and price; the terms of the sale; and the date.

The land transactions fell into several different categories, related to
how the land was used and how it was measured. For example, tierra de
pan llevar (grain-producing land) was used to grow cereal grains and was
measured in fanegas. A quiñón, measured indiscriminately in fanegas or
aranzadas, was a share in a piece of grain land. Viticulture accounted for
three categories of land: viñas (vineyards), majuelos (young vineyards
just starting to produce), and parrales (grape arbors or wild vines). Viñas
and parrales were commonly measured in aranzadas, while majuelos
were measured by the number of vines (*vides*, or *cepas*) they contained.
Similarly, olive groves (olivares) were sold by the number of trees. Occasionally, a bill of sale would also mention the land measure of an olivar
in aranzadas.

The other categories of land sold enjoyed a distinctly minor importance compared to these. Huertas were generally used for vegetables
(*hortalizas*) or fruit trees, but they could contain grains, olive trees, or
other plants. Like quiñones, huertas were measured in either fanegas or
aranzadas in bills of sale. Herrenales were sown with a mixture of grains
(called *herrén*, or maslin) for animal fodder; when the measurements
were given, they were in fanegas. The last category, the zumacares (sumac fields), were rare in Ciudad Real. Often several categories of land
shared the same parcel. In these cases, I listed the sale according to its
most important part. A vineyard with a border of olive trees remained a
vineyard and a large parcel of tierra with a garlic field (*ajar*) inside remained tierra.

Unlike some of the other categories of land, the tierra sales varied
widely in size and value. Sometimes the largest sales neglected to note
how many parcels were involved, and in one case this meant a sale of 240
fanegas, ostensibly in 1 parcel. (APCR, leg. 199) As an experiment, I excluded from the calculations all sales that involved more than 20 fanegas
in 1 parcel. This eliminated both abnormally large parcels and also those
sales where a number of parcels were probably involved, but not differ-
entiated—a total of 1,309 fanegas in 15 parcels. Subtracting this from the
total left 2,353 fanegas in 474 parcels, for an average of 5.0 fanegas. This
seems to be a more realistic figure for the tierra parcels around Ciudad
Real, and it still allows for parcels up to 20 fanegas in size. In most tierra
transactions the price was paid in full at the time of sale. For other sales,
a portion was paid at the time of sale, with the remainder—often one-

half—to follow at a specified holy day a year or two in the future. When cash exchanged hands, it was sometimes described in detail. More often, it was given merely as "reales in cash" or "reales and other money." Curiously, the first specific mention of vellón (copper coinage) in a tierra sale was not until 1646, but it appeared consistently thereafter. This is curious because vellón seems to have been common currency elsewhere in Spain from the late 1620s (Hamilton, *American Treasure*, p. 212). Censos figured in 7 percent of the tierra sales. Some were mortgages taken out with the land as security, with yearly interest (réditos) due on the loan. Others were probably rental contracts, since the buyer merely took over the obligation to pay the réditos.

The 136 sales of quiñones involved an average-sized parcel of 3.85 fanegas with an average value per fanega of 6,000 maravedís. Mortgaged parcels were a scant 5.9 percent of the total and most bills of sale indicated a cash payment in full. Vellón first appeared in 1658; it was specified frequently until 1681 and exclusively thereafter. For the viticulture lands that are discussed at some length in chapter 3, bills of sale also show a late appearance of vellón, and most of the transactions indicated that the purchase price was paid in full at the time of the sale.

Most of the transactions of olive groves also mentioned that full payment occurred at the time of the sale, but I am reluctant to accept this at face value for olivar sales or any others. In a few cases, there were letters of debt (cartas de obligación) relating to olivar sales that were supposedly paid in full at the time of sale. These documents clearly stated that although the bill of sale indicated full payment, the buyer in fact had paid only a part and still owed the rest. Since the debt agreements were usually made at the time of the sale or shortly thereafter, the whole exercise appears to have been a subterfuge. Unfortunately, there is no way of knowing how many presumed cash sales were handled in this way, without making a thorough search of the cartas de obligación. Those encountered by chance did not provide enough evidence to generalize about their incidence or their purpose. They merely cast doubt on the real frequency of nominal cash sales. A few olivar sales involved an explicitly delayed payment; half the purchase price was paid at the time of sale and the other half was to be paid at a specified date in the future (see especially APCR, legs. 121, 122, 146, 205). We can be sure that full payment changed hands only where the actual currency was described. In olivar sales, vellón was not mentioned until mid-century. After 1665 it appeared in nearly every bill of sale. Nonetheless, sales in 1683 and 1691 still noted payment "in doubloons of 8 [pieces] and 4 and vellón money" and "in silver money and vellón currency" (APCR, legs. 199, 217). Nearly 10 percent of the olivar transactions involved censo obligations, a somewhat higher figure than in other categories of land.

The huertas were also heavily indebted, perhaps because their value made them attractive as security for loans. About one-third of the huertas sold carried a financial obligation of some sort. Cash payments in full were noted in most of the bills of sale; vellón appeared first in 1651, and regularly after 1663. There were too few sales of other types of land to warrant detailed analysis.

Defining social categories for the buyers and sellers of land in Ciudad Real created some problems. Eventually I chose three groups: clergy and institutions, nobles, and nonnobles. Those in each group shared a traditional sociolegal status that defined them in the population, but they differed in other social measures, especially in wealth. Assigning individuals to a particular group was also difficult. The series of choices made in placing an individual in one group or another is valid for Ciudad Real, but it is not likely to find universal acceptance among historians of Habsburg Spain.

The first group—clergy and institutions—included clerics acting as individuals and institutions such as convents and charitable foundations. It did not include transactions of the church's patrimonial property, business that was handled by separate notaries. Clerics were identifiable from their titles and offices, and they were grouped with the clergy regardless of their social origins. The line between noble and nonnoble was much harder to draw. Only the higher nobility of Spain had explanatory titles after their surnames. The simple hidalgos at the bottom of the noble scale had to be content with the honorific "Don" or "Doña" before their Christian names. The terms have become almost meaningless now, except to indicate respect and, sometimes, deference. In the seventeenth century, however, they were still good indicators of hidalguía in Ciudad Real. Therefore, anyone referred to as "Don" or "Doña" in the bills of sale was placed with the nobles. Anyone lacking the honorific title was a nonnoble, despite occasional suspicions to the contrary. This is much more likely to have underestimated rather than inflated noble participation in the land sales.

In order to look more closely at members of the three social groups, all the buyers, sellers, and other participants in the land sales were arranged by name, and all transactions attributable to each individual were gathered together. The dates of the transactions were helpful in this process, as were the names of spouses, occupations, and places of residence. Because of the small number of Spanish surnames, linking the records could not be done on the basis of names alone. When in doubt, even though individuals had identical names, they were listed separately. Altogether there were 1,272 named individuals in the transactions, 1,240 as principals and the rest as witnesses, proxy holders, or minor parties to the sale. Of the 1,272 individuals, only 435 listed an occupation or other identifying information. The frequent appearance of some individuals may have been coincidental, but I have taken it to be a true reflection of their importance in landownership in Ciudad Real. It is conceivable that most, or even all, of the individuals who did not list an occupation were farmers. If so, then the high incidence of urban occupations I found would be a distortion of the true situation.

Table C.1. Cereal lands: Buyers and sellers by social group.

Land category and total sales	Clergy and institutions	Nobles	Nonnobles
Tierra (265)			
Percentage of buyers	4	8	88
Percentage of land bought	13	25	62
Percentage of sellers	6	20	74
Percentage of land sold	14	44	42
Quiñón (136)			
Percentage of buyers	15	5	80
Percentage of land bought	19	6	75
Percentage of sellers	8	21	71
Percentage of land sold	9	26	65

Table C.2. Viticulture lands: Buyers and sellers by social group.

Land category and total sales	Clergy and institutions	Nobles	Nonnobles
Viña (105)			
Percentage of buyers	11	2	87
Percentage of land bought	12	2	86
Percentage of sellers	9	17	74
Percentage of land sold	9	22	69
Majuelo (51)			
Percentage of buyers	10	15	75
Percentage of land bought	10	19	71
Percentage of sellers	10	10	80
Percentage of land sold	15	7	78
Parral (54)			
Percentage of buyers	2	2	96
Percentage of land bought	1	5	94
Percentage of sellers	4	9	87
Percentage of land sold	4	9	87

Table C.3. Other cultivated lands: Buyers and sellers by social group.

Land category and total sales	Clergy and institutions	Nobles	Nonnobles
Olivar (101)			
Percentage of buyers	18	9	73
Percentage of land bought	23	14	63
Percentage of sellers	11	23	66
Percentage of land sold	15	38	47
Huerta (45)			
Percentage of buyers	32	12	56
Percentage of land bought	56	9	35
Percentage of sellers	8	16	76
Percentage of land sold	3	14	83
Zumacar (8)			
Percentage of buyers	25	13	62
Percentage of land bought	49	22	29
Percentage of sellers	13	37	50
Percentage of land sold	29	28	43

Table C.4. Frequency of individuals in land sales, by social group.

Total individuals (with occupation)	Number of transactions[a]	Clergy and institutions	Nobles	Nonnobles
947 (293)	1	6	13	81
176 (78)	2	11	15	74
44 (23)	3	14	11	75
29 (17)	4	17	24	59
11 (6)	5	27	0	73
9 (4)	6	11	22	67
11 (8)	7	18	9	73
7 (1)	8	14	14	72
2 (2)	9	0	0	100
1 (1)	10	0	100	0
1 (1)	11	0	0	100
1 (0)	14	0	0	100
1 (1)	17	0	0	100

a. Average percentage in 1-8 transactions: clergy and institutions, 15; nobles, 13; nonnobles, 72.

FINANCIAL DOCUMENTS

APPENDIX D

D.1. MUNICIPAL INCOME AND EXPENDITURES: CIUDAD REAL, 1751

Various public agencies were budgeted separately from the city government and paid the salaries of their officials with the fees and fines they collected. These included the court of the Santa Hermandad Vieja; the royal tax collection agencies; the supervision of public sales of meat, grain, and other staples; the postal system; and royal monopolies such as the sales of tobacco and salt. The expenses of the city government alone were close to 1,500 ducados yearly (16,500 reales), based on a five-year average.

Expenditures	Amount (reales)
Salary of the king's representative (corregidor)	4,400 (unchanged since fifteenth century)
Salary of eighteen aldermen (regidores) (1,000 maravedís each)	270
Celebration of Corpus Christi (holy day)	2,200
Votive offering of the city and prayer fees for bad times, water shortage, health, and other reasons	1,500
Public streets and maintenance of fountains	600
Salary of notary of the city government	1,100
Salary of the city porter (*portero*)	330
Cleaning of drains and sewers (not counting contributions of manpower by the	

(cont.)

Expenditures	Amount (reales)
citizenry for such works, and bearing in mind that in years of bad flooding, these expenses could surpass 9,000 reales)	1,300
Raising abandoned children, repairs to orphanage facilities and maintenance of nurses, and the transportation of some of the orphans to Toledo (in addition to 660 reales that this charity received in interest on a censo of 2,000 ducados on the posito in the town of Alcolea and the rental of some land, also in Alcolea)	4,000
Salary of the common councilmen (*jurados*) (500 maravedís each)	45
Salary of the mace bearers (*maceros*)	220
Salary of the town crier (*pregonero*)	240
Salary of the person who cares for the city's clocks	150
Total	16,355

This list does not include one hundred ducados (1,100 reales) for the quartering and transit of troops, in addition to what the citizenry contributed in lodging.

The income of Ciudad Real flowed mainly from fees charged for services and pasturage in its término.

Income	Amount (reales)
Brokerage fees (*correduría*)	10,500
Fees for weighing (*peso real*)	500
Summer pasture to the north of city and in La Celada, both stubble areas. The order of Calatrava, owner of the sheep, paid monthly, according to a head count	4,500
Fees for entrails (*asaduras*) and just weights for meats sold in public market	1,000
Annual revenue from inspector of weights (*fiel almotacen*) of public meat market	1,000
Fishing licenses for the Guadiana	100
Rental on a piece of land owned by the city	50
Rental on two shares of summer pasture and stubble to south of city	3,000
Given total	20,550
Real total	20,650

Ciudad Real also had disposal and income rights for seven years (1750–1757) to two shares of mountainous winter pasture called *las Navas* and five shares of summer pasture and stubble. They produced 8,500 reales yearly, which the city used for its operating expenses, including a physician's salary. When the *contaduría de millones* (area tax collection for the millones) was in Ciudad Real, it produced 50,000 maravedís annually for the city. This occurred in the seventeenth century, but not in 1751. With what appears to be a healthy budget margin, Ciudad Real needed no municipal levies or loans from her citizenry, except for repairs to the city hall, public markets, and jail, and for hermitages in the outskirts, such as that of the patroness of the city. The full budget in 1751 appears in AGS, *RG*, lib. 468; questions 23-28. In addition, the municipal archive has numerous documents dealing with city government, income, and expenses throughout the period.

(cont.)

Table D.2. Tax-list (*padrón*), 1694.

	Percentage of householders paying a given amount		
Assigned tax (reales)	Nuestra Señora del Prado[a]	San Pedro[b]	Santiago[c]
Exempt			
Poor	7 ⎱	6 ⎱	9 ⎱
Noble	4 ⎬ 19	3 ⎬ 15	4 ⎬ 18
Unspecified	8 ⎰	6 ⎰	5 ⎰
1-10	67	73	72
11-20	9	10	7
21-30	4	2	2
Over 30	1	0.3	1

Source: AMCR, doc. 181. The list was probably for the servicios.

a. Total 423 householders, with one page missing from the list.

b. Total 377 householders.

c. Total 288 householders.

Table D.3. Juros held on the alcabalas of Ciudad Real's partido, 1620-1622.

Juros	Yearly interest (maravedís)
Perpetual	
The prior, monks, and convent of the order of Calatrava	2,000
Monastery of Santo Domingo el Real in Toledo	15,000
Perafan de Rivera, son of Don Hernando de Rivera and Doña María Tellez, his wife	20,000
Captain Cristóbal de Mena	3,000
Don Bernardino Manrique de Lara, successor in the entail of García Hernández Manrique	13,000
Doña María de Coca, widow of Luis de Avila	69,242
Hospital de la Concepción (Descalced Mercedarians) in the city of Ciudad Real	10,000
Juan Hernández de Herrera, householder of the city of Toledo	15,000
Redeemable	
Alonso de Oliver as patron of the charitable foundation (*patronazgo*) founded by Pedro Francés Caballero, householder of Ciudad Real	16,100
Assignees of the General Agreement of 14 May 1608	6,900
Administrator for the prayer fund instituted by Juan de Arévalo	35,000
Said assignees of the General Agreement	15,000
Hospital of San Juan Baptista, Toledo, founded by Cardinal Don Juan Taveras, Archbishop of Toledo	200,000
Said hospital, which is located outside the walls of the city of Toledo near the Bisagra gate	115,000
Don Bernardino de Alcaraz, schoolmaster in Toledo	40,000
Prioress, nuns, and convent of the Monastery of Nuestra Señora de Gracia (Dominicans) in Ciudad Real	15,400
Pedro López de Toledo (5 percent interest, dating from 20 Sept. 1577)	1,415
Prior of convent of Santo Domingo in Ciudad Real as testamentary executor and distributor of the prayer fund and charitable foundation that Pedro Hernández Conejero established in his will	51,000
Don Antonio de Galiana (5 percent interest, dating from 30 July 1583)	52,000
Don Antonio de Galiana (same as above)	13,647
Pedro Gómez and Doña María de Céspedes as patrons of the prayer fund left by Doña Beatriz de Céspedes	13,125
Executors of Cardinal Don Gaspar de Quiroga	55,000
Doña Gerónima de Treviño, widow of Don Juan Fernández Treviño	140,625

(cont.)

Table D.3.

Juros	Yearly interest (maravedís)
Fernan Suárez and Doña Beatriz de Critana, his wife, had 75,000 at 7.1 percent interest. By a pragmatic of 9 October 1621, their share was reduced to 52,500, with the remaining 22,500 going to the king.	52,500
Doña Antonia de Ulloa, Countess of Salinas had 150,000 at 7.1 percent interest. Reduced to 105,000, with 45,000 going to the king.	105,000
Juan Núñez del Aguíla had 159,600 at 7.1 percent interest. Reduced to 104,720, with 44,880 going to the king.	104,720
Don Lorenzo de Mendoza, householder of the city of Toledo, for himself and his successors in the entailed estate (*vínculo y mayorazgo*) founded by his father Don Alvaro de Luna had 223,387 at 7.1 percent interest. Reduced to 156,371, with 67,016 going to the king.	156,371
Licentiate Pereda de Velarde had 150 fanegas of wheat and the same amount of barley, and since the alcabalas and tercias were currently under royal administration, it was handed over without valuation.	
Prayer fund and pious foundation instituted by Don Antonio de Galiana	149,250
Patrons of the prayer fund and dispositions left by Captain Cristóbal de Mena and Doña Ana Mesía his wife	160,000
Doctor Juan de Rojas and the licentiate Gerónimo Jiménez, patrons of the prayer fund instituted by Andrés Montero	37,500
Don Francisco de Céspedes and Doña Florencia de Céspedes	84,000
Livia Balbi, Genoese, wife of Juan Francisco Palavesín	358,041
The Society of Jesus of San Eugenio in Toledo had 75,000, of which 57,692 were transferred to the alcabalas of Campos (Palencia) as of the first of January 1622.	75,000
Don Fernando Treviño and Don Cristóbal Bermúdez	3,026
Doña Francisca de Guevara, householder of Ciudad Real	21,750
Prayer fund and chaplaincy instituted by Diego de Soto	21,000
Lope de Guzmán y de Guevara for himself and those who will succeed him in the entailed estate (vínculo y mayorazgo) founded by Doña Marina de Padilla y Sarmiento and Don Carlos de Guevara, her husband	29,176
Prayer fund and pious foundation left by Juan de Narváez Marcos	109,550
Heirs of César Garvarino	225,000
Don Francisco de Salcedo Poblete, householder of Ciudad Real	112,500
Given total	2,802,624
Real total	2,721,838
[Dated Madrid, 14 December 1626]	
[Signed Alonso de Yepes, notary, and Juan Ladrón de Guevara]	

Source: AGS, *CMC 3a*, leg. 287.

NOTES

ABBREVIATIONS

AGI	Archivo General de Indias (Seville)
AGS	Archivo General de Simancas (Simancas, Valladolid)

	CG	*Contadurías Generales*
	CJH	*Consejo y Juntas de Hacienda*
	CMC 3a	*Contaduría Mayor de Cuentas, 3a Época*
	RG	*Respuestas Generales*
	TMC	*Tribunal Mayor de Cuentas*

AHN	Archivo Histórico Nacional (Madrid)
AMCR	Archivo Municipal de Ciudad Real (Ciudad Real)
APCR	Archivo Provincial de Ciudad Real (Ciudad Real)
APNSP	Archivo Parroquial de Nuestra Señora del Prado (Ciudad Real)
APSP	Archivo Parroquial de San Pedro (Ciudad Real)
BN	Biblioteca Nacional (Madrid)
RAH	Real Academia de la Historia (Madrid)

doc.	document
leg.	*legajo* (bundle)
lib.	*libro* (book)
tít.	*título* (heading)

CURRENCY

Sums of money in the text and in the notes are given in the units in which they appeared in the documents. See Appendixes B and C for the contemporary value of money in terms of wages and land prices.

escudo: a gold coin with a legal value of 440 maravedís from 1609 onward.

ducado: a unit of account worth 375 maravedís or 11 reales.

real: a coin made of silver or a mixture of silver and copper worth 34 maravedís.

maravedí: the basic unit of account in Castile.

vellón: currency made of copper or a mixture of copper and silver and appearing in various denominations, especially in the seventeenth century.

I. THE PHYSICAL AND HISTORICAL SETTING

1. The best overall surveys of the Spanish economy in this period are José Gentil da Silva, *En Espagne: Développement économique, subsistance, déclin* (Paris, 1965), and Jaime Vicens Vives with Jorge Nadal Oller, *An Economic History of Spain*, 3rd ed., trans. Frances M. Lopez-Morillas (Princeton, N.J., 1969).

2. See Julius Klein, *The Mesta* (Cambridge, Mass., 1920; reprint ed. Port Washington, N.Y., 1964), for the best study of this institution, which was formed under royal auspices in the late Middle Ages. The Mesta regulated the biannual transhumance of the sheep and had jurisdiction over disputes arising over land use along the sheepwalks. La Mancha, a favored grazing area, was called the Campus Espartarium by the Romans, and even today, some of the natural grasses can still be seen in the Campo de Calatrava and the Campo de Montiel in the south of Ciudad Real province. See Charles Julian Bishko, "The Castilian as Plainsman: The Medieval Ranching Frontier in La Mancha and Extremadura," in *The New World Looks at Its History*, ed. Archibald R. Lewis and Thomas F. McGann (Austin, Tex., 1963), pp. 48-50.

3. Matias Gotor Mestre, "La Mancha, a Sea Made of Land," *Oro Verde* (*Green Gold*): *Revista de Turismo* 70 (Oct. 1969):25. The mean altitude of the Manchegan plain is from 680 to 700 meters above sea level. *Diccionario geográfico de España*, 17 vols. (Madrid, 1958), 8:348.

4. François Bertaut, "Diario del viaje de España," in *Viajes de extranjeros por Espana y Portugal*, ed. José García Mercadal, 3 vols. (Madrid, 1952), 2:575.

5. Rainfall usually ranges from about 350 millimeters a year in eastern La Mancha to about 480 millimeters a year in the west. *Anuario estadístico de España, 1972* (Madrid, 1973), pp. 19-23. An anonymous Moroccan ambassador to the court of Charles II in 1690 was dismayed by the arid appearance of La Mancha in comparison to Andalusia. García Mercadal, *Viajes*, 2:1233.

6. Bertaut, "Diario," in García Mercadal, *Viajes*, 2:614. Each escudo was worth 440 maravedís.

7. Hereafter the unmodified name Ciudad Real will refer to the city, capital of the present day province of the same name.

8. The 1575 inquiry, which contained fifty-seven questions, was sent to Ciudad Real, according to Luis Delgado Merchán, *Historia documentada de Ciudad Real*, 2nd ed. (Ciudad Real, 1907), p. 331. A 1578 version, with forty-five questions, probably was not. Replies from the area around Ciudad Real have survived and reside in the Biblioteca del Monasterio de San Lorenzo del Escorial, *Relaciones topográficas*. They have recently been published as *Relaciones histórico-geográfico-estadísticas de los pueblos de España hechas por iniciativa de Felipe II: Ciudad Real*, ed. Carmelo Viñas and Ramón Paz (Madrid, 1971); all references in this section can be found readily there.

9. Pedro de Medina, *Libro de grandezas y cosas memorables de España*

(Alcalá de Henares, 1566), fol. 83v. Like other cities on the plains, Ciudad Real faced chronic danger from flooding, plus the additional threat of malaria and other diseases from stagnant water. The maintenance of storm drains was a key item of city council business throughout the early modern period and an important part of the municipal budget (see Appendix D, Table D.1). Unfortunately, drainage projects on a larger scale always foundered from a lack of funds. Not until the mid-nineteenth century could Ciudad Real afford to construct an adequate drainage system. See Delgado Merchán, *Historia documentada,* pp. 331-340, and AMCR, docs. 63 and 238, among others.

10. AGS, *RG,* lib. 468, question 20. The *Respuestas* were responses to the government inquiry now called the *Catastro de Ensenada,* ordered in 1749 but answered in Ciudad Real in 1751. Ensenada (Don Cenón de Somodevilla) was secretary of the Despacho de Hacienda under King Ferdinand VI. His inquiry was designed to gather information about the Spanish economy, with the end of establishing a single tax (*única contribución*) for Castilian taxpayers. The *Catastro de Ensenada* included answers to forty general questions on each town's economy and a separate description of the wealth and holdings of its largest landowner (*mayor hazendado*). A copy of the *Respuestas* is conserved in the Archivo General de Simancas. In addition, there is a résumé of all the responses in the Archivo Histórico Nacional (AHN, *Hacienda: Catastro*), as well as detailed and lengthy responses from individual taxpayers in many local archives. See Antonio Matilla Tascón, *La única contribución y el Catastro de Ensenada* (Madrid, 1947), for a discussion of these sources.

11. Gaspar Barreiros, "Corografía de algunos lugares," in García Mercadal, *Viajes,* 1:955.

12. AGS, *RG,* lib. 468, question 20. See also chapter 3.

13. An anonymous traveler called M***, in García Mercadal, *Viajes,* 3:95.

14. AGS, *RG,* lib. 468, question 3.

15. A fanega is the amount of land needed to sow one fanega (55 liters) of seed, about 0.65 hectares, in modern terms.

16. AGS, *RG,* lib. 468, question 10. Slightly different figures for land-use patterns are given in the "Resumen General de las Cuerdas de Tierra," which is appended to the local responses to the *Catastro* in APCR, leg. 616, but the overall pattern is the same. See chapter 3 for a discussion of the land and its productivity.

17. José María Martínez Val, *Ciudad Real: Estudio geográfico y económico* (Ciudad Real, 1972). Some of the largest municipal términos in Spain are found in La Mancha. Twenty-two are each larger than 30,000 hectares, and Almodóvar del Campo, which contains over 120,000 hectares, is the third largest in Spain. The national average is quite small, about 5,833 hectares. *Anuario estadístico,* 1972, p. 11; *Reseña estadística de la provincia de Ciudad Real* (Madrid, 1960), pp. 10-12.

18. Town charter (*carta puebla*) of Villa Real, in *La fundación de Ciudad Real,* ed. Margarita Peñalosa Esteban-Infantes (Ciudad Real, 1955), p. 9. The best source for the early history of Calatrava is Manuel Danvila y Collado, "Origen, naturaleza y extensión de los derechos de la Mesa Maestral de la Orden de Calatrava," *Boletín de la Real Academia de la Historia* 12 (1888):116-163. Also

useful is François Gutton, *La chevalerie militaire en Espagne: L'ordre de Cala-trava* (Paris, 1955; Spanish trans. Madrid, 1969); and L. P. Wright, "The Military Orders in Sixteenth- and Seventeenth-Century Spanish Society," *Past and Present* 43 (May 1969):34-70.

19. Peñalosa, *Fundación de Ciudad Real*, p. 9, prints the text of this reference as "grand villa é bona que corriesen todos por fuero é que fuese cabesza de toda aquella tierra . . . é púsele nombre Real" (from AMCR, doc. 1). There is some confusion over the true date of the city's foundation. The carta puebla is clearly from 1255, but one local historian argues that this only indicated Alfonso's intention to establish the new town, and that the actual foundation did not occur until 1262. Delgado Merchán, *Historia documentada*, chap. 5. The 1255 foundation date is accepted by the city itself, which celebrated its 700th anniversary in 1955.

20. It is unclear whether these walls were ever completed, though references to their construction and repair appear in the local archives from 1297 onward. Inocente Hervás y Buendía, *Diccionario histórico, geográfico . . . de Ciudad Real* (Ciudad Real, 1890), p. 215. The walls were evidently in disrepair by 1476, and in 1489 the crown authorized a local assessment to patch them (AMCR, doc. 34). Flooding of the Guadiana in 1508 probably damaged them irreparably, and by 1600 only the gates of Toledo and Alarcos remained standing. *Diccionario geográfico*, 8:382-384.

21. See Delgado Merchán, *Historia documentada*, chap. 5, for the early history of the city.

22. See Tomás Muñoz y Romero, comp., *Colección de fueros municipales y cartas-pueblas de los reinos de Castilla, León, Corona de Aragón y Navarra* (Madrid, 1847), for studies of the fuero of Cuenca.

23. Carta puebla in Peñalosa, *Fundación de Ciudad Real*, p. 10, from AMCR, doc. 1. "Et do á esta villa sobredicha que haya por Aldeas ó por término Zuhéruela é Villar del Pozo é la Figueruela et Poblet é Alvala con todos sus términos yermos é poblados é con todos sus derechos, con monetes, con fuentes, con ríos, con pastos, con todas sus entradas é con todas sus salidas é con todas sus pertenencias assí como las han estos lugares sobre dichos é las deven aver."

24. Juan de la Jara de Santa Teresa, *Historia de la imagen de Nuestra Señora del Prado, fundadora y patrona de Ciudad Real* (Ciudad Real, 1880), excerpted in Peñalosa, *Fundación de Ciudad Real*, p. 16. Settlers were often attracted by tax exemptions for new arrivals. AMCR, doc. 7.

25. Florencio Janer, *Condición social de los moriscos de España: Causas de su expulsion y consequencias que ésta produjo en el orden económico y político* (Madrid, 1857), p. 205, printed the pertinent document. "Invitación hecha á los sarracenos en el año 1279 para que fuesen á poblar á Villareal," from the Archivo General de la Corona de Aragon, no. 44, fol. 193.

26. These and other rights were granted in 1266, according to Jara in Penalosa, *Fundación de Ciudad Real*, pp. 15-16. See AMCR, doc. 6.

27. Hervás, *Diccionario histórico*, p. 341. Gutton, *Chevalerie militaire*, has the most detailed descriptions of the struggles between Calatrava and Ciudad Real.

28. Villa Real laid claim to Batanejo, Corralejo, and Navas de Ucendo in

Miguelturra's término, in addition to Picon (a village of Piedrabuena) and Porzuna. See Hervás, *Diccionario histórico*, pp. 344, 386, 394; Danvila, "Origen de Calatrava," p. 129; Gutton, *Chevalerie militaire*, pp. 74-75; AMCR, docs. 15, 17.

29. Danvila, "Origen de Calatrava," pp. 129-131. See also AMCR, doc. 18.

30. Inocente Hervás y Buendía, "Documentos originales del Sacro Convento de Calatrava, que atesora el archivo de Hacienda en Ciudad Real," *Boletín de la Real Academia de la Historia* 20 (June 1892):570.

31. Francisco Rades y Andrada, *Crónica de las tres órdenes y cavallerías de Santiago, Calatrava y Alcántara* (Toledo, 1572). See Delgado Merchán, *Historia documentada*, pp. 182-187, for a good brief summary of this encounter. Ciudad Real's support of Ferdinand and Isabella was based purely on their legal possession of the monarchy. The city had supported Henry IV against his rivals and would have supported his daughter as well, had she been recognized as queen by the Cortes of Castile. AMCR, docs. 25, 28.

32. [Lope de Vega] Lope Félix de Vega Carpio, *Fuente Ovejuna*, trans. Roy Campbell, in *Masterworks of World Drama*, ed. Anthony Caputi, vol. 3 (Boston, 1968), 352-405; references are to act and line.

33. In the play, Rodrigo blamed the weakness of the walls and the enemy's strength for his defeat.

34. Calatrava was incorporated into the royal patrimony temporarily during the reign of Henry IV and habitually from 1487 onward. Pope Adrian VI (Adrian of Utrecht, former tutor of Charles I) permanently joined the headships (*maestrazgos*) of all the military orders with the crowns of Castile and Leon in 1523, specifically to avoid the potential scandal of noble rebellion against the crown. Danvila, "Origen de Calatrava," pp. 125, 133-134. Throughout the period under study, however, Calatrava and the city of Ciudad Real continued to battle in the courts, mostly over the city's firewood and pasture rights in the Campo de Calatrava. AMCR, docs. 26, 67, 129, 131, 133, 136, 138, 142, 147-149, 170 bis, 185, 353. For the most part, the city's claims were upheld time after time. See BN, ms. 2431, fol. 111, for an appeal by Calatrava in 1600.

35. Marvin Lunenfeld, *The Council of the Santa Hermandad: A Study of the Pacification Forces of Ferdinand and Isabella* (Coral Gables, Fla., 1970), pp. 85-98, has a good description of the hermandad of Ciudad Real. See also María del Carmen Pescador del Hoyo, "Los origenes de la Santa Hermandad," *Cuadernos de la Historia de España* 55-56 (1972):400-443. Medina, *Libro de grandezas*, pp. 83v-84v, has a laudatory view of the role of the hermandades in keeping order in the countryside.

36. Much of Delgado Merchán, *Historia documentada*, is devoted to the ancient Jewish community in Ciudad Real. See also Hervás, "Documentos de Calatrava," p. 570, and passing references in his *Diccionario histórico*. It seems that the legal prohibitions against Jews were not always enforced. RAH, *Salazar*, I-41, fols. 100-101, 154v-155, concern property owned by Jewish residents of Ciudad Real in the mid-fourteenth century.

37. Delgado Merchán, *Historia documentada*, pp. 66-67, 135-136, contains a description of the 1391 pogrom, but information on the Jewish and converso community appears throughout pp. 15-194. See also Philippe Wolff, "The 1391

Pogrom in Spain: Social Crisis or Not?" *Past and Present* 50 (Feb. 1971):4-18.

38. Delgado Merchán, *Historia documentada*, pp. 180-181; a contemporary description of the pogrom is given in AMCR, doc. 22.

39. Henry Charles Lea, *A History of the Inquisition in Spain*, 4 vols. (New York, 1906-1907), 1:166-68, 3:82-84, 4:520, generally follows the analysis of Delgado Merchán, *Historia documentada*, pp. 195-271, although he also used the records in AHN, *Inquisition de Toledo*. Recently these records have been published as *Records of the trials of the Spanish Inquisition in Ciudad Real*, ed. Haim Beinart, vol. 1 (Jerusalem, 1974).

40. Paul J. Hauben, ed., *The Spanish Inquisition* (New York, 1969), presents excerpts from major interpretations of the Inquisition.

41. Delgado Merchán, *Historia documentada*, pp. 272-277.

42. Wladimiro Piskorski, *Las Cortes de Castilla en el período de tránsito de la Edad Media a la Moderna* (Barcelona, 1930), pp. 38-42.

43. Numerous works on the comunero revolt are cited in John Lynch, *Spain under the Habsburgs*, 2 vols. (Oxford, England, 1964-1969), vol. 1, and several newer ones indicate a lively interest in the subject. Joseph Pérez, *La revolution des "comunidades" de Castille (1520-1521)* (Bordeaux, 1970), presents a convincing case that one key conflict in the comunero revolt was between the cloth producing towns and the exporters of raw wool.

44. Felipe Ruiz Martín, "La población española al comienzo de los tiempos modernos," *Cuadernos de historia: Anexos de la revista Hispania 1* (Madrid, 1967):189-202.

45. For the development of the European economy in this period see Immanuel Wallerstein, *The Modern World-System: Capitalist Agriculture and the Origins of the European World-Economy in the Sixteenth Century* (New York, 1974).

46. Gentil da Silva, *En Espagne: Développement économique, subsistance, déclin.*

II. POPULATION: STRUCTURE AND TRENDS

1. See the excellent bibliographical essay by Jaime Sobrequés Callicó, "La Peste Negra en la Península Ibérica," *Anuario de Estudios Medievales* 7 (1970-71):67-102. Recent articles that deal with the broader crisis of the fourteenth century include Emilio Mitre Fernández, "Algunas cuestiones demográficas en la Castilla de fines del siglo XIV," *Anuario de Estudios Medievales* 7 (1970-71):615-622; Julio Valdeón Baruque, "Aspectos de la crisis castellana en la primera mitad del siglo XIV," *Hispania* 29 (1969):5-25.

2. Felipe Ruiz Martín, "La población española al comienzo de los tiempos modernos," *Cuadernos de historia: Anexos de la revista Hispania 1* (Madrid, 1967):189-202. Ruiz discusses eight separate government population counts for the sixteenth century, but those for 1530 (actually 1528-1536 and often called the Relación de 1541) and 1591 are the only ones worthy of extensive analysis. Another good summary and analysis is Jorge Nadal, *La población española (siglos XVI a XX)* (Barcelona, 1966). His figures are about 30 percent higher in 1530 and 4.5 percent higher in 1591 than those of Ruiz, although both authors use the coef-

ficient 5.0 to calculate total population from the number of householders. This is a good choice for the sixteenth century, but in general modern researchers use 4.5 or at most 4.7 as the coefficient.

3. Martín González de Cellorigo (known as Cellorigo), *Memorial de la política necessaria y útil restauración política de España* . . . (Valladolid, 1600), prologue, n.p. Cellorigo was only one of a number of writers who analyzed Spain's economic troubles in the early seventeenth century and proposed remedies for them. Often scorned by those in power and ridiculed in the literature of the day, these *arbitristas* were nonetheless astute critics of their government's economic policy. See Jean Vilar, *Literatura y economía: La figura satírica del arbitrista en el Siglo de Oro*, trans. Francisco Bustelo García del Real (Madrid, 1973).

4. Emigration to the Indies claimed 4,000-5,000 persons a year, perhaps somewhat more in the mid-seventeenth century. Military losses accounted for about 12,000 a year, and that, too, increased after 1634. Antonio Domínguez Ortiz estimates that there were 288,000 Spaniards dead, missing, or imprisoned from the time of Spain's entry into the Thirty Years' War to the Peace of the Pyrenees in 1659. *La sociedad española en el siglo XVII*, 2 vols. (Madrid, 1963, 1970), 1:86-113. The total number of Moriscos expelled was about 275,000, according to the best recent work on the subject, Henri Lapeyre, *Géographie de l'Espagne morisque* (Paris, 1959), p. 205.

5. Agricultural and price historians often use a harvest year running from September to August. Earl J. Hamilton rejected this method for his classic studies of Spanish prices in the early modern period not only because seasonal calculations based on the calendar year are simpler to construct, but also because he felt they reflected the Spanish situation as well as or better than an artificial harvest year. See his *American Treasure and the Price Revolution in Spain, 1501-1650* (Cambridge, Mass., 1934; reprint ed. New York, 1965); *War and Prices in Spain: 1651-1800* (Cambridge, Mass., 1947; reprint ed. New York, 1969).

6. I have calculated conceptions by the simple expedient of moving the baptismal data back nine months, which is sufficiently accurate for my purposes. This assumes that all conceptions resulted in live births, and that a fall in births was due to a fall in conceptions. Neither assumption is tenable, but a more complex term, such as "fruitful conceptions," would hardly be an improvement.

7. The method is from D. E. C. Eversley, "Exploitation of Anglican Parish Registers by Aggregative Analysis," in *An Introduction to English Historical Demography from the Sixteenth to the Nineteenth Century*, ed. Edward Anthony Wrigley (New York, 1966), p. 75.

8. Jerónimo López-Salazar Pérez, "Evolución demográfica de la Mancha en el siglo XVIII," *Hispania* 36 (1976):233-299. Unless otherwise cited, the eighteenth-century population figures come from this article.

9. In the demographic Old Regime, a generation rarely reached age twenty with more than half of its original numbers, though we usually lack records complete enough to follow the process. Early death may have carried off one-fourth to one-third of all newborn, and stillborn children would raise the toll even higher. See Pierre Goubert, *Beauvais et le Beauvaisis de 1600 à 1730: Contribution à l'histoire sociale de la France du XVIIe siècle* (Paris, 1960).

10. Goubert, *Beauvais*, p. 51; Jean Meuvret, "Les crises de subsistances et la

démographie de la France d'Ancien Régime," *Population* (Oct.-Dec., 1946):43-50.

11. Carla Rahn Phillips, "Ciudad Real no período dos Habsburgos: um estudo demográfico," *Anaïs de historia* 7 (Dec. 1975):151-165.

12. Goubert, *Beauvais,* p. 47; Bartolomé Bennassar, *Valladolid au siècle d'or: Une ville de Castille et sa campagne au XVIe siècle* (Paris, 1967), pp. 197-198, 207.

13. André Vénard and Philippe Ariès, "Deux contributions à l'histoire des practiques contraceptives: I, Saint François de Sales et Thomas Sanchez; II, Chaucer et Madame de Sévigné," *Population* 9 (Oct.-Dec., 1954):688-692.

14. Domínguez Ortiz, *Sociedad española,* 1:68-70. See Bartolomé Bennassar, *Recherches sur les grandes épidémies dans le Nord de l'Espagne à la fin du XVIe siècle: Problemes du documentation et des méthodes* (Paris, 1969). Ciudad Real had a serious problem with flooding in 1596, but it does not seem to have bred disease. AMCR, *Libros Capitulares,* leg. 8, mentions the flooding and the measures taken by city officials to guard against plague.

15. Ruth Pike, *Aristocrats and Traders: Sevillian Society in the Sixteenth Century* (Ithaca, N.Y., 1972), p. 20.

16. The essential unity of climatic conditions in western Europe is discussed by Emmanuel Le Roy Ladurie, *Times of Feast, Times of Famine: A History of Climate since the Year 1000,* trans. Barbara Bray (Garden City, N.Y., 1971), pp. 288-308.

17. AMCR, doc. 192, dated 10 October 1606; See APCR, leg. 72, for the grain loans, and Hamilton, *American Treasure,* for Spanish prices.

18. AGS, *Cámara de Castilla,* leg. 2183, for 1581; AGS, *Estado,* leg. 227, for 1610. It is not clear to what extent the Moriscos were included in the 1591 total of householders (See Table 2.3).

19. Hervás, *Diccionario histórico,* p. 215. Hervás's figure is accepted by most scholars, including Domínguez Ortiz, *Sociedad española,* 1:149.

20. Many Moriscos returned illegally to the Ciudad Real area after being expelled, and it was not until late in 1613 that we can consider the expulsion accomplished in La Mancha. AGS, *Estado,* legs. 233, 234, 244, 246, 247, 250. I consider this problem in "The Moriscos of La Mancha, 1570-1614," forthcoming in *The Journal of Modern History* (demand reprints).

21. AHN, *Clero,* leg. 1867.

22. APCR, leg. 73.

23. Bennassar, *Valladolid,* p. 206. Hamilton, *American Treasure,* p. 363, indicates that wheat prices in Andalusia also were quite high from 1616 to 1619.

24. AMCR, doc. 200; AMCR, *Libros Capitulares,* leg. 10; AGS, *CMC 3a,* leg. 287.

25. Juan de la Jara, *Historia de la imagen de Nuestra Señora del Prado, fundadora y patrona de Ciudad Real* (Ciudad Real, 1880), p. 456.

26. Joaquín Villalba, *Epidemiología española u historia cronológica de las pestes contagios, epidemias y epizootias que han acaecido en España desde la venida de las Cartagineses hasta el año 1801,* 2 vols. in 1 (Madrid, 1803), 2:43-68. See also Domínguez Ortiz, *Sociedad española,* 1:71-75. In the Levant and Anda-

lusia, Domínguez estimates that 500,000 people died of the pestilence. It was probably true plague, though other diseases may have been present as well.

27. Nadal, *Población española*, pp. 58-59.

28. The city spent nearly 14,000 reales on locust control in 1648, raised by an assessment of the population according to wealth. AMCR, doc. 230. Hamilton, *American Treasure*, p. 220, discusses the disruptions in commerce during these disastrous years. Because plague was raging in places that habitually traded with Ciudad Real, local officials banned some merchandise from infected places in 1648. Since the ban was not complete, it could hardly have been effective against plague, but it did raise the price of the merchandise. AMCR, *Libros Capitulares*, leg. 10.

29. APCR, leg. 141.

30. Bernard H. Slicher van Bath, *The Agrarian History of Western Europe: A.D. 500-1850*, trans. Olive Ordish (London, 1963).

31. Henry Kamen, "The Decline of Castile: The Last Crisis," *Economic History Review* 17 (1964-65):72. See also Hamilton, *War and Prices*, p. 122.

32. AMCR, *Libros Capitulares*, leg. 17; AMCR, doc. 265.

33. Kamen, "Decline of Castile," p. 72.

34. AMCR, *Libros Capitulares*, leg. 18. See Hamilton's tables, *War and Prices*, following p. 232.

35. Kamen, "Decline of Castile," citing AGS, *CJH*, leg. 1007.

36. Domínguez Ortiz, *Sociedad española*, 1:36, quoting Galindo.

37. Villalba, *Epidemiología española*, 2:121, quoting from Juan Nieto de Valcarol, physician of the duke of Sesa y Baena.

38. Jara, *Historia de la imagen de Nuestra Señora del Prado*, pp. 458-459. AMCR, doc. 272, deals with the precautionary measures taken by local officials in May 1677 to avert contagion. Among other things, the city gates were manned around the clock, and the watch lists included numerous noblemen and many clerics.

39. John Colin Dunlop, *Memoirs of Spain during the Reigns of Philip IV and Charles II*, 2 vols. (Edinburgh, 1834), 2:226-227.

40. Luis Delgado Merchán, *Historia documentada de Ciudad Real*, 2nd ed. (Ciudad Real, 1907), p. 335. Some of it cost 65-70 reales a fanega, subsidized by private charity. AMCR, *Libros Capitulares*, leg. 18.

41. Hamilton, *War and Prices*, p. 126; Kamen, "Decline of Castile," pp. 73-75.

42. APCR, leg. 201. AMCR, *Libros Capitulares*, leg. 18, contains a litany of disaster in these years. One of the tragic consequences of the bad times was a great increase in the number of abandoned children (*niños expositos*) and the lack of adequate means to care for them.

43. Both of the city's doctors fell victim to the epidemic, and in September 1684 the municipal officials asked the king to send them a replacement from the University of Alcalá. Failing that, they borrowed a doctor from the neighboring town of Almagro, but he would not stay. A year later Ciudad Real was still looking for a permanent physician. AMCR, *Libros Capitulares*, leg. 18.

44. Kamen, "Decline of Castile," p. 74.

45. AMCR, *Libros Capitulares*, leg. 20.

46. López-Salazar, "Evolución demográfica," p. 269. AMCR, docs. 328, 329, 335, and 336, indicate that Ciudad Real contributed to the Bourbon war effort by supplying grain and other foodstuffs, horses, and billeting for passing troops.

47. AMCR, *Libros Capitulares*, leg. 20.

48. Hamilton, *War and Prices*, pp. 144-147.

49. López-Salazar, "Evolución demográfica," pp. 269-273. The difficulties of 1735 were the subject of a royal decree lowering taxes in Ciudad Real. AMCR, doc. 344. See the discussion in chapter 6.

III. THE RURAL ECONOMY

1. Noël Salomon, *La campagne de nouvelle Castille à la fin du XVIe siècle: D'après les "Relaciones topográficas"* (Paris, 1964), pp. 266-269, found this range for the number of labradores in most of New Castile near the end of the sixteenth century. Nearly 200 years later, the *Catastro* reported that 26 percent of Ciudad Real's householders were labradores. Isabel Pérez Valera, ed., *Ciudad Real en el siglo XVIII* (Ciudad Real, 1955), p. 58. Appendix B gives a detailed analysis of taxpaying householders in 1751.

2. Salomon, *Campagne de nouvelle Castille*, p. 257.

3. Pérez Valera, *Ciudad Real en el siglo XVIII*, pp. 53-57.

4. Fernand Braudel, *The Mediterranean and the Mediterranean World in the Age of Philip II*, 1966 rev. ed., trans. Siân Reynolds, 2 vols. (New York, 1972-73), 1:234-238.

5. J. M. Houston, *The Western Mediterranean World: An Introduction to its Regional Landscapes* (London, 1964), chap. 8.

6. A. Jouvin, "El viaje de España y Portugal," in *Viajes de extranjeros por España y Portugal*, ed. José García Mercadal, 3 vols. (Madrid, 1952), 2:762. In praise of the wines and the more dubious attractions of La Mancha, he added the old saying that "In La Mancha, the wine is good and the girls are bad" (p. 763).

7. Rodrigo Méndez Silva, *Población general de España* (Madrid, 1645), p. 28.

8. Carmelo Viñas and Ramón Paz, eds., *Relaciones histórico-geográfico-estadísticas de los pueblos de España hechas por iniciativa de Felipe II: Ciudad Real* (Madrid, 1971).

9. Salomon, *Campagne de nouvelle Castille*, p. 83.

10. Ibid., pp. 323-325.

11. Jerónimo López-Salazar is currently studying tithe returns for La Mancha that will allow us to trace year-to-year harvest fluctuations with some precision. I have relied upon tithe records available in the archive of Nuestra Señora del Prado, which cover eighteen years in the early seventeenth century, and 1555. APNSP, docs. 30, 297, 608.

12. In other words, 17,000 fanegas for grain, and 6,000 for other plants. AGS, *RG*, lib. 468, question 10. See chapter 1 for land quality in Ciudad Real and its surrounding area.

13. See Appendix C for the methods used to select and analyze these documents, and chapter 5 for a discussion of their significance.

14. Bartolomé Bennassar, *Valladolid au siècle d'or: Une ville de Castille et sa campagne au XVIᵉ siècle* (Paris, 1967), p. 315.

15. Pierre Goubert, *Beauvais et le Beauvaisis de 1600 à 1730: Contribution à l'histoire sociale de la France du XVIIᵉ siècle* (Paris, 1960), p. 101. Bernard H. Slicher van Bath has discussed yield ratios in his numerous works on agricultural history, especially *Yield Ratios, 810-1820, Afdeling Agrarische Geschiedenis Bijdragen* 10 (Wageningen, 1963). He has come under heavy criticism for attempting to categorize agricultural development on the basis of figures that are subject to numerous difficulties of interpretation.

16. Manuel Colmeiro y Penido, *Historia de la economía política en España,* 1863, 2 vols. (rev. ed. Madrid, 1965), 2:607. Colmeiro is here citing Eugenio Larruga y Boneta, *Memorias políticas y económicas sobre los frutos, comercio, fábricas y minas de España,* 45 vols. (Madrid, 1787-1800), 1:13.

17. APCR, leg. 152. The wage agreement could be either a flat rate paid to the contractor, with the amount of land area understood, or a fee (in one case seven reales) for each fanega of land to be harvested, out of which the contractor paid the wages of the crew.

18. Juan Dantín Cereceda, *La alimentación española: Sus diferentes tipos* (Madrid, 1934), pp. 12-20.

19. AGS, *RG,* lib. 468, question 17. There were 209,764 square meters of heras altogether: 27 percent first quality, 20 percent second quality, and 53 percent third quality.

20. AGS, *RG,* lib. 468, question 17. City residents also owned mills in nearby términos. See Viñas and Paz, *Relaciones Ciudad Real,* p. 280.

21. APCR, leg. 141; AGS, *RG,* lib. 468, question 17.

22. APCR, leg. 201; AGS, *RG,* lib. 468, question 17.

23. Viñas and Paz, *Relaciones Ciudad Real,* question 23.

24. Nearly every major town in the two Castiles maintained a pósito in this period, and the grain was often used to avert famine as well as to provide seed to local farmers. Earl J. Hamilton, *American Treasure and the Price Revolution in Spain* (Cambridge, Mass., 1934; reprint ed. New York, 1965), p. 257. For a brief historical résumé of the pósitos see Gonzalo Anes Alvarez, "Los pósitos en la España del siglo XVIII," *Moneda y crédito* 105 (June 1968):39-69. Reprinted in idem, *Economía e "ilustración" en la España del siglo XVIII* (Barcelona, 1969). City council records in Ciudad Real are full of pósito transactions, which were clearly at the center of business for the city government.

25. AHN, *Clero,* leg. 1867. This copy of the original donation is among the papers of the Descalced Mercedarians, now housed at the AHN in Madrid. Unless otherwise noted, all references to the pósito are from this document.

26. Borrowers had to own at least two pair of oxen or one pair of mules to be eligible, and their animals were security for the debt. This disqualified the poorest farmers, though it was perhaps a necessary precaution to assure the continuation of the pósito. The maximum grain loan would have been sufficient to sow about 35 fanegas of land.

27. For a time, the pósito occupied a building near the convent church of

the Descalced Mercedarians, also endowed by Don Alvaro Muñoz de Figueroa. When Ciudad Real became the capital of its own province in 1691, the pósito building helped to house the provincial assembly. Luis Delgado Merchán, *Historia documentada de Ciudad Real*, 2nd ed. (Ciudad Real, 1907), p. 335. The pósito's terms were strictly enforced. Doña María Catalina brought suit against one administrator in 1727 for using her gift of 312 fanegas to finance repairs to the building.

28. See the *Novísima recopilación*, lib. 7, tít. 20, *ley* (law) 3, for the Bourbon law of 19 October 1735; Inocente Hervás y Buendía, *Diccionario histórico geográfico . . . de Ciudad Real* (Ciudad Real, 1890), p. 238, for the nineteenth-century history of the pósito.

29. Des Essarts, "Diario del viaje hecho en el año 1659, de Madrid a Alicante y de Valencia a Madrid," in *Viajes de extranjeros por España y Portugal*, ed. José García Mercadal, 3 vols. (Madrid, 1952), 2:690.

30. Salomon, *Campagne de nouvelle Castille*, pp. 328-329. Viticulture was a mainstay of Miguelturra's economy, dating from its foundation in the thirteenth century by the order of Calatrava. Those receiving land allotments were forced to plant vines or lose the land. Charles Julian Bishko, "The Castilian as Plainsman: The Medieval Ranching Frontier in La Mancha and Extremadura," in *The New World Looks at Its History*, ed. Archibald R. Lewis and Thomas F. McGann (Austin, Tex., 1963), p. 54, n. 16.

31. APNSP, docs. 30, 297, 608, for tithes; AGS, *CG*, leg. 2304, for alcabalas.

32. AGS, *RG*, lib. 468, questions 10, 13. Each *arroba* weighed 25 pounds, or 11.4 kilos.

33. See Hamilton, *American Treasure*; Earl J. Hamilton, *War and Prices in Spain: 1651-1800* (Cambridge, Mass., 1947; reprint ed. New York, 1969), for wine prices in New Castile.

34. Miguel de Cervantes Saavedra, *The Adventures of Don Quixote*, trans. J. M. Cohen (Baltimore, Md., 1950), pt. 2, chap. 13, p. 549.

35. Bennassar, *Valladolid*, p. 314. An aranzada was a surface measure of 400 square *estadales* (20 per side), each linear estadal being equivalent to about 3.3 meters in modern terms. The aranzada was subject to regional variation, however, and that in Ciudad Real was about 8 percent smaller than the standard. It was used almost exclusively as a measure for viticulture lands.

36. Des Essarts, "Diario," pp. 689-690. García Mercadal's anonymous Moroccan ambassador also remarked on the use of mules in La Mancha. "Viaje a España (1690-91)," in *Viajes de extranjeros por España y Portugal*, ed. José García Mercadal, 3 vols. (Madrid, 1952), 2:251. Shortly thereafter the king granted a perpetual privilege to Ciudad Real and other towns in the region for the conservation of various breeds of mules. AMCR, doc. 302, dated 29 January 1692.

37. Braudel, *Mediterranean*, 1:241, 426, 589; Salomon, *Campagne de nouvelle Castille*, p. 95, n. 2; Gonzalo Anes Alvarez, *Las crisis agrarias en la España moderna* (Madrid, 1970), pp. 120-122.

38. Diego Medrano y Treviño, *Consideraciones sobre el estado económico moral y político de la provincia de Ciudad Real . . .* (Madrid, 1843; reprint ed. Madrid, 1972), p. 26.

39. Salomon, *Campagne de nouvelle Castille*, pp. 86-87. The anonymous *Memorial por la agricultura* (1633), pp. 1v-2v, blamed the expansion of vineyards for a presumed decline in olive culture. The author deplored the change, since it raised labor costs, reduced forage areas for cattle, and sacrificed a crop favored by climatic advantage for one with keen international competition and high risk.

40. Antonio Matilla Tascón, *La única contribución y el Catastro de la Ensenada* (Madrid, 1947), p. 80. AGS, *RG*, lib. 468, question 15, gives the figures for the city of Ciudad Real.

41. AGS, *RG*, lib. 468, question 13. The individual owners were Don Alvaro Muñoz y Torres, the wealthiest man in the city; Don Ignacio Palacios, an alderman of the city council and a functionary in the royal bureaucracy; Don Bernardino Muñoz de Loaisa, an alderman and major livestock owner; Don Francisco Treviño Calderón, also a major livestock owner; the licentiate Don Antonio de Torres, a priest; and the heirs of Don Felipe Muñoz Salcedo, a royal tax collector. The convents of Franciscan nuns and Dominican monks owned the other two mills.

42. AGS, *RG*, lib. 468, questions 4, 6, 8, 12.

43. Salomon, *Campagne de nouvelle Castille*, p. 87.

44. AGS, *RG*, lib. 468, question 13.

45. See Salomon, *Campagne de nouvelle Castille*, p. 74.

46. J. M. Houston, *The Western Mediterranean World*, chap. 9, discusses why the soil types, climate, and topography of Castile have lent themselves to migratory flocks, probably since the Bronze Age. See Julius Klein, *The Mesta* (Cambridge, Mass., 1920; reprint ed. Port Washington, N.Y., 1964), the classic study of this important institution. The map between pages 18 and 19 shows the sheepwalks of Castile.

47. In the early sixteenth century Ciudad Real rented some of its fall and winter pasture to 2,000 Mesta sheep. AMCR, docs. 71, 75. Royal privilege allowed the rental and established rules for relations between the Mesta and the city.

48. APNSP, docs. 30, 297, 608. Salomon, *Campagne de nouvelle Castille*, pp. 66-69, gives tithe figures for the Ciudad Real area ca. 1575.

49. See chapter 5, and Pérez Valera, *Ciudad Real*, pp. 30-39.

50. AGS, *RG*, lib. 468, questions 23-25.

IV. INDUSTRY, COMMERCE, TRADE

1. See chapter 1, n. 10 for a discussion of the *Catastro* and its various parts.

2. AHN, *Hacienda: Catastro*, lib. 7465, question G, fol. 1; lib. 7466, question F, fol. 2.

3. The broad categories were adapted from Louis Henry, *Manuel de démographie historique* (Paris, 1967), pp. 46-48. In general French researchers prefer broad categories for village economies and a more detailed listing of occupations for larger cities.

4. AGS, *RG*, lib. 468, question 33.

5. Artisans accounted for 18 percent of the vecinos listed in the *Catastro* (316 of 1,752). This was six times higher than Noël Salomon's overall estimate of artisan strength in New Castile in 1575-1580. *La campagne de nouvelle Castille à la fin du XVIe siècle: D'après les "Relaciones topográficas"* (Paris, 1964), pp. 285-286. See chapter 2 for the population of the city in various times.

6. José Gentil da Silva, *En Espagne: Développement économique, subsistance, déclin* (Paris, 1965), pp. 26-27. In Valladolid, on the other hand, agricultural income was strong in the sixteenth century. Industry was predictably weak and atomized, although it comprised a large number of people. See Bartolomé Bennassar, *Valladolid au siècle d'or: Une ville de Castille et sa campagne au XVIe siècle* (Paris, 1967), pp. 329, 348.

7. See chapter 1.

8. Inocente Hervás y Buendía, *Diccionario histórico geográfico de . . . Ciudad Real* (Ciudad Real, 1890), p. 220.

9. Gentil da Silva, *Espagne: Développement*, p. 168.

10. Ibid., p. 48. Artisans' wage rates in 1751 are listed in Appendix B. In the seventeenth century, there may have been more payments in kind than there were later. Even the workers in as large a concern as the mercury mines of Almadén (present-day Ciudad Real Province) were sometimes paid in food, though most of the time they collected weekly wages for their work. Antonio Matilla Tascón, *Historia de las minas de Almadén* (Madrid, 1958), p. 78. It is therefore very difficult, if not impossible, to set a money value on all wages before the eighteenth century at the earliest. See Earl J. Hamilton, *War and Prices in Spain: 1651-1800* (Cambridge, Mass.; reprint ed. New York, 1969), p. 205; Pierre Vilar, "Remarques sur l'histoire des prix," *Annales: Économies, Sociétés, Civilisations* (Jan.-Feb. 1961), pp. 110-115, for cautionary notes about the use of wage statistics in this period.

11. Salomon, *Campagne de nouvelle Castille*, pp. 98-99.

12. Each textile manufacturing city of Spain became known for a particular kind and quality of cloth. For example, Segovia produced a fine broadcloth for the export market, and Cuenca was known for coarse cloth destined for the local market. See Paulino Iradiel Murugarren, *Evolución de la industria textil castellana en los siglos XIII-XVII: Factores de desarrollo, organización y costas de la producción manufactura en Cuenca* (Salamanca, 1974). "And the little birds of the fields have God to provide for them and feed them; and four yards of Cuenca shoddy will warm you more than any four of Segovia broadcloth," Sancho Panza in Miguel de Cervantes Saavedra, *The Adventures of Don Quixote*, trans. J. M. Cohen (Baltimore, Md., 1950), pt. 2, chap. 33, p. 688.

13. Juan de la Jara, *Historia de la imagen de Nuestra Señora del Prado, fundadora y patrona de Ciudad Real* (Ciudad Real, 1880), chap. 10, reprinted in *La fundación de Ciudad Real: Antología de textos históricos*, ed. Margarita Peñalosa Esteban-Infantes (Ciudad Real, 1955), p. 16.

14. Ramón Carande Thobar, *Carlos V y sus banqueros, 1516-1556*, 3 vols. (Madrid, 1943-1967), 1:172, 189.

15. Hervás, *Diccionario histórico*, p. 220. See chapter 6 for taxes.

16. Hervás, *Diccionario histórico*, p. 220.

17. Luis Delgado Merchán, *Historia documentada de Ciudad Real*, 2nd ed. (Ciudad Real, 1907), p. 331.

18. Jara, "Historia de la imagen," in Peñalosa, *Fundación de Ciudad Real*, p. 16. Also mentioned in Carande, *Carlos V y sus banqueros*, 1:209. It is possible that glove making was in decline by the 1680s. No glover was chosen to represent his fellows to the city council in 1684 "por no aver personas," though the epidemic of that year may have caused the apparent lack of people in the trade. AMCR, *Libros Capitulares*, leg. 18.

19. APCR, legs. 150, 151, transactions from September 1660 to July 1665.

20. It is likely that population growth and handicraft industry reinforced one another up to a point in preindustrial Europe, though the exact mechanism is not yet clear. The best starting point for the literature concerned with this topic and others under the heading of protoindustrialization is Rudolf Braun, "The Impact of the Cottage Industry on an Agricultural Population," in David Landes, ed., *The Rise of Capitalism* (New York, 1966). Also useful is Franklin F. Mendels, "Proto-industrialization: The First Phase of the Industrialization Process," *Journal of Economic History* 32 (March 1972):241-261.

21. Gentil da Silva, *Espagne: Développement*, pp. 48-49.

22. See chapter 5.

23. David R. Ringrose, *Transportation and Economic Stagnation in Spain, 1750-1850* (Durham, N.C., 1970).

24. Felipe Ruiz Martín, "Un testimonio literaria sobre las manufacturas de paños en Segovia por 1625," in *Homenaje al Profesor Alarcos*, 2 vols. (Valladolid, 1966), 2:1-21.

25. Gentil da Silva, *Espagne: Développement*, pp. 125-128, 153; see also Antonio Domínguez Ortiz, *The Golden Age of Spain 1516-1659*, trans. James Casey (New York, 1971), pp. 182-187, for a clear summary of the reasons usually given for Spain's industrial decline. The body of laws enforcing the guilds' control over production and the service trades are collected in the *Novísima recopilación*, lib. 8, tít. 10-25, most easily accessible in *Los códigos españoles concordados y anotados*, 12 vols. (Madrid, 1847-1851). For prices see Earl J. Hamilton, *American Treasure and the Price Revolution in Spain, 1501-1650* (Cambridge, Mass.; reprint ed. New York, 1965), pp. 206-207.

26. Michael Weisser, "The Decline of Castile Revisited: The Case of Toledo," *Journal of European Economic History* (Winter 1973), pp. 631-632.

27. Manuel Colmeiro y Penido, *Historia de la economía política en España*, 2 vols. (Madrid, 1863; reprint ed., Madrid, 1965), 2:204.

28. Francisco Martínez de Mata, *Memorial en razón del remedio de la despoblación, pobreza, y esterilidad de España* (ca. 1655), in *Apéndice de la educación popular* by Pedro Rodríguez Campomanes, 4 vols. (Madrid, 1775-1777), 4:1-418.

29. Carande, *Carlos V y sus banqueros*, 2:238.

30. See chapter 6 for royal taxes.

31. Tercias (literally, thirds) were the royal share of the church tithe, legally one-third, actually two-ninths; they were collected with the alcabalas.

32. Hervás, *Diccionario histórico*, p. 220.

33. See chapter 2 and my forthcoming "The Moriscos of La Mancha, 1570-1614," *The Journal of Modern History* (demand reprints).

34. AGS, *Cámara*, leg. 2160, fol 66; *Expedientes de Hacienda*, leg. 83.

35. José Antonio Vizcaíno, *Los caminos de la Mancha* (Madrid, 1966), pp. 88-89.

36. AGS, *CG*, leg. 2304; *Expedientes de Hacienda*, leg. 81.

37. Real wages in New Castile hit their highest level between 1500 and 1650 in 1605-1619. Hamilton, *American Treasure*, p. 279.

38. Delgado Merchán, *Historia documentada*, p. 330.

39. See the *Novísima recopilación*, lib. 8, tit. 24, leyes 1 and 3 for Bourbon textile laws.

40. Appendix B. Hervás, *Diccionario histórico*, p. 221, and Delgado Merchán, *Historia documentada*, p. 339, also mention the industrial revival of the city.

41. The roads of the province are mentioned in numerous works: Antonio Blázquez, "Vías romanas de la provincia de Ciudad Real," *Boletín de la Real Sociedad Geográfica* 32 (1892):366-382; Manuel Corchado Soriano, *El camino de Toledo a Córdoba*, new ed. (Jaén, 1969); Manuel Corchado Soriano, "Pasos naturales y antiguos caminos entre Jaén y la Mancha," *Boletín del Instituto de Estudios Giennenses* 38 (Oct.-Dec. 1963): 9-37. Juan de Villuga, *Reportorio de todos los caminos de España* (Madrid, 1546); Gonzalo Menéndez Pidal, *Los caminos en la historia de España* (Madrid, 1951); José Canga Argüelles, *Diccionario de hacienda*, 5 vols. (London, 1826-27), 2:12.

42. Madame d'Aulnoy [Marie Catherine le Jumelle de Berneville, Comtesse d'Aulnoy], "Relación del viaje de España . . . ," in *Viajes de extranjeros por España y Portugal*, ed. José García Mercadal, 3 vols. (Madrid, 1952), 2:1045-46.

43. Villuga, *Reportorio*, n.p. Menéndez Pidal, *Caminos*, includes maps based on Villuga's book, as well as on later descriptions of the Spanish road network. In all cases Ciudad Real was shown located on a secondary route.

44. Delgado Merchán, *Historia documentada*, pp. 331, 335. The city of Ciudad Real made it through the grain scarcity of 1679-1680 with imports from Extremadura. The citizens of Ciudad Real sometimes resented their close ties to Portugal, particularly when Portuguese merchants resided in the city without becoming citizens and when cheap Portuguese cloth flooded the local market. See AMCR, *Libros Capitulares*, leg. 9, for the former complaint in 1613.

45. Hervás, *Diccionario histórico*, pp. 221-222. See Ladislas Reitzer, "Some Observations on Castilian Commerce and Finance in the Sixteenth Century," *Journal of Modern History* 32 (1960):213-223, for a description of the larger fairs of Castile.

46. Salomon, *Campagne de nouvelle Castille*, pp. 128-130. Some Manchegan towns did sell wine and other products to Madrid. See chapter 3.

47. See David R. Ringrose, "Carting in the Hispanic World: An Example of Divergent Development," *Hispanic American Historical Review* (Feb. 1970), pp. 30-51; and Ringrose, *Transportation and Economic Stagnation in Spain*, especially chaps. 3 and 4.

48. AGS, *RG*, lib. 468, questions 17, 31, and 32. All references to commer-

cial transport in Ciudad Real have been taken from this source, unless otherwise noted.

49. AHN, *Clero*, leg. 1867.

50. Ringrose, *Transportation*, p. 64, shows a range between 20 and 120 carts per owner in the largest carting enterprises.

51. Ibid., p. 71.

52. Ibid., p. 63, lists the average number of carts per owner as 1.43 in La Mancha and 35.5 in Cuenca. The Cuenca average was heavily influenced by 350 carts owned by seven carters in Almodóvar del Pinar.

53. Bennassar, *Valladolid*, p. 94.

54. AGS, *RG*, lib. 468, question 31.

55. Ibid., question 32.

56. Pérez Valera, *Ciudad Real*, pp. 32-36. The four were Don Francisco Bustillo, Don Mathias Bustillo, Don Esteban de Aguirre, and Don Fernando Espinosa.

57. AHN, *Hacienda: Catastro*, lib. 7466, pt. 2, lists the income of all whole-sale and retail merchants as 80,620 reales a year.

58. AGS, *RG*, lib. 468, question 32.

59. Ibid., question 29.

60. APCR, legs. 141, 147, 152.

61. Ibid., leg. 152.

62. Ruth Pike, *Aristocrats and Traders: Sevillian Society in the Sixteenth Century* (Ithaca, N.Y., 1972). See also the excellent study by William James Callahan, *Honor, Commerce, and Industry in Eighteenth-Century Spain* (Boston, 1972).

63. Marriage registers at San Pedro and Nuestra Señora del Prado.

64. APCR, leg. 105.

65. See, for example, Z. P. Pach, "Sixteenth-century Hungary: Commercial Activity and Market Production by the Nobles," in *Economy and Society in Early Modern Europe*, ed. Peter Burke (New York, 1972), pp. 113-133.

66. Salomon, *Campagne de nouvelle Castille*, p. 249.

67. APCR, legs. 72, 73.

68. Ibid., leg. 139. A village in Burgos bought 150 fanegas of grain from Don Cristóbal Treviño Velarde of Ciudad Real in 1644. The final purchase price had to be paid within a month. Other grain sales were of similarly short and precise terms. Ibid., legs. 147 bis, 152.

69. Hamilton, *American Treasure*, pp. 258-259, found that more than half of the annual wheat and barley prices in New Castile illegally exceeded the tasa.

70. APCR, leg. 141.

71. Ibid., leg. 36.

72. Ibid., leg. 152.

73. One horse was sold to a priest in Leganés by his counterpart in Ciudad Real for 1,000 reales. Its trappings cost another 1,300 reales. Transaction in 1646, ibid., leg. 152.

74. Ibid., leg. 36.

75. Ibid., leg. 152.

76. Felipe Ruiz Martín, "La Banca en España hasta 1782," in *El Banco de España: Una historia económica* (Madrid, 1970), p. 138. See also Earl J. Hamilton's several articles on the unsuccessful attempts at founding a national banking system in Spain during the Habsburg period, in the *Journal of Political Economy* between 1945 and 1949.

77. Bernard Schnapper, *Les rentes au XVIe siècle: Histoire d'un instrument de crédit* (Paris, 1957), p. 64.

78. Felipe Ruiz Martín, "Banca en España," pp. 139-140.

79. AGS, *CG*, leg. 2304. Chapter 6, Table 6.1. Bennassar noted similar activity in Valladolid in the same period. *Valladolid*, pp. 258-264.

80. Ibid., pp. 24, 140-144. Bennassar, *Valladolid*, pp. 259-260, 271, discusses the debt structure in Valladolid. Interest rates for *rentes* near Paris in the same period were considerably higher than those in Castile (Schnapper, *Rentes*, pp. 100-102), though French rates steadily declined during the seventeenth century, largely because of the volume of credit available.

81. Helen Nader, "The Nobility as Borrowers and Lenders: A New Look at the *Censos*," paper presented to the American Historical Association Convention, Washington, D.C., Dec. 1976. See also Bartolomé Bennassar, "En Vieille-Castille: Les ventes de rentes perpétuelles," *Annales: Économies, Sociétés, Civilisations* (Nov.-Dec. 1960), pp. 1115-1126.

82. Ruiz Martín, "Banca en España," p. 141.

83. Carmelo Viñas y Mey, *El problema de la tierra en la España de los siglos XVI-XVII* (Madrid, 1941); Pierre Goubert, *Beauvais et le Beauvaisis de 1600 à 1730: Contribution à l'histoire sociale de la France du XVIIe siècle* (Paris, 1960), traced the pattern of peasant ruin through debt in France during the same period.

84. Ruiz Martín, "Banca en España," pp. 143-145.

85. APCR, legs. 10, 11, 20 bis, 36, 148, 152, and others. See also Bennassar, *Valladolid*, pp. 260-272, and Goubert, *Beauvais*, pp. 185-188, for similar findings in Valladolid and the French Beauvaisis.

86. Ringrose, *Transportation*, pp. 132-141.

87. Diego Medrano y Treviño, *Consideraciones sobre el estado económico moral y político de la provincia de Ciudad Real . . .* (Madrid, 1843; reprint ed. Madrid, 1972).

88. Eugenio Larruga y Boneta, *Memorias políticas y económicas sobre los frutos, comercio, fábricas y minas de España . . .*, 45 vols. (Madrid, 1787-1800), vols. 17 and 18.

V. CHANGING PATTERNS OF LANDOWNERSHIP IN THE SEVENTEENTH CENTURY

1. By the late seventeenth century, clergy and religious accounted for about 2 percent of the total Spanish population. Their numbers had increased somewhat over the course of the century. See Antonio Domínguez Ortiz, *La sociedad española en el siglo XVII*, 2 vols. (Madrid, 1963-1970), 2:8. The nobility accounted for about 10 percent of the total population in this period, although

their numbers could vary considerably in the diverse regions of Spain. Domín-guez Ortiz, *Sociedad española*, 1:169. The remaining 88 percent were commoners of all degrees.

2. See chapter 7.

3. A detailed tabular summary of the buyers and sellers by occupation appears in my earlier article on this topic, "Urban Control of the Castilian Countryside: Additional Evidence from Seventeenth Century Ciudad Real," *Societas—A Review of Social History* (Autumn 1973):313-335.

4. APCR, legs. 195, 197, 198, 201, 219.

5. Ibid., legs. 199, 215, 243.

6. Ibid., legs. 201, 217, 218.

7. Ibid., legs. 147, 149, 150 bis, 201, 211.

8. Ibid., legs. 119, 120, 122, 123, 141, 195, 196, 196 bis, 198, 214, 216.

9. Lucas de la Fuente, transactions in January 1662, October 1662, and January 1665. Ibid., legs. 150 bis, 151.

10. Antonio de Cárdenas, transactions in September 1660, September 1662, and July 1665. Ibid., legs. 150, 150 bis, 151.

11. Transaction of February 1679. Ibid., leg. 198.

12. Transactions of May 1683, August 1683, and February 1684. Ibid., legs. 199, 215.

13. Transactions from March 1650 to April 1676. Ibid., legs. 146, 149, 159 bis, 197.

14. Transactions from January 1601 to February 1607. Ibid., legs. 11, 13, 14, 15, 17.

15. Transactions from May 1652 to April 1666. Ibid., legs. 150 bis, 151.

16. Transactions from October 1689 to August 1697. Ibid., legs. 216, 218, 219.

17. Ibid., leg. 106.

18. Farmers may actually have been more numerous than those with exclusively urban occupations, if the proportion of the population in agriculture is any guide. See Appendix D.

19. Juan de Salcedo, transactions from April 1662 to March 1684. APCR, legs. 150 bis, 151, 198, 199, 215.

20. Ibid., legs. 120, 151, 195, 196, 216, 218.

21. Antonio Ponz, *Viaje de España* . . . , 18 vols. (Madrid, 1777-1794), 16: 34-50.

22. Jean Sarrailh, *L'Espagne éclairée de la seconde moitié du XVIIIᵉ siècle* (Paris, 1964), p. 17.

23. Noël Salomon, *La campagne de nouvelle Castille à la fin du XVIᵉ siècle: D'après les "Relaciones topográficas"* (Paris, 1964), pp. 243-244.

24. Martín González de Cellorigo, *Memorial de la política necesaria, y útil restauración a la república de España* . . . (Valladolid, 1600), fol. 24. See chapter 2, n. 3.

25. Salomon, *Campagne de nouvelle Castille*, pp. 249-250.

26. Ibid., pp. 182-184.

27. An anonymous observer writing in 1633 deplored the excessive conver-

sion of land to vineyards, blaming it for a decline in olive oil production and available grazing land and an increase in overall labor costs. *Memorial por la agricultura* (Madrid, 1633), pp. 1v-2v.

28. APCR, legs. 150, 151.

29. Gonzalo Anes Alvarez and Jean-Paul Le Flem found some evidence of soil exhaustion in the Segovia area during the seventeenth century, which could help to explain the continuing expansion of landholdings in the area. Wheat and barley production declined over the course of the century, whereas that of rye and oats increased. Since rye takes less care than wheat or barley and can thrive on poorer land, this suggests that even the better lands were exhausted. "Las crisis del siglo XVII: Producción agrícola, precios e ingresos en tierras de Segovia," *Moneda y crédito* 93 (June, 1965):3-55.

30. APCR, legs. 151, 196, 197, 198, 214, 219. See also Bernard H. Slicher van Bath, *The Agrarian History of Western Europe: A.D. 500-1850*, trans. Olive Ordish (New York, 1963), p. 213, for the low price of land all over Europe after 1650.

31. In 1751 nearly 77 percent of the término of Ciudad Real was cultivated, and 20 percent served as pasture. AGS, *RG*, lib. 468, question 10. In 1958, with a much higher population and vastly higher productivity, only 48 percent of the término was considered fit for cultivation. *Reseña estadística de la provincia de Ciudad Real* (Madrid, 1958), pp. 312-313.

32. Complaints of usurped common lands in Ciudad Real exist from as early as 1474, and they appear often thereafter. See AMCR, docs. 29, 42, 47, 88. Useful modern discussions of the problem are David E. Vassberg, "The *tierras baldías:* Community Property and Public Lands in Sixteenth-Century Castile," *Agricultural History* 48 (July 1974):383-401; idem, "The Sale of 'tierras baldías' in Sixteenth-Century Castile," *Journal of Modern History* 47 (Dec. 1975):629-654; Felipe Ruiz Martín, "La Banca en España hasta 1782," in *El Banco de España: Una historia económica* (Madrid, 1970), pp. 145-147.

33. AMCR, doc. 303; APCR, leg. 201. The place was named Santa María de Guadiana, or Nuestra Señora de Guadiana.

34. AGS, *RG*, lib. 468, question 28.

35. See particularly the series of documents dealing with the rental of part of the city's lands (*tierras concejiles*) in the 1630s. AMCR, docs. 211, 212, 217, 218.

36. See David Ringrose, *Transportation and Economic Stagnation in Spain, 1750-1850* (Durham, N.C., 1970), maps, for the principal lines of supply to the capital in the mid-eighteenth century.

37. The new landholding bourgeoisie in Castile often used revenue from lands, censos, and juros to affect an aristocratic style of life. Rarely did they reinvest their money in agriculture or in industry. In short, they did not recognize their potential as protocapitalists. This "defection of the bourgeoisie," in Braudel's famous phrase, helped to perpetuate backward methods of production in Spain. Fernand Braudel, *The Mediterranean and the Mediterranean World in the Age of Philip II*, 1966 rev. ed., trans. Siân Reynolds, 2 vols. (New York, 1972-73), 2:725-734. We should not forget, however, that in many cases there was no viable alternative to the unproductive use of capital.

38. Ciudad Real province is now one of the richest agricultural areas in the

country, largely because of wine production. See the *Reseña estadística de la provincia de Ciudad Real* and the *Anuario estadístico de España, 1972* (Madrid, 1973) and subsequent years, to examine the modern economy of Ciudad Real.

VI. ROYAL TAXATION

1. *Preconditions of Revolution in Early Modern Europe*, ed. J. P. Greene and Robert Forster (Baltimore, Md., 1971), provides the best short summaries and recent interpretations of each of these revolts. J. W. Smit on the Netherlands, John H. Elliott on the other rebellions against Spain, Roland Mousnier on France, and Lawrence Stone on England, each an expert in the field, provide the best starting places for further research.

2. John Lynch, *Spain under the Habsburgs*, 2 vols. (Oxford, 1964, 1969), vol. 1.

3. Charles J. Jago, "Aristocracy, War and Finance in Castile, 1621-1665," Ph.D. thesis, Cambridge University, 1969; Charles J. Jago, "The Influence of Debt on the Relations between Crown and Aristocracy in Seventeenth-Century Castile," *Economic History Review* 26 (May, 1973):218-236.

4. Wladimiro Piskorski, *Las Cortes de Castilla en el período de tránsito de la Edad Media a la Moderna* (Barcelona, 1930); Lynch, *Spain under the Habsburgs*.

5. See Noël Salomon, *La campagne de nouvelle Castille à la fin du XVIᵉ siècle: D'après les "Relaciones topográficas"* (Paris, 1964), pp. 219-222, for diezmos in 1575-1580. Salomon found wide variation in the tithe rate in New Castile, although most towns did pay close to one-tenth. Laws concerning the diezmos can be found in the *Novísima recopilación*, lib. 1, tít. 6, most readily available in *Los códigos españoles concordados y anotados*, 12 vols. (Madrid, 1847-1851).

6. See Miguel Angel Ladero Quesada, *La hacienda real de Castilla en el siglo XV* (La Laguna: Universidad de La Laguna, 1973); Bartolomé Bennassar, "Impôts et crédit public en Espagne du XVIᵉ siècle à nos jours (traits dominants d'une mutation)," in *Finances Publiques d'Ancien Régime* (Brussels, 1972).

7. Ramón Carande Thobar, *Carlos V y sus banqueros, 1516-1556*, 3 vols. (Madrid, 1943-1967).

8. See Salvador de Moxó, *La alcabala: Sobre sus orígenes, concepto y naturaleza* (Madrid, 1963).

9. Modesto Ulloa, *La hacienda real de Castilla en el reinado de Felipe II* (Rome, 1963), pp. 105, 122-127.

10. Ibid., pp. 317-332. See Antonio Domínguez Ortiz, *Política y hacienda de Felipe IV* (Madrid, 1960), for millones and other taxes under Philip III and Philip IV.

11. Domínguez Ortiz, *Política y hacienda*, p. 186.

12. Ibid., pp. 22-27, 235, 338. See Jago, "Aristocracy, War and Finance," pp. 132-135, for some of the ill-fated tax reform plans.

13. Although legally associated with the alcabalas, the unos por ciento in their origin had more to do with the millones. Under royal pressure, the Cortes enacted successive unos por ciento to help pay for successive additions to the mil-

lones. See *Escrituras, acuerdos, administraciones y súplicas de los servicios de 24 millones* (Madrid, 1734).

14. Domínguez Ortiz, *Política y hacienda*, p. 229. See the *Novísima recopilación*, lib. 10, tít. 24, for laws dealing with papel sellado.

15. Domínguez Ortiz, *Política y hacienda*, pp. 229-238, 297-315. For the alienation of the aristocracy see Jago, "Aristocracy, War and Finance," chap. 3.

16. The fiscal policy of Charles II is still awaiting its historian; useful discussions can be found in Antonio Domínguez Ortiz, "La crisis de Castilla en 1677-1688," *Revista portuguesa de historia* 10 (1962):435-445, reprinted in idem, *Crisis y decadencia de la España de los Austrias* (Barcelona, 1969); Gabriel Maura y Gamazo, *La vida y reinado de Carlos II*, 2nd ed., 3 vols. (Madrid, 1954), 2:188-192. Also useful is the contemporary manual by Juan de la Ripia, *Práctica de la administración y cobranza de las rentas reales* . . . (Madrid, 1695; the edition cited here was reprinted in 5 vols. and updated in Madrid, 1795), 1:266-267.

17. Salomon, *Campagne de nouvelle Castille*, p. 234, gives the following estimates for yearly taxes per householder in New Castile (1575-1580): seigneurial charges, including the *alcabalas*, 40-50 maravedís; diezmos (plus at least 7.5 fanegas of bread grain), 466 maravedís; royal taxation (both *servicios* and the *millones*, which began in 1594), 472 maravedís. Salomon considered the alcabalas as seigneurial dues, since they were often held by the great lords of Castile. Technically, however, the alcabalas were royal taxes, and they will be so considered for Ciudad Real.

18. Earl J. Hamilton, *American Treasure and the Price Revolution in Spain, 1501-1650* (Cambridge, Mass., 1934; reprint ed., New York, 1965), pp. 342-345.

19. According to the *Catastro*, the city's diezmos were 40,000 reales (1.36 million maravedís), plus 3,883 fanegas of wheat; 4,388 fanegas of barley; and 496 fanegas of rye a year, divided among 1,752 households. AGS, *RG*, lib. 468, question 16.

20. AGS, *CG*, leg. 768.

21. Ibid., leg. 2303. In 1491 Ciudad Real had paid a total of nearly 1.23 million maravedís in farmed taxes, which probably included servicios as well as alcabalas and tercias. Ladero Quesada, *Hacienda real*, pp. 50-53. The rise in these basic taxes, then, had hardly been dramatic since the end of the fifteenth century.

22. AGS, *CMC 3a*, leg. 3023; AMCR, docs. 73, 98, 137. The state bankruptcy of 1557 was an obvious reason for the increase in royal taxes. Ulloa, *Hacienda real*, pp. 305-306, has some figures for Ciudad Real in the late sixteenth century, but they cannot be trusted.

23. AGS, *Expedientes de Hacienda (Ciudad Real)*, leg. 81. I have used five-year averages for better comparison with the 1557-1561 returns. For the years between 1593 and 1597, there was very little variation for most taxable items. Only wine and vinegar, property sales, and salt showed a wide range, and their averages are still representative of the five-year period.

24. AGS, *Cámara*, leg. 2162, fol. 1.

25. Fernand Braudel, *The Mediterranean and the Mediterranean World in the Age of Philip II*, 1966 rev. ed., trans. Siân Reynolds, 2 vols. (New York, 1972-73), 1:570-606.

26. AGS, *CG*, leg. 2973.

27. Ibid., leg. 799, gave the city's total population as 2,049 vecinos in 1591. A count for about 1527 had reported 1,146 taxpaying householders (*vecinos pecheros*) (ibid., leg. 768), or a total population of 1,252 vecinos, based on the proportions used in Felipe Ruiz Martín, "La población española al comienzo de los tiempos modernos, "*Cuadernos de historia: Anexos de la revista Hispania* 1 (Madrid, 1967):189-202.

28. Alvaro Castillo, "Population et 'richesse' en Castile durant la seconde moitié du XVIe siècle," *Annales: Économies, Sociétés, Civilisations* (July-August 1965), pp. 731-732.

29. AGS, *CMC 3a*, leg. 287. AMCR, doc. 199, contains servicios figures for 1597 to 1616, which averaged 355,284 maravedís a year. In 1621 they were lowered to 282,267 maravedís a year, plus expenses, in recognition of the city's distress and loss of inhabitants. AMCR, doc. 201.

30. AGS, *CMC 3a, leg*. 278. See Domínguez Ortiz, *Política y hacienda*, pt. 2, for financiers of the crown in the seventeenth century.

31. AGS, *CMC 3a*, legs. 287, 2092, 3097.

32. Ibid., leg. 3097.

33. Hamilton, *American Treasure*, p. 217.

34. See chapter 2.

35. Antonio Domínguez Ortiz, *La sociedad española en el siglo XVII*, 2 vols. (Madrid, 1963-1970), 1:25-28.

36. AGS, *CMC 3a*, legs. 2181, 2071. See also AMCR, doc. 215.

37. AGS, *CMC 3a*, leg. 287.

38. Hamilton, *American Treasure*, pp. 217-219.

39. Ibid., pp. 219-220.

40. AGS, *CMC 3a*, leg. 2642.

41. Ibid., legs. 289, 294.

42. See Domínguez Ortiz, *Politica y hacienda*, pp. 318-321, for juro reductions in this period; Ripia, *Práctica . . . de las rentas reales*, 2:174-193, for juro reductions from 1621 to 1722.

43. AGS, *CMC 3a*, leg. 1927. See Geoffrey Parker, *The Army of Flanders and the Spanish Road, 1567-1659* (Cambridge, 1972).

44. AGS, *CG*, leg. 3545. See Domínguez Ortiz, *Política y hacienda*, pp. 235-237, for additions to the millones. Contributors to the 1636-37 voluntary gift (*donativo*) in Ciudad Real are listed in AMCR, doc. 216, nearly a roster of the city's elite.

45. AGS, *CG*, leg. 3545.

46. APCR, leg. 141; AGS, *CMC 3a*, legs. 2456, 2487, 2498, 2542, 2652, 3158.

47. Domínguez Ortiz, *Política y hacienda*, pp. 236-237.

48. AGS, *CMC 3a*, legs. 546, 2339, 3052, 3306, 3465. Domínguez Ortiz, *Sociedad española*, 1:325-337, listed 167 distressed towns, 10 of them near Ciudad Real.

49. AGS, *CMC 3a*, legs. 546, 2218, 2219, 2576, 2620, 3052; APCR, leg. 140.

50. AGS, *CMC 3a*, legs. 535, 1545, 1829, 1973, 2033, 2040, 2047, 2140,

2143, 2146, 2148, 2273, 2274, 2313, 2482, 2810, 2917, 2923, 2958, 2962, 2978, 3006, 3030, 3070, 3082, 3089, 3091, 3096, 3251, 3306, 3372, 3390, 3392, 3422, 3456, 3498.

51. Ibid., legs. 2181, 2247, 2294, 2620, 3010, 3221, 3328.

52. Ibid., leg. 2247.

53. *Actas de las Cortes de Castilla* 58 (1) (Madrid, 1962):137-138.

54. AGS, *CMC 3a*, leg. 2735.

55. Ibid., leg. 2620.

56. Ibid., legs. 2247, 2746, 2878, 3036.

57. Ibid., legs. 564, 1687, 1922, 2062, 2248, 2293, 2304, 2526, 2564, 2776, 3379, 3480.

58. Ibid., leg. 3379. Part was due in silver, the rest in vellón.

59. Ibid., legs. 1922, 2293.

60. Ibid., leg. 3328.

61. Ibid., legs. 564, 2293.

62. Ibid., legs. 511, 1531, 2936.

63. Ibid., leg. 2642.

64. Ibid., leg. 2109.

65. Ibid., leg 3379; APCR, leg. 201.

66. AGS, *CMC 3a*, legs. 564, 2304.

67. Hamilton, *American Treasure*, pp. 216-221; Earl J. Hamilton, *War and Prices in Spain, 1651-1800* (Cambridge, Mass., 1947; reprint ed. New York, 1969), pp. 121-136.

68. Hamilton, *War and Prices*, pp. 121-128.

69. AGS, *CMC 3a*, legs. 1810, 2316, 2489.

70. Ibid., *legs.* 2248, 2564, 2776. See AMCR, doc. 263, for servicios, 1669-1671.

71. Collection expenses were raised to 5-6 percent in 1687. See Ripia, *Práctica de las rentas reales*, and Maura, *Vida y reinado de Carlos II* for tax policies under the last Habsburg. AMCR, doc. 256, contains records of legal action against taxpayers in Ciudad Real who avoided paying millones on meat sales.

72. AMCR, docs. 275, 280.

73. AGS, *TMC*, leg. 2581.

74. Ibid. Summary accounts for Ciudad Real from 1688 to 1692 show an average yearly collection of 1.52 million maravedís in alcabalas and 515,786 maravedís in unos, which may not have included collection expenses. AMCR, *Libros Capitulares*, leg. 19.

75. AGS, *CMC 3a*, legs. 3196, 3240. An interesting tax list (*padrón*) from 1694, probably for the servicios, exempted 17.3 percent of the householders from any payment, either for poverty, for nobility, or for other reasons. Another 70.6 percent of the householders paid 1-10 reales each, and the remainder paid 11-56 reales, nearly all of them at the lower part of the range. AMCR, doc. 181. The list is analyzed in Appendix D, Table D.4. There is no necessary connection between assessed tax and wealth, but this list agrees well with the social structure revealed by the *Catastro*. See Appendixes B and D.

76. AMCR, docs. 344, 361.

77. AHN, *Catastro*, lib. 7466, question E, and AGS, *RG*, lib. 468, question 2. See chapter 7, n.59 for the offices and their owners.

78. Taking the diezmos as one-tenth of agricultural production and agricultural production as two-thirds of total production, Domínguez Ortiz arrives at a figure of 180 million ducados a year for Spain's national income during the reign of Philip IV. Royal taxes, at 20 million ducados a year, would then have been only 11 percent of the total. Domínguez Ortiz, *Política y hacienda*, pp. 177-183. Using this method, total royal taxes in Ciudad Real in 1751 would have been worth from 4 to 8 percent of total production, depending on how the grain diezmos are figured.

VII. THE URBAN ELITE

1. See Antonio Domínguez Ortiz, *La sociedad española en el siglo XVII*, 2 vols. (Madrid, 1963, 1970), Volume 2 for the most complete treatment of the Spanish ecclesiastical establishment. The clergy in Ciudad Real included representatives from several of the city's major noble families. APNSP, lib. 1018. Local nobles were also prominent in the various monastic foundations in the area and as secular and clerical members of the military orders. For example, Hermann Kellenbenz, *Die Fuggersche Maestrazgopacht* (Tübingen, 1967), p. 67, mentions a Coca and a Treviño as friars in the order of Calatrava in the early sixteenth century.

2. The licentiate Bartolomé de Leon, a beneficed priest of Nuestra Señora del Prado, owned forty-five pieces of land when he died in 1676, plus houses, credit paper, and substantial household furnishings. Since he died unexpectedly and without a will, his entire estate went to the church. APNSP, doc. 121.

3. See Annie Molinié-Bertrand, "Le clergé dans le royaume de Castille à la fin du XVIe siècle: Approche cartographique," *Revue d'histoire économique et sociale* 51 (1973):5-53, for an interesting attempt to map the location of the clergy in 1591; Felipe Ruiz Martín, "Demografía eclesiástica de España hasta el siglo XIX," in *Diccionario de historia eclesiástica de España*, ed. by Quintín Aldea Vaquero, Tomás Marín Martínez, and José Vives Gatell, 3 vols. (Madrid, 1972-73), 2:682-733.

4. APCR, leg. 197. The same convent received, among its other gifts, a yearly donation from the order of Santiago of 6,000 maravedís plus the market value of 10 fanegas of wheat. Kellenbenz, *Fuggersche Maestrazgopacht*, pp. 60, 157, 202, 217, 241, 267-268, 276.

5. Gerónimo de Uztáriz, *Theórica y práctica de comercio y de marina* (Madrid, 1724), p. 79.

6. Bartolomé Bennassar, *Valladolid au siècle d'or: Une ville de Castille et sa campagne au XVIe siècle* (Paris, 1967), p. 390.

7. For 1591 see AGS, *Dirección General del Tesoro*, leg. 1301, printed in Manuel Fernández Álvarez, *La sociedad española del Renacimiento* (Salamanca, 1970), p. 81; Molinié-Bertrand, "Clergé dans le royaume de Castille," pp. 12-17. For 1751 see Isabel Pérez Valera, ed., *Ciudad Real en el siglo XVIII* (Ciudad Real, 1955), pp. 77-94.

8. Luis Delgado Merchán, *Historia documentada de Ciudad Real*, 2nd ed. (Ciudad Real, 1907), pp. 332-335. See also Inocente Hervás y Buendía, *Diccionario histórico geográfico de . . . Ciudad Real* (Ciudad Real, 1890), p. 236. Law-

suits over the building and maintenance of monasteries were frequent and often bitterly contested. See RAH, *Salazar*, U-12, fols. 321-331, 397-400; X-39, fols. 146-154, for other disputes of this sort in Ciudad Real. The proliferation of monastic foundations and the acrimony surrounding them helped convince Philip II to restrict the establishment of new convents. A copy of his 1593 instruction to Castile's cities appears in AMCR, doc. 163.

9. Pérez Valera, *Ciudad Real en el siglo XVIII*, pp. 91-93. See also AGS, *RG*, lib. 468, question 39.

10. Delgado Merchán, *Historia documentada*, p. 332; Pérez Valera, *Ciudad Real en el siglo XVIII*, pp. 93-94; AGS, *RG*, lib. 468, question 39.

11. Lozano's will and an inventory of his goods are in AGI, *Casa de Contratación*, leg. 300, no. 10. A clear copy of the will is filed with the papers of the Descalced Mercedarians, AHN, *Clero*, leg. 1867.

12. APNSP, docs. 303, 452.

13. Bill of sale for the house purchased from Doña Estefania de Prado, widow of Antonio de Oliver. AHN, *Clero*, 1867. See also the record of testimony by concerned clerics in AMCR, *Libros Capitulares*, leg. 19, pp. 118r-121. A suit over the terms of the will is in RAH, *Salazar*, X-39, fols. 146-154.

14. AHN, *Clero*, leg. 1867. The convent church later became a parish of Nuestra Señora del Prado, now the cathedral of Ciudad Real.

15. The annual income of the foundations suggests an endowment of nearly 375,000 ducados, at 6 percent interest. Antonio de Torres Treviño's share was apparently 94,000 ducados, and 50,000 of that provided the entire endowment of the monks' convent and hospital. AGI, *Casa de Contratación*, leg. 403, pt. 1, no. 3. Much of the total endowment was invested in juros. AGS, *CMC 3a*, legs. 511, 1531.

16. AGS, *RG*, lib. 468, question 30. See also Delgado Merchán, *Historia documentada*, p. 335.

17. Juan de la Jara, *Historia de la imagen de Nuestra Señora del Prado, fundadora y patrona de Ciudad Real* (Ciudad Real, 1880), pp. 363-365. Antonio de Poblete y Loaisa, a young noble disowned by his family for an inappropriate marriage, emigrated to the New World and took with him a copy of the statue of the Virgen del Prado. Many people later attributed miracles to the Virgen's intervention. Ibid., pp. 281-286, 455-456.

18. APNSP, docs. 303, 452, 671.

19. Hervás, *Diccionario histórico*, pp. 225-226, and Delgado Merchán, *Historia documentada*, pp. 238-239, each have summaries of pious donations in Ciudad Real. Their sources were hundreds of documents dealing with such donations, especially from local nobles. See APNSP, docs. 567, 581, 221-236, 898, 899, 929, as a representative sample. In addition, docs. 316, 346, 305, and 894 record expenditures for church construction and repair, and doc. 299 gives a detailed inventory of the silver objects owned by the church in 1601.

20. Hervás, *Diccionario histórico*, p. 239.

21. AMCR, docs. 247, 249, 250.

22. APCR, legs. 105, 107, 119, 149 bis; APNSP, doc. 69.

23. Letter from Don Pedro de Arandía to Don Bartolomé de Valencia, dated

Almagro, 21 May 1750. This and other documents are printed in Pérez Valera, *Ciudad Real en el siglo XVIII*, pp. 16-19.

24. AHN, *Hacienda: Catastro*, libs. 7466, 7467, question E.

25. AGS, *RG*, lib. 468, question 32.

26. Noël Salomon, *La campagne de nouvelle Castille à la fin du XVIe siècle: D'après les "Relaciones topográficas"* (Paris, 1964), p. 298.

27. Domínguez Ortiz, *Sociedad española*, 1:209-220. Claims and provisions about hidalguía appear habitually in the municipal records of Ciudad Real. See, for example, AMCR, docs. 101, 111, 113, 121, 125, 127, 164, 177. The most interesting is doc. 209 from 1630-31, which reports the city council's review of all claims to nobility in the city. The councillors found that all but four of the city's nobles had undisputable claims based on birth, royal grants, or service. The four disputed cases claimed noble status from their advanced university degrees.

28. Pérez Valera, *Ciudad Real en el siglo XVIII*, pp. 30-36, lists 40 of 1,752 householders as nobles, most of whom expressly claimed noble status.

29. Ildefonso Romero García, "Los hidalgos de San Benito," *Cuadernos de estudios manchegos* 6 (1953):8.

30. José Gentil da Silva, *En Espagne: Développement économique, subsistance, déclin* (Paris, 1965), p. 110. Domínguez Ortiz, *Sociedad española*, 1:167-169, estimates that one of ten persons was noble in seventeenth-century Castile.

31. Josephe Díaz Jurado, "Historia de Ciudad Real" (unpublished manuscript in the APCR, written ca. 1750), pp. 80-109.

32. Ibid., pp. 93-95. See also AHN, *Mayorazgos*, leg. 37, 833; RAH, *Salazar*, D-25, fol. 194v; D-35, fol. 172; D-54, fols. 49-49v.

33. APCR, legs. 141, 195, 198.

34. APCR, legs. 205, 214. See RAH, *Salazar*, D-27, fols. 113r-116v, for the Aguileras and D-25, fol. 90v; D-42, fols. 315-321v, for the Messías (sometimes spelled Mesía or Mexía).

35. See RAH, *Salazar*, D-28, fol. 187; I-27, fols. 96v-97, 103v-104v, for Antonio Galiana y Bermudez. APNSP, doc. 580, contains his will, dated 26 December 1592. In addition to the family mayorazgo, he left a dozen houses and shops, thirteen censos, forty-five pieces of land containing about 1,500 aranzadas, and an impressive collection of movable goods.

36. Díaz Jurado, "Historia de Ciudad Real," pp. 83-84. See also APNSP, doc. 898, and AMCR, doc. 358, for the Velardes' continued prominence in the eighteenth century.

37. APCR, legs. 195, 198, 214, 216-218.

38. Díaz Jurado, "Historia de Ciudad Real," pp. 83-86. RAH, *Salazar*, I-27, fols. 96v-97, contains the Bermúdez genealogy. See n. 34 for the Messías.

39. Díaz Jurado, "Historia de Ciudad Real," pp. 89-90. RAH, *Salazar*, C-34, fols. 95-104; D-26, fol. 240.

40. AGS, *RG*, lib. 474. See chapter 3 for his livestock holdings, and RAH, *Salazar*, D-27, fols. 113-116, for his genealogy.

41. Díaz Jurado, "Historia de Ciudad Real," pp. 83-84. See Pérez Valera, *Ciudad Real en el siglo XVIII*, introduction, for Doña María Catalina's social gatherings.

42. Don Antonio de la Cueva Laso de la Vega, householder and perpetual alderman of Ciudad Real, sold five large pieces of land between 1656 and 1683. APCR, legs. 149, 150, 195, 199, 215.

43. Díaz Jurado, "Historia de Ciudad Real," p. 87.

44. Peter Boyd-Bowman, *Índice geobiográfico de cuarenta mil pobladores españoles de América en el siglo XVI*, 2 vols. (Bogotá, 1964, Mexico, 1968), 1:xii.

45. Roger Bigelow Merriman, *The Rise of the Spanish Empire in the Old World and the New*, 4 vols. (New York, 1918-1934), 3:448-449.

46. Unfortunately he does not appear in the standard sources for colonial Latin America.

47. Hervás, *Diccionario histórico*, pp. 240-244.

48. Delgado Merchán, *Historia documentada*, pp. 334-336.

49. Domínguez Ortiz, *Sociedad española*, 1:86-91.

50. Raimundo de Lencastre, the Portuguese duke of Aveiro, was given the title of duke of Ciudad Real for services to the Spanish crown while Portugal was under Spanish rule. When Portugal broke away in 1640, prominent residents of the city complained to the king that the title should not be allowed to stand. See below for the full delegation.

51. Bartolomé Arzáns de Orsúa y Vela, *Historia de la Villa Imperial de Potosí*, ed. Lewis Hanke and Gunnar Mendoza, 3 vols. (Providence, R.I., 1965), 1:150; 2:113-114, 117-120, 121, 123, 125, 127, 128, 131, 134, 141, 155, 166, 168, 182-183, 188, 203-205, 218, 356, 409. The official inquiry and sentencing are in AGI, *Escribanía de Cámara*, legs. 865B, 865C, 1190.

52. Domínguez Ortiz, *Sociedad española*, 1:197. At the time of the *Relaciones topográficas* (1575-1580), the town of Picón was under the jurisdiction of a resident of Ciudad Real, Luis Alfonso Destrada, who had purchased the rights from the crown in 1562. Carmelo Viñas and Ramón Paz, eds., *Relaciones histórico-geográfico-estadísticas de los pueblos de España hechas por iniciativa de Felipe II: Ciudad Real* (Madrid, 1971), p. 367. Other residents of the city owned land and houses in Picón and in other smaller towns.

53. Salomon, *Campagne de nouvelle Castille*, pp. 202-209, 316-317. See also Viñas and Paz, *Relaciones Ciudad Real*.

54. Domínguez Ortiz, *Sociedad española*, 1:190.

55. John Lynch, *Spain under the Habsburgs*, 2 vols. (Oxford, 1964-69), 2:234-235; Domínguez Ortiz, *Sociedad española*, 1: 253-258. The nobles of Ciudad Real upheld their right to run the city, even against the king's representative. See AMCR, docs. 157, 189, 196.

56. Bennassar, *Valladolid*, pp. 407-408.

57. Delgado Merchán, *Historia documentada*, p. 333. Those nobles left outside the administrative hierarchy did not always take their exclusion quietly. During the Corpus Christi procession in 1534 a violent quarrel broke out between the noble aldermen and other nobles over the right to bear the statue of the city's patroness. AMCR, doc. 78.

58. Domínguez Ortiz, *Sociedad española*, 1:185-188, discusses the role of cofradías in assigning municipal offices. In Ciudad Real the church of Nuestra Señora del Prado was called simply Santa María del Prado in 1751 (Pérez Valera, *Ciudad Real en el siglo XVIII*, p. 64). Membership lists for the Slaves of Nuestra

Señora del Prado in 1633, 1634, and 1690 show that ordinary citizens, and even paupers, could join along with the city's nobles, and quite often entire families would join together. APNSP, lib. 546.

59. AHN, *Hacienda: Catastro*, lib. 7468, p. 22; AGS, *RG*, lib. 468, questions 17, 20, 32. Individual owners of offices were the following: *regidores* (aldermen)—Don Diego Muñoz, Don Bernardino Loaisa, Don Pedro Díaz de la Cruz, Juan de Arenas y San Martín, Don Tomás de Aguilera, Don Josephe Sanz de Torres, Don Lorenzo del Valle, Don Juan Folgar y Varela, Don Luis Treviño, Don Bernabé Francés, Don Narciso de la Cueva, Don Ignacio Palacios, Don Alvaro Muñoz, Don Gerónimo Vendejo Vicario, Don Luis Velarde; *jurados* (common councilmen)—Francisco Valverde, Francisco Delgado, Don Juan de Azañón, Don Josephe Poblete Naranjo, Cristóbal Sánchez Savariegos, Francisco Díaz de la Concha; *escribanos del numero* (numbered scriveners)—Juan de Arenas y San Martín, Jacinto García Prieto, Francisco Peñuela, Lorenzo Gil de Almansa, Juan Cavello, Juan Díaz de la Cruz, Vicente Alises y Talavera, Nicanor Calahorra, Francisco Ruiz Carneras, Don Pedro Fernández Moreno; other scriveners —Juan de Arenas y San Martín, Jacinto García Prieto, Joseph Cordobés, Don Josephe Velarde Muñoz (3 offices), Don Diego Almansa; *procuradores* (solicitors) —Manuel Cándido Guzmán, Joseph López de Arias, Antonio Ruiz Delgado, Julián Jiménez, Juan Manuel Barona, Julián de Calcerrada; judicial officials— Don Josephe Velarde (3 offices), Don Cristóbal Muñoz Treviño, Eusebio Sánchez, Don Rodrigo Bermúdez, Don Luis Velarde.

60. AGS, *Estado*, leg. 40, fol. 53.

61. APCR, leg. 73, and Delgado Merchán, *Historia documentada*, app. 2, pp. 358-360.

62. Ibid., p. 333. Partial lists of officials appear throughout AMCR, *Libros Capitulares*.

63. Jara, *Historia de la imagen*, p. 463. See also Delgado Merchán, *Historia documentada*, pp. 74-75.

64. Antonio Domínguez Ortiz, *Política y hacienda de Felipe IV* (Madrid, 1960), pp. 297-313; AMCR, doc. 209.

65. Salomon, *Campagne de nouvelle Castille*, pp. 91, 253.

66. Domínguez Ortiz, *Sociedad española*, 1:162-178. See also Albert A. Sicroff, *Les controverses des Statuts de "Pureté de Sang" en Espagne, du XVe au XVIIe siècle* (Paris, 1960).

67. Miguel de Cervantes Saavedra, *The Adventures of Don Quixote*, tr. J. M. Cohen (Baltimore, Md., 1950), pt. 1, chap. 28, p. 239; pt. 2, chap. 21, p. 602.

68. Ibid., pt. 2, chap. 19, p. 588; pt. 2, chap. 2, p. 483.

69. Pérez Valera, *Ciudad Real en el siglo XVIII*, pp. 32-36; Domínguez Ortiz, *Sociedad española*, 1:223-224.

70. See chapter 4 and Pérez Valera, *Ciudad Real en el siglo XVIII*, for merchants in Ciudad Real. Domínguez Ortiz, *Sociedad española*, 1:181-184, describes the sale of patents of nobility.

71. See Richard L. Kagan, *Students and Society in Early Modern Spain* (Baltimore, Md., 1974).

72. Alvaro Castillo Pintado, "Los juros de Castilla: Apogeo y fin de un in-

strumento de crédito," *Hispania* 23 (1963):43-70. See also Domínguez Ortiz, *Política y hacienda,* pp. 51-62, 81-87, 315-329, for juros in the reign of Philip IV.

73. AGS, *CMC 3a,* leg. 1821.

74. Bennassar, *Valladolid,* p. 257.

75. AGS, *CMC 3a,* leg. 287.

76. Felipe Ruiz Martín, "Los hombres de negocios genoveses de España durante el siglo XVI," in *Fremde Kaufleute auf der Iberischen Halbinsel,* ed. Hermann Kellenbenz (Cologne, 1970), pp. 84-99. Credit paper was particularly popular with foreign investors. Its average return in the mid-sixteenth century was about 10 percent.

77. Alvaro Castillo, " 'Decretos' et 'medios generales' dans le système financier de la Castille: La crise de 1596," in *Mélanges en l'honneur de Fernand Braudel,* 2 vols. (Paris, 1973), pp. 138-139. See idem, "Dette flottante et dette consolidée en Espagne de 1557 à 1600," *Annales: Économies, Sociétés, Civilisations* (July-August 1963), pp. 745-759; and Domínguez Ortiz, *Política y hacienda,* pt. 2, for the public debt under Philip IV.

78. AGS, *CMC 3a,* legs. 294, 511. See chapter 6.

79. Most of the income from the 1660-1662 tax, for example, went to Bernardino Garrimendi for supplying money for the Spanish army in Milan, and to Clemente Clemente for similar services in Flanders. AGS, *CMC 3a,* leg. 511.

80. Earl J. Hamilton, *War and Prices in Spain: 1651-1800* (Cambridge, Mass., 1947; reprint ed. New York, 1969), pp. 13-16. See Octavio Gil Farrés, *Historia de la moneda española* (Madrid, 1959), pp. 242-243 for the actual coins involved.

81. APCR, leg. 201.

82. AGS, *CMC 3a,* legs. 511, 1531.

83. Diego Medrano y Treviño, *Consideraciones sobre el estado económico, moral y político de la Provincia de Ciudad Real* (Madrid, 1843), pp. 19-21.

84. Pierre Vilar, "Le temps du Quichotte," *Europe* 34 (Jan.-Feb. 1956):3-16. Translated and reprinted in *Crecimiento y desarrollo: Economía e historia: Reflexiones sobre el caso español* (Barcelona, 1964), pp. 431-448, and in English in Peter Earle, ed., *Essays in European Economic History, 1500-1800* (Oxford, 1974).

85. See Ruth Pike, *Enterprise and Adventure: The Genoese in Seville and the Opening of the New World* (Ithaca, N.Y., 1966); Ruth Pike, *Aristocrats and Traders: Sevillian Society in the Sixteenth Century* (Ithaca, N.Y., 1972).

86. Castillo, " 'Decretos' et 'medios generales.' "

BIBLIOGRAPHY

PRINTED SOURCES

Actas de las Cortes de Castilla. Madrid, 1861-1936.

Alonso de Herrera, Gabriel. *Obra de agricultura copilada de diversos auctores.* Alcalá de Henares, 1513. Recently reprinted as *Obra de agricultura. Biblioteca de autores españoles.* Vol. 225. Madrid, 1970.

Arzáns de Orsúa y Vela, Bartolomé. *Historia de la Villa Imperial de Potosí.* Edited by Lewis Hanke and Gunnar Mendoza. 3 vols. Providence, 1965.

d'Aulnoy, Madame [Marie Catherine le Jumelle de Berneville, Comtesse d'Aulnoy]. "Relación del viaje de España." In *Viajes de extranjeros por España y Portugal.* Vol. 2. Edited by José García Mercadal. Madrid, 1952.

Beinart, Haim, ed. *Records of the Trials of the Spanish Inquisition in Ciudad Real. I:1483-1485.* Jerusalem, 1974.

Bertaut, Francisco (François). "Diario del viaje de España." In *Viajes de extranjeros por España y Portugal.* Vol. 2. Edited by José García Mercadal. Madrid, 1952.

Cervantes Saavedra, Miguel de. *The Adventures of Don Quixote.* Translated by J. M. Cohen. Baltimore, 1950.

Los códigos españoles concordados y anotados. 12 vols. 2nd ed. Madrid, 1872-73.

Des Essarts. "Diario del viaje hecho en el año 1659, de Madrid a Alicante y a Valencia y de Valencia a Madrid." In *Viajes de extranjeros por España y Portugal.* Vol. 2. Edited by José García Mercadal. Madrid, 1952.

Dunlop, John Colin. *Memoirs of Spain during the Reigns of Philip IV and Charles II.* 2 vols. Edinburgh, 1834.

Elies y Robért, Antonio. *Discurso sobre el origen, antigüedad y progresos de los pósitos o graneros públicos en los pueblos.* Cervera, 1787.

Fernández Navarrete, Pedro. *Discursos políticos. Biblioteca de autores españoles.* Vol. 25. Madrid, 1947.

Gallardo Fernández, Francisco. *Origen, progresos y estado de las rentas de la Corona de España, su gobierno y administración.* 7 vols. Madrid, 1805.

García Mercadal, José, ed. *Viajes de extranjeros por España y Portugal.* 3 vols. Madrid, 1952.

González de Cellorigo, Martín. *Memorial de la política necesaria, y útil restauración a la república de España . . .* Valladolid, 1600.

Joly, Barthélemy, "Voyage de Barthélemy Joly en Espagne." *Revue hispanique* 20 (1909):460-618.

Jouvin, A. "El viaje de España y Portugal (1672)." In *Viajes de extranjeros por España y Portugal.* Vol. 2. Edited by José García Mercadal. Madrid, 1952.

Larruga y Boneta, Eugenio. *Memorias políticas y económicas sobre los frutos, comercio, fábricas y minas de España, con inclusión de los reales decretos, órdenes, cédulas, aranceles y ordenanzas expedidos para su gobierno y fomento.* 45 vols. Madrid, 1787-1800.

M***. "Viajes hechos en diversos tiempos." In *Viajes de extranjeros por España y Portugal*. Vol. 3. Edited by José García Mercadal. Madrid, 1952.

Martínez de Mata, Francisco. *Memorial en razón del remedio de la despoblación, pobreza, y esterilidad de España* (ca. 1655). In Pedro Rodríguez Campomanes, *Apéndice a la educación popular*. 4 vols. Madrid, 1775-1777. 4:1-418.

Martínez Val, José María, and Peñalosa Esteban-Infantes, Margarita, eds. *Un epistolario inédito del reinado de Felipe IV. Correspondencia del Venerable Fray Tomás de la Virgen*. Ciudad Real, 1961.

Mascareñas, Jerónimo. *Definiciones de la orden y caballeriá de Calatrava conforme al capítulo general celebrado en Madrid MDCLII*. Madrid, 1660.

Medina, Pedro de. *Libro de las grandezas y cosas memorables de España*. Alcalá de Henares, 1566. First published 1543.

Memorial por la agricultura. Madrid, 1633.

Méndez Silva, Rodrigo. *Población general de España*. Madrid, 1645.

Mercado, Luis de. *El libro de la peste*. Madrid, 1921. A contemporary account of the 1599 plague in Valladolid.

[Millones]. *Escrituras, acuerdos, administraciones y súplicas de los servicios de veinte y quatro millones . . . que el reyno hizo a su Magestad, en las Cortes . . . en 8 de febrero de 1649 . . .* Madrid, 1734 rev. ed.

Moncada, Sancho de. *Restauración política de España*. Madrid, 1619.

[A Moroccan ambassador]. "Viaje a España (1690-91)." In *Viajes de extranjeros por España y Portugal*. Vol. 2. Edited by José García Mercadal. Madrid, 1952.

Navagero, Andrés. "Cartas." In *Viajes de extranjeros por España y Portugal*. Vol. 1. Edited by José García Mercadal. Madrid, 1952.

———— "Viaje por España." In *Viajes de extranjeros por España y Portugal*. Vol. 1. Edited by José García Mercadal. Madrid, 1952.

Novísima recopilación de las leyes de España. 12 bks. in 6 vols. Madrid, 1567. Rev. ed. Madrid, 1805-1807. Reprinted in *Los códigos españoles concordados y anotados*. 12 vols. 2nd ed. Madrid, 1872-73.

Ortega y Cotes, Ignacio José de; Alvarez Baquedano, Juan Francisco de; Ortega Zúñiga, Pedro de. *Bullarium Ordinis Militiae Calatravae*. Madrid, 1761.

Peñalosa Esteban-Infantes, Margarita, ed. *La fundación de Ciudad Real: Antología de textos históricos*. Ciudad Real, 1955.

Pérez Valera, Isabel, ed. *Ciudad Real en el siglo XVIII*. Ciudad Real, 1955.

Rades y Andrada, Francisco. *Crónica de las tres órdenes y cavallerías de Santiago, Calatrava y Alcántara*. Toledo, 1572.

Ripia, Juan de la. *Práctica de la administración y cobranza de las rentas reales y visitas de los ministros que se ocupan de ellas*. 5 vols. Madrid, 1795 ed. Originally written 1675.

Sánchez, Tomás. *De sancto matrimonii sacramento . . .* 2 vols. Antwerp, 1600.

Sarmiento de Acuña, Diego (Conde de Gondomar). "Cartas." II. *Colección de documentos inéditos para la historia de España*. N.S. 4 vols. Madrid, 1936-1945, 2:131-147.

Uhagón y Guardamino, Francisco Rafael de. *Relaciones históricos de los siglos XVI y XVII*. Madrid, 1896.

Uztáriz, Gerónimo de. *Theórica y prática de comercio y de marina.* Madrid, 1724.

Vega Carpio, Lope Félix de. *Fuente Ovejuna.* Translated by Roy Campbell. In *Masterworks of World Drama.* Edited by Anthony Caputi. Vol. 3. Boston, 1968.

Villuga, Juan de. *Reportorio de todos los caminos de España.* Madrid, 1546.

Viñas, Carmelo, and Paz, Ramón, eds. *Relaciones histórico-geográfico-estadísticas de los pueblos de España hechas por iniciativa de Felipe II: Ciudad Real.* Madrid, 1971.

SECONDARY WORKS

Anes Alvarez, Gonzalo. *Las crisis agrarias en la España moderna.* Madrid, 1970.
———— "Los pósitos en la España del siglo XVIII." *Moneda y crédito* 105 (June 1968):39-69. Reprinted in idem, *Economía e "ilustración" en la España del siglo XVIII.* Barcelona, 1969.

Anes Alvarez, Gonzalo, and Le Flem, Jean-Paul. "Las crisis del siglo XVII: Producción agrícola, precios e ingresos en tierras de Segovia." *Moneda y crédito* 93 (June, 1965):3-55.

Aníbal, C. E. "The historical elements of Lope de Vega's *Fuenteovejuna.*" *Publications of the Modern Language Association* 49 (1934):657-718.

Arribas Arranz, Filemón. "Repercusiones económicas de las Comunidades de Castilla." *Hispania* 18 (1958):505-47.

Bennassar, Bartolomé. "Être noble en Espagne. Contribution à l'étude des comportements de longue durée." In *Mélanges en l'honneur de Fernand Braudel.* 2 vols. Paris, 1973, 1:95-106.
————"Impôts et crédit public en Espagne du XVIe siècle à nos jours (traits dominants d'une mutation)." *Finances Publiques d'Ancien Régime. Finances Publiques Contemporaines. Processus de Mutation. Continuités et Ruptures.* Papers of an International Colloquium held at Spa, 1971. Brussels, 1972.
———— *Recherches sur les grandes épidémies dans le Nord de l'Espagne à la fin du XVIe siècle: Problèmes du documentation et des méthodes.* Paris, 1969.
———— *Valladolid au siècle d'or: Une ville de Castille et sa campagne au XVIe siècle.* Paris, 1967.
————"En Vieille-Castille: Les ventes de rentes perpétuelles." *Annales: Économies, Sociétés, Civilisations* 6 (1960):1115-26.

Beraza, María Luisa Guadalupe. *Diezmos de la sede toledana y rentas de la mesa arzobispal (siglo XV).* Salamanca, 1972.

Bishko, Charles Julian. "The Castilian as Plainsman: The Medieval Ranching Frontier in La Mancha and Extremadura." *The New World Looks at Its History.* Edited by Archibald R. Lewis and Thomas F. McGann. Austin, Tex., 1963.

Blázquez y Delgado, Antonio. *Apuntes para la historia de la provincia de Ciudad Real.* Ciudad Real, 1888.
———— *Apuntes para las biografías de hijos ilustres de la provincia de Ciudad*

Real. Avila, 1888.

——— *Historia de la provincia de Ciudad Real.* 2 vols. Avila, 1898.

——— "Vías romanas de la provincia de Ciudad Real." *Boletín de la Real Sociedad Geográfica* 32 (1) (1892):366-382.

Boyd-Bowman, Peter. *Índice geobiográfico de cuarenta mil pobladores españoles de America en el siglo XVI.* 2 vols. Vol. 1. Bogotá, 1964. Vol. 2. Mexico, 1968.

Braudel, Fernand. "Conflits et refus de civilisation: Espagnols et Morisques au XVIe siècle." *Annales: Économies, Sociétés, Civilisations* (Oct.-Dec. 1947), pp. 397-410.

——— *The Mediterranean and the Mediterranean World in the Age of Philip II.* 2 vols. Translated by Siân Reynolds from the 1966 rev. ed. New York, 1972-73.

Braudel, Fernand, and Spooner, F. C. "Prices in Europe, 1450-1750." *Cambridge Economic History of Europe,* Vol. 4. Edited by E. E. Rich and C. H. Wilson. Cambridge, 1967.

Braun, Rudolf. "The Impact of the Cottage Industry on an Agricultural Population." In *The Rise of Capitalism.* Edited by David Landes. New York, 1966.

Bustelo García del Real, Francisco. "Algunas reflexiones sobre la población española a principios del siglo XVIII." *Anales de economía* 13 (1972).

——— "La transformación de vecinos en habitantes. El problema del coeficiente." *Estudios geográficos* 130 (Feb. 1973):154-164.

Cabrillana, Nicolás. "La crisis del siglo XIV en Castilla: La peste negra en el obispado de Palencia." *Hispania* (1968), pp. 245-258.

Callahan, William J. *Honor, Commerce, and Industry in Eighteenth-Century Spain.* Boston, 1972.

Camilleri Lapeyre, A. "Spain." In *World Atlas of Agriculture under the Aegis of the International Association of Agricultural Economists.* 3 vols. Novara, Italy, 1969, 1:370-392.

Canga Argüelles, José. *Diccionaria de hacienda.* 5 vols. London, 1826-27.

Carande Thobar, Ramón. *Carlos V y sus banqueros, 1516-1556.* 3 vols. Madrid, 1943-1967.

Carrera Pujal, Jaime. *Historia de la economía española.* 5 vols. Barcelona, 1943-1947.

Castillo Pintado, Alvaro. " 'Decretos' et 'medios generales' dans le système financier de la Castille: La crise de 1596." In *Mélanges en l'honneur de Fernand Braudel.* 2 vols. Paris, 1973, 1:137-144.

——— "Dette flotante et dette consolidée en Espagne de 1557 à 1600." *Annales: Économies, Sociétés, Civilisations* (July-Aug. 1963), pp. 745-759.

——— "Los juros de Castilla. Apogeo y fin de un instrumento de crédito." *Hispania* 23 (1963):43-71.

——— "Population et 'richesse' en Castille durante la seconde moitié du XVIe siècle." *Annales: Économies, Sociétés, Civilisations* (July-Aug. 1965), pp. 719-733.

Ciudad Real: El sector agraria en el conjunto de la economía nacional (1961-1970). Ciudad Real, 1971.

Clavero, Bartolomé. *Mayorazgo: Propiedad feudal en Castilla (1369-1836).* Madrid, 1974.

Colmeiro y Penido, Manuel. "Discurso sobre los políticos y arbitristas de los siglos XVI y XVII y su influencia en la gobernación del estado." In *Discursos leídos en las sesiones públicas de la Real Academia de la Historia,* pp. 403-427. Madrid, 1858.

────── *Historia de la economía política en España.* 2 vols. 1863. Rev. ed. Madrid, 1965.

Corchado Soriano, Manuel. *El camino de Toledo a Córdoba.* Rev. ed. Jaén, 1969.

────── "La Mancha en el siglo XVI." *Hispania* 33 (Jan.-April 1973):141-158.

────── "Pasos naturales y antiguos caminos entre Jaén y la Mancha." *Boletín del Instituto de Estudios Giennenses* 38 (Oct.-Dec. 1963):9-37.

Dantín Cereceda, Juan. *La alimentación española: Sus diferentes tipos.* Madrid, 1934.

────── *Las plantas cultivadas.* Madrid, 1946.

────── *La población de la Mancha española.* Madrid, 1932.

────── *Regiones naturales de España.* 2nd ed. Madrid, 1942.

Danvila y Collado, Manuel. "Origen, naturaleza y extensión de los derechos de la Mesa Maestral de la Orden de Calatrava." *Boletín de la Real Academia de la Historia* 12 (1888):116-163.

Delgado Merchán, Luis. *Historia documentada de Ciudad Real.* 2nd ed. Ciudad Real, 1907.

Diccionario de historia eclesiástica de España. 3 vols. to date. Directed by Quintín Aldea Vaquero, Tomás Marín Martínez, and José Vives Gatell. Madrid, 1972-73.

Domínguez Ortiz, Antonio. "La conspiración del duque de Medina Sidonia y el marqués de Ayamonte." *Archivo hispalense* 106 (1961):133-159. In idem, *Crisis y decadencia en la España de los Austrias.* Barcelona, 1969.

────── "La crisis de Castilla en 1677-1688." *Revista portuguesa de historia* 10 (1962):435-451.

────── "La desigualdad contributiva en Castilla durante el siglo XVII." *Anuario de historia del derecho español* 22 (1951):1222-68.

────── "Los gastos de Corte en la España del siglo XVII." In *Homenaje a Jaime Vicens Vives.* 2 vols. Barcelona, 1965-1967, 2:113-124.

────── *The Golden Age of Spain, 1516-1659.* Translated by James Casey. New York, 1971.

────── *Política y hacienda de Felipe IV.* Madrid, 1960.

────── "La ruina de la aldea castellana." *Revista internacional de sociología* 24 (1948):99-124.

────── *La sociedad española en el siglo XVII.* 2 vols. Madrid, 1963-1970. Abridged as *Las clases privilegiadas en la España del antiguo régimen.* Madrid, 1973.

────── *La sociedad española en el siglo XVIII.* Madrid, 1955.

────── "Ventas y extensiones de lugares durante el reinado de Felipe IV." *Anuario de historia del derecho español* 34 (1964):163-207.

Elliott, John H. "The Decline of Spain." *Past and Present* 20 (1961):52-75.

────── *Imperial Spain 1469-1716.* New York, 1963.

"El empleo del Don en los documentos hasta el siglo XVIII y su presunción de califacción de nobiliaria." In *Hidalguía* 16 (1968):9-12.

Fernández Alvarez, Manuel. *Economía, sociedad y corona: Ensayos históricos sobre el siglo XVI.* Madrid, 1963.

———— *La sociedad española del Renacimiento.* Salamanca, 1970.

Fontecha y Sánchez, Ramón de. *La moneda de vellón y cobre de la monarquía española (años 1516 a 1931).* Madrid, 1968.

García Sainz de Baranda, Julián. *La hidalguía en las merindades antiguas de Castilla: Genealogía y heráldica de las familias más importantes de ellas y de las jurisdicciones limítrofes.* Burgos, 1969.

Gentil da Silva, José. *En Espagne: Développement économique, subsistance, déclin.* Paris, 1965.

Gil Farrés, Octavio. *Historia de la moneda española.* Madrid, 1959.

González, Tomás. *Censo de población de las provincias y partidos de la corona de Castilla en el siglo XVI, con varios apéndices para completar la del resto de la península en el mismo siglo, y formar juicio comparativo con la del anterior y siquiente, según resulta de los libros y registros que se custodian en el Real Archivo de Simancas.* Madrid, 1829.

Goubert, Pierre. *Beauvais et le Beauvaisis de 1600 à 1730: Contribution à l'histoire sociale de la France du XVIIe siècle.* Paris, 1960.

Granjel, Luis [Sánchez]. "Las epidemias de peste en España durante el siglo XVII." *Cuadernos de historia de la medicina española* 3 (1964):19-40.

Greene, J. P., and Forster, Robert, eds. *Preconditions of Revolution in Early Modern Europe.* Baltimore, Md., 1971.

Guilarte, Alfonso María. *El régimen señorial en el siglo XVI.* Madrid, 1962.

Gutton, François. *La chevalerie militaire en Espagne: L'ordre de Calatrava.* Paris, 1955.

Hamilton, Earl J. *American Treasure and the Price Revolution in Spain, 1501-1650.* Cambridge, Mass., 1934. Reprint ed. New York, 1965.

———— "The Decline of Spain." *Economic History Review* 8 (1938):168-179.

———— "The First Twenty Years of the Bank of Spain." *Journal of Political Economy* 54 (1946):17-37, 116-140.

———— "The Foundation of the Bank of Spain." *Journal of Political Economy* 53 (1945):97-114.

———— "Money and Economic Recovery in Spain under the First Bourbon." *Journal of Modern History* 15 (1943):192-206.

———— "Plans for a National Bank in Spain, 1701-83." *Journal of Political Economy* 57 (Aug. 1949):315-336.

———— "Spanish Banking Schemes before 1700." *Journal of Political Economy* 57 (April 1949):134-156.

———— *War and Prices in Spain: 1651-1800.* Cambridge, Mass., 1947. Reprint ed. New York, 1969.

Hauben, Paul J., ed. *The Spanish Inquisition.* New York, 1969.

Henry, Louis. *Manuel de démographie historique.* Paris, 1967.

Hervás y Buendía, Inocente. *Diccionario histórico geográfico . . . de Ciudad Real.* Ciudad Real, 1890.

———— "Documentos originales del Sacro Convento de Calatrava, que atesora el archivo de Hacienda en Ciudad Real." *Boletín de la Real Academia de la Historia* 20 (June 1892):545-572.

Hosta, José de. "Crónica de la Provincia de Ciudad-Real." In *Crónica general de*

España. 2nd ed. Madrid, 1865.

Houston, J. M. *The Western Mediterranean World: An Introduction to its Regional Landscapes*. London, 1964.

Hoyos Sancho, Nieves de. "La vida pastoril en la Mancha." *Estudios geográficos* 9 (1948):623-636.

Iradiel Murugarren, Paulino. *Evolución de la industria textil castellana en los siglos XIII-XVII: Factores de desarrollo, organización y costas de la producción manufactura en Cuenca*. Salamanca, 1974.

Jago, Charles J. "Aristocracy, War and Finance in Castile, 1621-1665." Ph.D. thesis, Cambridge University, 1969.

―――― "The Influence of Debt on the Relations between Crown and Aristocracy in Seventeenth-Century Castile." *Economic History Review* 26 (May 1973): 218-236.

Janer, Florencio. *Condición social de los moriscos de España: Causas de su expulsión y consequencias que ésta produjo en el orden económico y político*. Madrid, 1857.

Jara, Juan de la (de Santa Teresa, Augustín Recoleto). *Historia de la imagen de Nuestra Señora del Prado, fundadora y patrona de Ciudad Real*. Ciudad Real, 1880. Chap. 10 reprinted in *La fundación de Ciudad Real: Antología de textos históricos*. Edited by Margarita Peñalosa Esteban-Infantes. Ciudad Real, 1955.

Jessen, Otto. "La Mancha: Contribución al estudio geográfico de Castilla la Nueva." Translated by Joaquin Gómez de Llarena. *Estudios geográficos* 7 (1946):269-312, 479-524.

Kagan, Richard L. *Students and Society in Early Modern Spain*. Baltimore, 1974.

Kamen, Henry. "The Decline of Castile: The Last Crisis." *Economic History Review* 17 (1964-65):63-76.

―――― *The War of Succession in Spain 1700-15*. Bloomington, Ind., 1969.

Kellenbenz, Hermann. *Die Fuggersche Maestrazgopacht (1525-1542): Zur Geschichte der spanischen Ritterorden im 16. Jahrhundert*. Tubingen, 1967.

Klein, Julius. *The Mesta*. 1920. Port Washington, N.Y., 1964.

Konetzke, Richard. "Entrepreneurial Activities of Spanish and Portuguese Noblemen in Medieval Times." *Explorations in Entrepreneurial History* 6 (Dec. 1953):115-120.

Ladero Quesada, Miguel-Angel. *La hacienda real castellana entre 1480 y 1492*. Valladolid, 1967.

―――― *La hacienda real de Castilla en el siglo XV*. La Laguna, 1973.

Lapeyre, Henri. *Géographie de l'Espagne morisque*. Paris, 1959.

Lea, Henry Charles. *A History of the Inquisition in Spain*. 4 vols. New York, 1906-7.

―――― *The Moriscos of Spain: Their Conversion and Expulsion*. London, 1901.

Le Flem, Jean-Paul. "Las cuentas de la Mesta, 1510-1709." *Moneda y crédito* 121 (1972):23-104, plus graphs.

Le Roy Ladurie, Emmanuel. *Les paysans de Languedoc*. 2 vols. Paris, 1966.

―――― *Times of Feast, Times of Famine: A History of Climate since the Year 1000*. Translated by Barbara Bray from the 1967 French edition. New York, 1971.

Livi-Bacci, Massimo. "Fertility and Population Growth in Spain in the Eighteenth and Nineteenth Centuries." *Daedalus* (Spring 1968), pp. 523-535.

López de Ayala, F. *Contribuciones e impuestos en León y Castilla durante la Edad Media.* Madrid, 1896.

López-Salazar Pérez, Jerónimo. "Evolución demográfica de la Mancha en el siglo XVIII." *Hispania* 36 (1976):233-299.

Lourie, Elena. "A Society Organized for War: Medieval Spain." *Past and Present* 35 (1966):54-76.

Lunenfeld, Marvin. *The Council of the Santa Hermandad: A Study of the Pacification Forces of Ferdinand and Isabella.* Coral Gables, Fla., 1970.

Lynch, John. *Spain under the Habsburgs.* 2 vols. Oxford, 1964-1969.

Maldonado Cocat, Ramón José. *El escudo de Ciudad Real.* Ciudad Real, 1972.

——— "Expedientes de hidalguía para la vecindad con esta calidad, en Ciudad Real." *Hidalguía* 7 (1959):233-240.

Marcos González, María Dolores. *Castilla la Nueva y Estremadura. La España del Antiguo Régimen*, part 6. Edited by Miguel Artola. *Acta salmanticensia* 64. Salamanca, 1971.

Martínez y González, F. *Participación de los hijos de la Mancha en el descubrimiento, conquista y dominación de América.* Baena, Spain, 1908.

Matilla Tascón, Antonio. *Historia de las minas de Almadén.* Madrid, 1958.

——— *La única contribución y el Catastro de Ensenada.* Madrid, 1947.

Maura y Gamazo, Gabriel. *La vida y reinado de Carlos II.* 2nd ed. 3 vols. Madrid, 1954.

Medrano y Treviño, Diego. *Consideraciones sobre el estado económico, moral y político de la provincia de Ciudad Real . . .* Madrid, 1843. Reprint ed. Madrid, 1972.

Mendels, Franklin F. "Protoindustrialization: The First Phase of the Industrialization Process." *Journal of Economic History* 32 (March 1972):241-261.

Menéndez Pidal, Gonzalo. *Los caminos en la historia de España.* Madrid, 1951.

Merriman, Roger Bigelow. *The Rise of the Spanish Empire in the Old World and the New.* 4 vols. New York, 1918-1934.

Meuvret, Jean. "Les crises de subsistances et la démographie de la France d'Ancien Régime." *Population* (Oct.-Dec. 1946), pp. 643-650.

Mitre Fernández, Emilio. "Algunas cuestiones demográficas en la Castilla de fines del siglo XIV." *Anuario de estudios medievales* 7 (1970-71):615-622.

Molinié-Bertrand, Annie. "Le clergé dans le royaume de Castille à la fin du XVIe siècle: Approche cartographique." *Revue d'histoire économique et sociale* 51 (1973):5-53.

Mousnier, Roland. *Peasant Uprisings in Seventeenth-Century France, Russia, and China.* Translated by Brian Pearce. New York, 1972.

Moxó, Salvador de. *La alcabala: Sobre sus orígenes, concepto y naturaleza.* Madrid, 1963.

Muñoz y Romero, Tomás. *Colección de fueros municipales y cartas-pueblas de los reinos de Castilla, León, Corona de Aragón y Navarra.* Madrid, 1847.

Nadal, Jorge. *La población española (Siglos XVI a XX).* Barcelona, 1966.

——— "La revolución de los precios españoles en el siglo XVI: Estado actual de la cuestión." *Hispania* 19 (1959):503-529.

Nadal, Jorge, and Giralt, Emilio. *La population catalane de 1553 à 1717: L'immigration française et les autres facteurs de son développement.* Paris, 1960.
Nomenclator de las ciudades, villas, lugares, aldeas y demas entidades de población de España: Provincia de Ciudad Real. Madrid, 1950.
Olagüe, Ignacio. *La decadencia española.* 4 vols. San Sebastian, 1939-1951.
——— "El paisaje manchego en tiempos de Cervantes." *Anales cervantinos* 3 (1953):215-279.
Pach, Z. P. "Sixteenth-century Hungary: Commercial Activity and Market Production by the Nobles." In *Economy and Society in Early Modern Europe,* pp. 113-133. Edited by Peter Burke. New York, 1972.
Parker, Geoffrey. *The Army of Flanders and the Spanish Road, 1567-1659.* Cambridge, 1972.
Parker, William, ed. *European Peasants and Their Markets.* Princeton, N.J., 1975.
Pérez, Joseph. *La revolution des "comunidades" de Castille (1520-1521).* Bordeaux, 1970.
Pérez, Ural A. "El precio de los granos en la península ibérica, 1585-1650." *Anuario del Instituto de Investigaciones Históricas* 6 (1962-1963).
Pérez Valera, Isabel, ed. *Índice de los documentos del Archivo Municipal de Ciudad Real, 1255-1899.* Ciudad Real, 1962.
Pescador del Hoyo, María del Carmen. "Los orígenes de la Santa Hermandad." *Cuadernos de la historia de España* 55-56 (1972):400-443.
Phillips, Carla Rahn. "Ciudad Real no período dos Habsburgos: um estudo demográfico." *Anaïs de historia* 7 (Dec. 1975):151-165.
——— "Urban Control of the Castilian Countryside: Additional Evidence from Seventeenth Century Ciudad Real." *Societas—A Review of Social History* (Autumn 1973):313-335. Translated into Castilian as "La propiedad urbana en Castilla." *Moneda y crédito* 140 (March 1977):49-65.
Pike, Ruth. *Enterprise and Adventure: The Genoese in Seville and the Opening of the New World.* Ithaca, N.Y., 1966.
——— *Aristocrats and Traders: Sevillian Society in the Sixteenth Century.* Ithaca, N.Y., 1972.
Piskorski, Wladimiro. *Las Cortes de Castilla en el período de tránsito de la Edad Media a la Moderna.* Barcelona, 1930.
Ponz, Antonio. *Viaje de España* . . . 18 vols. Madrid, 1777-1794, 16:34-50.
Reitzer, Ladislas. "Some Observations on Castilian Commerce and Finance in the Sixteenth Century." *Journal of Modern History* 32 (1960):213-223.
Ringrose, David R. "Carting in the Hispanic World: An Example of Divergent Development." *Hispanic American Historical Review* (Feb. 1970), pp. 30-51.
——— *Transportation and Economic Stagnation in Spain, 1750-1850.* Durham, N.C., 1970.
Romero García, Ildefonso. "Los hidalgos de San Benito." *Cuadernos de estudios manchegos* 6 (1953):7-18.
Ruiz Martín, Felipe. "La Banca en España hasta 1782." In *El Banco de España: Una historia económica.* Madrid, 1970.
——— "Demografía eclesiástica de España hasta el siglo XIX." In *Diccionario de*

historia eclesiástica de España. 3 vols. Edited by Quintín Aldea Vaquero, Tomás Marín Martínez, and José Vives Gatell. Madrid, 1972-73, 2:682-733.

———— "Los hombres de negocios genoveses de España durante el siglo XVI." In *Fremde Kaufleute auf der Iberischen Halbinsel*. Cologne, 1970, pp. 84-99.

———— "La población española al comienzo de los tiempos modernos." In *Cuadernos de historia: Anexos de la revista Hispania* 1 (Madrid, 1967):189-202.

———— "Un testimonio literaria sobre las manufacturas de paños en Segovia por 1625." In *Homenaje al Profesor Alarcos*. 2 vols. Valladolid, 1966, 2:1-21.

Ruwet, J. "Crises démographiques—problèmes économiques ou crises morales?" *Population* 9 (1954):451-476.

Salomon, Noël. *La campagne de nouvelle Castille à la fin du XVIe siècle: D'après les "Relaciones topográficas."* Paris, 1964.

Santa María, Ramón. "La Inquisición de Ciudad Real: Proceso original del difunto Juan González Escogido (Agosto 1484-15 Marzo 1485)." *Boletín de la Real Academia de la Historia* 22 (1893):189-204.

———— "Ritos y costumbres de los hebreos españoles." *Boletín de la Real Academia de la Historia* 22 (1893):181-188.

Sarrailh, Jean. *L'Espagne éclairée de la seconde moitié du XVIIIe siècle*. Paris, 1964.

Schnapper, Bernard. *Les rentes au XVIe siècle: Histoire d'un instrument de crédit*. Paris, 1957.

Sicroff, Albert A. *Les controverses des statuts de "pureté de sang" en Espagne, du XVe au XVIIe siècle*. Paris, 1960.

Slicher van Bath, Bernard H. *The Agrarian History of Western Europe: A.D. 500-1850*. Translated by Olive Ordish. London, 1963.

———— *Yield Ratios, 810-1820*. In *Afdeling Agrarische Geschiedenis Bijdragen* 10. Wageningen, 1963.

Sobrequés Callicó, Jaime. "La peste negra en la península ibérica." *Anuario de estudios medievales* 7 (1970-71):67-102.

Ulloa, Modesto. *La hacienda real de Castilla en el reinado de Felipe II*. Rome, 1963.

Valdeón Baruque, Julio. "Aspectos de la crisis castellana en la primera mitad del siglo XIV." *Hispania* 29 (1969):5-25.

Vassberg, David E. "The Sale of 'tierras baldías' in Sixteenth-Century Castile." *Journal of Modern History* 47 (Dec. 1975):629-654.

———— "The *tierras baldías:* Community Property and Public Lands in Sixteenth-Century Castile." *Agricultural History* 48 (July 1974):383-401.

Vénard, André, and Philippe Ariès. "Deux contributions à l'histoire des practiques contraceptives: I. Saint François de Sales et Thomas Sánchez; II. Chaucer et Madame de Sévigné." *Population* 9 (Oct.-Dec. 1954):683-692.

Vicens Vives, Jaime. *Aproximación a la historia de España*. 2nd ed. Barcelona, 1960. Translated (as *Approaches to the History of Spain*) by Joan Connelly Ullman. Berkeley and Los Angeles, Calif., 1967.

Vicens Vives, Jaime, with Jorge Nadal Oller. *An Economic History of Spain*. Translated by Frances M. López-Morillas. Princeton, N.J., 1969.

Vilar, Jean. *Literatura y economía: La figura satírica del arbitrista en el Siglo de Oro*. Translated from the French by Francisco Bustelo García del Real. Madrid, 1973.

Vilar, Pierre. *Crecimiento y desarrollo: Economía e historia: Reflexiones sobre el caso español*. Essays translated from the original French. Barcelona, 1964.

———— "Problem of the Formation of Capitalism." *Past and Present* 10 (1956): 15-38. Translated in *Crecimiento*.

———— "Remarques sur l'histoire des prix." *Annales: Economies, Sociétés, Civilisations* (Jan.-Feb. 1961), pp. 110-115. Translated in *Crecimiento*.

———— "Le temps du Quichotte." *Europe* 34(1956):3-16. Translated in *Crecimiento*.

Villalba, Joaquín. *Epidemiología española u historia cronológica de las pestes contagios, epidemias y epizootias que han acaecido en España desde la venida de las cartagineses hasta el año 1801*. 2 vols. in 1. Madrid, 1803.

Viñas Mey, Carmelo. *El problema de la tierra en la España de los siglos XVI-XVII*. Madrid, 1941.

Vincent, Bernard. "Les pestes dans le royaume de Grenade aux XVIe et XVIIe siècles." *Annales: Économies, Sociétés, Civilisations* (Nov.-Dec. 1969), pp. 1511-13.

Wallerstein, Emmanuel. *The Modern World-System: Capitalist Agriculture and the Origins of the European World-Economy in the Sixteenth Century*. New York, 1974.

Weisser, Michael. "The Decline of Castile Revisited: The Case of Toledo." *Journal of European Economic History* (Winter 1973), pp. 614-640.

———— "Les marchands de Tolède dans l'économie castillane, 1565-1635." *Mélanges de la Casa de Velázquez* 7 (1971):223-236.

———— *The Peasants of the Montes: The Roots of Rural Rebellion in Spain*. Chicago, 1976.

Wolff, Philippe. "The 1391 Pogrom in Spain: Social Crisis or Not?" *Past and Present* 50 (Feb. 1971):4-18.

Wright, L. P. "The Military Orders in Sixteenth and Seventeenth Century Spanish Society: The Institutional Embodiment of a Historical Tradition." *Past and Present* 43 (May 1969):34-70.

INDEX